G
7/08

956.70443
Lacey, Jim, 1958-
Takedown : the 3rd Infantry
 Division´s twenty-one day
c2007

Discarded by
Santa Maria Library

09
1

SANTA MARIA PUBLIC LIBRARY

D1603080

TAKEDOWN

The 3rd Infantry
Division's
Twenty-One Day
Assault on
Baghdad

TAKEDOWN

by
Jim Lacey

NAVAL INSTITUTE PRESS
Annapolis, Maryland

Naval Institute Press
291 Wood Road
Annapolis, MD 21402

© 2007 by Jim Lacey
All rights reserved. No part of this book may be reproduced or utilized in
any form or by any means, electronic or mechanical, including photocopying
and recording, or by any information storage and retrieval system, without
permission in writing from the publisher.

LIBRARY OF CONGRESS CATALOGING-IN-PUBLICATION DATA
Lacey, Jim, 1958–
    Takedown : the 3rd Infantry Division's twenty-one day assault on Baghdad
/ James G. Lacey.
        p. cm.
    Includes index.
    ISBN-13: 978-1-59114-458-8 (alk. paper)
    ISBN-10: 1-59114-458-2 (alk. paper)
    1. Iraq War, 2003–   2. United States. Army. Infantry Division, 3rd.
I. Title.
DS79.76.L325 2006
956.7044'34—dc22

                                                    2006036392

Printed in the United States of America on acid-free paper

13 12 11 10 09 08 07   8 7 6 5 4 3 2
First printing

All maps courtesy of the Center for Army Lessons Learned at
Fort Leavenworth.

All photos are from the author's personal collection and are available at the
Military History Institute in Carlisle, Pennsylvania.

Contents

Maps

Acknowledgments

No book of this type can be written without the help and support of many others. First, I want to thank Brigadier General Anthony Cucolo, without whose support and indulgence this book would not have been written. I also want to thank my family and all the friends who were continuing sources of encouragement to finish it. I particularly want to thank Dr. Williamson Murray and Sharon Moore, who made several painstaking edits of the manuscript. If this book succeeds as a well-told narrative of the events of the Third Infantry Division during Operation Iraqi Freedom, they are the primary reason.

I also have to thank all of the officers and soldiers of the 3rd ID whose names the reader will find throughout this book. These great soldiers gave the gift of their precious time, without which this book would have been a much inferior product, assuming it could have been done at all. What the soldiers of the 3rd ID collectively accomplished should be ranked as one of the greatest military achievements of all time, and I only hope I can do it and them justice. For many of them, the retelling of their personal stories took a serious emotional effort; like countless silent heroes before them, many were initially reluctant to tell their stories. Most were convinced to do so only by my appeals that they owed an accurate history to their comrades in arms and the families of those soldiers who together sacrificed so much.

I want to apologize to all those whose stories I did not tell. Many times, I had to use the fight of a single platoon or company in order to present a detailed personal view of various combat actions. Usually, the unit selected was representative of fights that twenty or more other nearby platoons were fighting at the same time.

A Note on Sources

In putting this book together I had the full support of the 3rd ID chain of command that fought the war. Many of the quotes and remembrances in this book come from dozens of interviews and hundreds of hours spent talking with the soldiers and leaders of the division. Virtually every battalion commander and above in the division's maneuver elements gave freely of their time to answer my questions and in some cases review the manuscript for grievous errors (though all responsibility for any error of fact that still remains rests solely with me).

This book benefited greatly from a unique project that was instituted even before the war ended. The Army instituted a massive lessons-learned effort, led by Brigadier General Mark O'Neill and Mr. Greg Fontenot, to capture the events of the invasion. As part of this effort, the Operation Iraqi Freedom Study Group collected battle histories of every unit in the 3rd ID and conducted hundreds of interviews with participants in the invasion. These records and interviews were critical for me to develop a thorough understanding of confusing events and timelines. Much of this research has been published in Gregory Fontenot's book *On Point*.

Many units sent me unofficial histories they compiled after the war. Moreover, I received dozens of personal reminiscences from soldiers, with detailed stories I did not see or read in any other source. One thing I greatly regret was not using the poignant stories sent by family members who waited at home as the minute-by-minute actions of their loved ones were beamed into their living rooms from embedded journalists. There is another major story to be told about what these families endured, but it will have to wait for another historian to take up the challenge.

By far my most important resource was a collection of videotapes made by the participants themselves. Less than two weeks after Baghdad fell, the 3rd ID commander had soldiers and leaders brought back to the sites of most of the events found in this book to tell their full stories directly on the ground where they had fought. Each of these descriptions was filmed. Taken together these sixty hours of tapes told almost the entire story of the invasion as it was seen by the direct participants. These narratives were told in the presence of others who had been present at each fight. So each story was corrected or clarified as it was told, and thereby much of the bias that so often finds its way into narratives written or told in isolation was removed.

Because they were told so soon after the end of the war, these stories were still fresh in the minds of the participants. Also, they had not been greatly enhanced by repeated retelling. In multiple phone conversations two years after the invasion, new story elements were introduced that did not appear in the person's early narrative of the event. Usually if I presented their earlier words, a more accurate memory of the event would be sparked, and that is what is in this history. In nearly every case where later versions disagreed with what was said earlier, I went with the earliest version.

The sheer volume of information I was able to obtain and the publisher's space limitations forced me to prune many interesting details of this fight. For instance, I collected enough information on engineer and artillery units for separate histories of each of them, and anyone interested in undertaking the task will find electronic copies of all my research, including copies of the videos, at the Military History Institute at Carlisle, Pennsylvania.

I found only two books that dealt specifically with the 3rd ID's march to Baghdad. Both are superlative but narrow in scope. *Thunder Run*, by David Zucchino, provides a detailed account of the two thunder runs launched by the 3rd ID's 2nd brigade into the heart of Baghdad. *Heavy Metal*, by Jason Conroy and Ron Martz, presents a view of the invasion from the perspective of a company commander.

Finally, what sets this book apart from every other history of the war is that it includes a detailed look at the Iraqi side of the conflict. Kevin Woods and his research team spent two years studying the Iraqi regime and its decisions. A great deal of this information has been published in *The Iraqi Perspective Report*, which I coauthored. Anyone looking for a detailed account of the inside workings of Saddam's regime and his military is urged to pick up a copy.

Author's Note: Throughout this book I refer to battalions and brigades because I believe it enhances the clarity of the battle descriptions. In fact, battalions in this war were actually task forces and brigades are more properly referred to as brigade combat teams (BCT). At its home-station an infantry battalion consists of several infantry companies. In combat, though, infantry battalions often receive attachments of armor companies from pure armor battalions, and the armored units have infantry attached to them. These attached companies are often broken down further to put tank platoons with infantry companies and vice versa. These mixed companies are referred to as teams. Brigades often receive so many additional support units and attached task forces that they become BCTs, which barely resemble their basic home-station organization. This is a greatly simplified explanation, but I believe it suffices to enlighten the reader.

The 3rd ID moved combat power between companies, battalions, and brigades so often and so rapidly that trying to explain it as it was happening would leave those not fully indoctrinated in military jargon dazed. Thus, for the sake of simplicity I talk only about the basic units. Those readers who insist on knowing which companies were cross attached to what battalions on any particular day are free to consult my research notes at the Military History Institute.

Finally, because of the sensitivities of cavalry officers everywhere, I use their terms for units when discussing 3-7 CAV operations. Therefore, I use "squadron" to denote a battalion (task force) sized unit, and "troop" for a company (team) sized unit.

TAKEDOWN

Introduction

Staff Sergeant Dillard Johnson was nearing exhaustion at the end of a 180-mile nonstop run across the Iraqi Desert. In front of him stood the city of As Samawah. He had been told to expect an effusive welcome from the population and probably a parade in America's honor. Spotting a large number of armed men on the bridge leading into the city, Sergeant Johnson followed instructions and signaled them to surrender. When the Iraqis opened fire, he discovered there would be no parade.

Ordered to seize the bridge, Johnson, joined by an Abrams M-1 main battle tank, raced his Bradley forward. As they closed on the bridge Johnson noticed that the tank's .50-caliber machine gun was not having much effect so he opened up on the enemy with the Bradley's 25mm main gun. According to Johnson, "That laid them out quick enough." Laid them out it did. The next morning other members of the company counted sixty-five bodies on the bridge.

Crossing the bridge, Johnson ordered the tank to stay on the road while his vehicle pulled flank security in an adjoining field. Almost immediately, an Iraqi army truck came hurtling down the road, spotted the Americans, and, using a civilian vehicle to mask them from U.S. fire, made a hasty departure back into town. Unwilling to let the vehicle escape, Johnson gave chase and followed it inside a walled compound, while the M-1 tank waited at the gate.

Trapped, the Iraqis in the back of the truck opened up with small arms and RPGs (rocket-propelled grenades). One of them caught on fire from the back blast of the RPG and fell to the road in flames. Another jumped off the truck and carrying an RPG ran into a nearby bunker. He died there when the tank fired its 120mm main gun into the bunker at point-blank range. Johnson returned fire on the truck, which exploded into flames after absorbing four rounds from his 25mm cannon.

As Johnson tells it, "That is when all hell broke loose. Close to two hundred of these guys poured out of a nearby building and swarmed around us." The enemy was so close that dozens of RPG rounds were slamming into the Bradley without detonating—the Iraqis were shooting so close that the rounds did not have time to arm themselves before impact. The Bradley's observer began engaging with the M-240 machine gun while the vehicle's gunner fired the 25mm. Johnson's own machine gun had been smashed by Iraqi fire, so he was fighting with his rifle and later his pistol. After he had killed three or four Iraqis at close range with his pistol, the fighting stopped. Johnson reported there were thirteen prisoners and the rest were dead. A later count put the number of Iraqi dead at 167.

As Johnson was dismounting from his vehicle to give first aid to the wounded Iraqis, he was shot in the chest. Thinking he was a dead man because he did not have armored plates in his protective vest, Johnson slumped into the vehicle. Surprised to find himself alive but very sore at the point of impact, he managed to pull himself together and then, with the vehicle's driver, got out of the Bradley and started helping the men who had only moments ago been doing their best to kill him.

As he was tending to wounded Iraqis, eight trucks filled with armed enemy raced down the road and stopped just outside the compound. At first the Iraqis failed to notice Johnson and his vehicle only 30 yards from them and instead opened fire on the rest of Johnson's platoon, which was some distance away. Johnson's gunner turned each vehicle into a wreck with a dozen high explosive rounds each, while Johnson himself destroyed one truck with the grenade launcher on his rifle; then, spotting two guys about to engage the Bradley with an RPG, he killed both with a rifle.

While he was taking the two best-dressed prisoners back to his vehicle (under the assumption they were likely to be officers and possess valuable information), close to seventy more Iraqis stormed out of a nearby building and rushed the M-1 tank at the gate. They were cut to ribbons by the tank's .50-caliber and its coax machine gun. At the same moment, an Iraqi mortar round struck the center of the prisoners Johnson had just tended to, killing them all. Johnson looked at the pile of dead Iraqis and to his two remaining prisoners, obviously scared almost senseless, and gestured for them to run away. They did.

Johnson remounted his vehicle and was about to drive off when a second mortar round exploded in the palm tree directly above him. Biting down, Johnson ignored the pain from a burst eardrum and shrapnel wounds in both legs and both arms as he ordered the driver to get going. A second mortar round hit the vehicle as it retreated out of the compound, causing the loss of the vehicle's one remaining machine gun, Johnson's night vision goggles, their radio antennas, and all of the team's personal equipment stored on top of the vehicle.

At first Johnson parked his vehicle directly behind the M-1 to shield its vulnerable engine area from RPG attacks. For the next ten minutes enemy fire continued to increase, and Johnson finally signaled to the M-1 commander to pull back. Back on the American side of the bridge, Johnson was able to replace his antennas and make contact with his platoon. He was told to stay put and help would come to him. While waiting for the promised help he called in his own mortars on the enemy mortar positions, wiping them out. At the same time he and another crewmember performed first aid on their own wounds while the driver and loader refilled the ammo canisters.

After a few long minutes, the rest of the platoon came up and the Iraqis began to withdraw. Unfortunately, one of the reinforcing Bradleys hit a mortar crater and then slipped into a ravine at such an angle that it could not fire any of its weapons. Seeing this, the Iraqis swarmed back to their fighting positions and began plastering the trapped Bradley with small arms and RPG fire. Johnson watched as an ambulance with the Red Crescent roared up and disgorged ten armed men into a building. He let the ambulance leave but destroyed the building in a fusillade of 25mm high explosive rounds. That done, he raced up to the stricken Bradley, dropped his ramp while under intense fire, and rescued the trapped crew. After wiping out another vehicle full of Iraqi fighters, Johnson took his vehicle to the rear to replenish ammo and seek medical treatment for his several wounds.

Later that evening Sergeant Johnson took his vehicle back to the river to protect the stuck Bradley. The next day 221 bodies were found in his immediate vicinity. All of them were killed during the night by Johnson and his crew. Other soldiers in the unit swear Johnson killed over a thousand of the enemy that day. The official total was 488, and the enemy wounded went uncounted.

Johnson would go on to further heroics along "ambush alley," at Najaf, and finally around Baghdad. Not every soldier in the 3rd ID was a Sergeant Johnson, but he was not exceptional. As one officer said, the real weapon of mass destruction in Iraq was the 3rd ID, and it was a few thousand soldiers like Sergeant Johnson at the tip of the spear that made the 3rd ID the most awesome weapon of war America has ever placed on the battlefield. They were men who proved absolutely ruthless in fight, but a moment later would start helping enemy wounded, even at great personal risk.

One further story from Sergeant Johnson's experience around As Samawah gives insight into the character of the men who fight America's wars. In his own words:

> We were in an overwatch position after the battle of As Samawah. I was watching through the thermals and I see this Iraqi attempting to sneak up on us in the dark. He gets about seventy-five meters away when all of a sudden this bull comes out of nowhere and demolishes the guy. Really lays him out and thrashes him. The whole platoon is watching and is in absolute hysterics. Then somehow the guy manages to stab the bull and it bellows and runs away. Using his rifle as a crutch he then starts back towards my vehicle! He then falls down and begins to crawl towards us. When he is about thirty-five meters away he aims the rifle at us so we killed him with the coax. His rifle was a really nice .303 British so I kept it for a while. Later in the war I was shooting RPG guys from two hundred plus meters away. When that .303 hit them they stayed down for good. Anyway later that night the bull came back and stomped on this guy for hours. He would gore him, throw him up in the air, and then stomp on him some more. The next day the guy was about three inches thick! We later protected the bull the whole time he was there. We conducted first aid for his wounds and gave him all the water and vegetables we could find. We also protected him from other Iraqis and other soldiers.

This was the 3rd ID's war, and this is their story. It is not a happy story. There were no parades or welcoming crowds. Iraqi units did not all melt away or surrender as the troops had been led to believe they would. Rather, tens of thousands of Iraqis fought with fanatical, even suicidal, intensity. They were met by dedicated, hard-fighting American soldiers. Sergeant Johnson's story is typical of the hundreds of engagements the 3rd ID fought before it finally stormed into Baghdad. It is a story of twenty-one days of brutal fighting, a story that until now has remained largely untold. Mostly it is the story of American soldiers who killed in order to do what America asked them to do, but as one officer stated, "My men could not wait to stop killing and start helping people." It is a special breed of man that can fight America's wars one day and turn to repairing schoolhouses the next.

1

The Colonels' War

AFTER DESERT STORM, Bernard Trainor and Michael Gordon wrote a history of the conflict titled *The Generals' War*. Their basic premise was that Vietnam had been directed by politicians, but this time around the politicians let the generals plan and wage the kind of war they wanted. Desert Storm turned out to be as textbook a military exercise as had ever been dreamed up at any military staff college. A multi-Corps attack with massed divisions charging directly at and around the flank of a befuddled Iraqi army made it truly a generals' war.

If Desert Storm was a generals' war, Operation Iraqi Freedom was definitely a colonels' war. The massed divisions on line rushing across the desert to smash into the Iraqi Republican Guard were gone. Instead, just one Army division was going to sweep up the west side of the Euphrates River and one Marine division was going to do the same on the east side. For most of their respective marches to Baghdad they would be separated by more than one hundred miles and two major rivers. Behind them would come the 82nd Airborne Division and the 101st Airborne Division (AASLT), whose main job would be protecting lines of communications back to Kuwait and mopping up pockets of resistance left in the wake of the onrushing assault divisions.

When the 3rd ID crossed the border it had only three general officers: Major General Buford Blount, the division commander, Brigadier General Lloyd Austin, the assistant division commander for maneuver, and Brigadier General Louis Weber, the assistant division commander for support.

General Blount is well over six feet tall with close-cropped silver hair. Most agree the best word to describe this quiet and thoughtful man is laconic. Many find their first meeting with him a puzzling experience, and it takes some time to get used to his speech pattern. He has a habit of pausing in mid-conversation and often in mid-sentence for a prolonged period of time. More than one person has mistaken his pauses as a cue he was finished and begun to depart just when he started speaking again. And one of his brigade commanders has said of him, "Even when he is not speaking you can tell he is thinking and that something good is going to come out."

His subordinates agreed that he gave them a lot of leeway in how they got things done. His method was to give up-front intent and expect his colonels to know what to do. They were told he would be there when he thought they were doing something wrong, but if he was not present they should not interpret that as him not caring. His commanders gave him credit for being the one person during the war constantly pressing higher headquarters to be aggressive and maintain the momentum. In fact, the decisive moment of the war resulted from his push to keep moving when the situation was unclear and many of those above him were beginning to clamor for a lengthy operational pause. He convinced the wavering souls above that the enemy was breaking; to keep the 3rd ID waiting one hundred miles south of Baghdad for weeks while reinforcing divisions arrived would just give the enemy time to recover. It was Blount who forced the decision to drive on to Baghdad.

Blount came from a family steeped in military tradition: a great grandfather was wounded in the Civil War; his grandfather had been an Army surgeon in the Philippines; his own father had been a career officer, serving in the Pacific, Korea, and Vietnam. Still, Blount had not intended a long stay in the military. In 1972 his plan was to meet his two-year military commitment and then attend medical school. Two years turned into thirty and Blount, still in uniform, was being told he was going to take command of the 3rd Infantry Division, where he had served five of his previous thirty years. Upon his assuming command, Army Chief of Staff General Erik Shinseki told him that the division had been focused on peacekeeping in Kosovo for too long. He was instructed, "Get the division back home and focus them on war. You will probably take them to war before your command tour ends."

Blount spent the next year thinking and planning for war. This paid off when he saw the plans that higher headquarters had developed for the 3rd ID's operations in Iraq. That original plan called for the division to assault up between the Euphrates and Tigris Rivers, a canal-laden route inhospitable to tanks. The plan was changed only months before the war during a major simulation exercise held in Germany. Everyone present at that time now credits Blount with forcing the change that allowed the division to sweep rapidly through the desert west of the two rivers. An officer who was present said, "He was constantly selling the final plan to Vth Corps Commander Lieutenant General Wallace," much to the chagrin of Vth Corps planners who were telling the division staff to "pound sand"—the Army term for get lost. Along with their own commander, many 3rd ID officers continue to sing the praises of General Wallace, who had the tactical competence to know a good plan when he saw it and overrule his own staff.

When the war started, Blount could usually be found with his command post riding in the midst of the lead brigade. According to his division operations officer, being up front gave him a feel for the fight that superior officers mostly way to the rear did not have. When the 3-7 Cavalry was in dire straits outside Najaf and everyone in higher headquarters was saying to pull them out, Blount said, "That will send a terrible message to the Iraqis and our own troops. We are going to reinforce them." Later, when he was at the recently seized crossing site over the Euphrates, he was the first to realize that the Iraqis were on their heels and ordered his 1st Brigade to renew the attack immediately towards the Baghdad airport. The Corps and other higher headquarters were warning him against the move saying there was still trouble behind him and his lines of communications were not secure. He persisted and the airport was seized. It was this same feel for the fight that made him comfortable enough to deviate from all prior planning and order the two thunder runs into Baghdad that brought down Saddam's horrific regime. He had that intuitive feel for the right thing to do because he was constantly up forward where his soldiers were fighting.

As one officer said, "Great commanders don't decide all the time. They know when to keep their fingers out of the pie, and when they decide they made sure it was the important things with the biggest impact. Blount was a master of this."

It is said that no man is a hero to his valet. In the military the closest approximation to a valet is the general's aide, who says this of General Blount:

He was cool as a cucumber. During the entire fight I never once saw him apprehensive. When we were paused during the sand storm he showed a bit of impatience to get started again, but also knew it was a good idea to let some of our logistics to catch up. One thing that amazed me about him was that he could go without sleep forever. He was twenty years older then me and his endurance almost put me to shame. He also never worried about his own personal safety on the battlefield. He always wanted to be upfront seeing the soldiers. Four or five times we had to break contact under direct fire. I told him a number of times that the commanding general could not get himself killed. He ignored me, which caused me a great deal of personal angst for his safety.

The man General Blount trusted to make the minute-to-minute decisions was Brigadier General Lloyd Austin, a giant of a man who, if he had not become a soldier, would probably have been a great linebacker. General Blount trusted him completely and, while reserving the critical decisions to himself, he mostly left Austin to run the war. Driving from hot spot to hot spot in a small but efficient assault command post, Austin was the man who kept all the balls in the air and maintained the momentum of the fight. As one brigade commander said of him, "No matter what time of the day or night you called him, he had a constant grasp of what was going on all over the battlefield. He always knew what was available to help if I needed it and he always knew what I had available to give up if someone else needed help."

When subordinate commanders are asked to talk about Austin, the praise turns effusive: awesome, a great leader, voice of reason in the division, decisive, will talk to you anytime about anything. Austin was a constant presence for all the brigade and battalion commanders on the battlefield. When he was not right there beside them he was on the radio with them. As one commander said, "He was incredible even in the tightest situations. He was a very calming influence. When you talked to him you knew everything would be all right."

One company commander relates, "We were at the Kufa bridge after relieving an exhausted 3-7 CAV. We were under heavy fire from the enemy and Colonel Perkins and General Austin just drive up alone. General Austin just wanted to chat and see how things were going. Every time you saw Austin on the battlefield, which was often, you could just tell he wanted to be in the fight."

General Austin was the first African American to maneuver a division in combat. By unanimous acclaim he did it superbly, something the Army surely recognized, since after the war he was promoted, given command of the 10th Mountain Division, and ordered to take it to Afghanistan. There he planned that country's first democratic election. As this book is being written General Austin has been awarded his third star and has been selected to command the XVIII Airborne Corps.

Brigadier General Louis Weber had what constitutes the most thankless job in any war—he had to keep a fast-moving division supplied with food, fuel, and ammo. It was a horrendous undertaking whose story may never be justly told. As one brigade commander said, "He was the one guy in charge of supply whose head was constantly in the fight. He made everything the maneuver commanders did possible." Weber ensured that tens of thousands of tons of supplies moved along 400 miles of broken desert road and got to the combat units in time to win the fight. He accomplished this despite having less than 70 percent of the transport assets required to support a division and having to share some of his limited supply of trucks with the Marines. Logistics, though it is the most important element of war, is often overlooked because it lacks the glamor and intensity of the close combat fight. Hence, General Weber's contribution to victory has been obscured. He is truly the great unsung hero of this war. As one battalion commander said, "I was attacking and the entire battalion was almost out of fuel. I had no idea where more was going to come from when I looked up and saw General Weber setting up a massive gas station in the middle of the desert and not far from the enemy. He was CINC [commander in chief] gas stations and he was the man who kept the attack going."

All three generals made major impacts on the conduct of the war, but the real fighting in Iraq was conducted by its three brigade combat teams with their associated maneuver task forces, and these were commanded by colonels and lieutenant colonels. As we will see, the 3rd ID fight in Iraq was not a textbook division fight. Rather, it was a series of individual brigade and sometimes battalion fights, often spread out over hundreds of miles. Division's main role in each of these fights was to allocate supporting assets among the brigades and often to remove combat power from one brigade and give it to another that needed it. The direction of these fights was almost entirely left up to the colonels in command.

It is almost impossible to understand how the 3rd ID accomplished what it did without knowing a little bit about these men and their relationships with one another. The single most important thing to know about them is that they knew and trusted one another implicitly. Trust is a crucial and mostly overlooked element in modern war. It gives men courage to do what, without the support of others, they might not dare.

It is often forgotten that early in the Civil War, General Sherman became so worried about the imagined threat of massive Confederate armies swamping his department that he suffered a nervous breakdown. It took General Grant's strong influence to give him another chance and to mend his psyche. Later in the war he wrote a note telling Grant that, "all he [Sherman] had accomplished was because he knew that if he ever got in trouble Grant would come immediately to his support . . . if alive."

Every single commander in the 3rd ID knew that if he got in trouble, his brothers in arms would come with everything at their disposal to help him. After the war a company commander talked about this:

> Knowing the risks involved and knowing what may lay ahead I think there was an intangible from having worked together for six months in the desert. We took comfort and trust in knowing the other commanders would be there if you needed them. It came from working together and hearing how others handled the situations. We would know how the other guys were feeling just by hearing their voice on the radio as he was getting shot at throughout this war. The battalion commander had this unique calming effect on the radio. He could tell when you stressed and he was firm with you but lets you know it's going to be all right. I had to pick that up at the company level and let people know that getting excited wasn't going to help. Knowing that there was always someone who had your back before you started was comforting.

The three key individuals in this war were the commanders of the three maneuver brigade combat teams (BCT): Colonel William Grimsley, Colonel David Perkins, and Colonel Daniel Allyn.

Trying to sketch an outline of a commander's personality is a very difficult thing for a historian to do. Any man can often hide his true nature and character from his superiors or those with whom he has only sporadic contact. However it is almost impossible for a commander to hide from peers and subordinates with whom he is in almost daily contact—men who see him up close, enduring under the stress of combat. With that in mind we will look at these men through the eyes of those who fought with them. No two quotes below are from the same person.

COLONEL WILLIAM GRIMSLEY (1ST BCT)

"Grimsley is the most amazing officer I have ever worked for—awesome in fact. He creates an environment where you want to be part of his team and are ready to follow him anywhere."

"He fostered a command climate where it was okay to make mistakes, as long as you learned from them."

"He was out in front in every fight the Brigade had. He was very courageous, but does not fit the stereotype of a combat commander's persona. He was very humble and never sought any limelight. He was just a tactical genius who had mastered the art of warfighting and applied it on the battlefield."

"He was a very calm intellectual type. He never got hung up on details though, and he was very comfortable with ambiguity."

"He always gave me more latitude as a battalion commander then I probably deserved. He did not micromanage me. All he did was give me a mission and the tools to get it done. I will say that I love him like a brother . . . truly."

"He was always in the middle of the fight. The troops always saw him on the battlefield."

COLONEL DAVID PERKINS (2ND BCT)

"Perkins was a very practical and pragmatic commander. If something helps his ability to fight, he takes an interest. If it does not, then he does not concern himself."

"A great commander. Every time I saw him he was covered in dirt and grime and looking for ways to attack."

"He is so likeable and so intelligent that he sometimes intimidated people. He could blow you away with his intellect. It shocked all of the company commanders that this reserved intellectual was a wild man in combat. He was always up front."

"I was always on the radio telling him we could not afford him getting hit and not to stay so close to the fight. He would assure me that he was far from the danger and then I would hear his .50-caliber engaging targets."

"If there was a knife fight [slang for close combat] he always wanted to be in the middle of it. He amazed everyone with his warrior mentality. He was incredibly aggressive in combat."

"He never spoke unless he had something important to say."

"He had big balls and was always willing to take a bold but well-calculated risk."

COLONEL DANIEL ALLYN (3RD BCT)

"Simply a great commander."

"He was brilliant at quickly assessing a situation and then instinctively doing the right thing."

"He pushed the idea that if there was a chance to train for war you took it. Administrative and housekeeping tasks could always wait."

"Every interaction I had with him was positive, even if he had the right to be upset. His never-ending optimism, even under the most trying conditions, was infectious."

"He was great at listening to subordinates and getting information from lots of sources, but as soon as he thought he had enough info he would act decisively."

"If he called me to come halfway around the world to change his tires, I would be on my way before he hung up the phone. He was the best commander imaginable and I would do anything for him."

LIEUTENANT COLONEL PHILLIP DECAMP (4-64 ARMOR)

"A hyperactive guy with a great heart. He was an incredibly hard worker who often drove the staff nuts."

"He was a very smart guy with a lot of energy. He drove his staff hard and his commanders harder, but he had great people who were impossible to burn out. In the long run his battalion was a lot better prepared because he pushed them."

LIEUTENANT COLONEL JEFFREY SANDERSON (2-69 ARMOR)

"In a tough fight Sanderson is a great guy to have on your flank, unless you can have him in front of you."

"He was very demanding in holding us to standards during training. We had no idea we could train as hard as we did. We were tired and looking for a rest and he kept us going by sheer force of his will."

"He spent a lot of time working with his subordinate commanders, making us think intellectually about the upcoming fight. He seemed to have known that the war would be a long series of company level fights and made sure we were ready. He spent two or three hours every day beating the basics into us, no matter how tired we were."

"He looks like the stereotype of the southern redneck, with a slow drawl. The troops liked him because he dipped tobacco and they could identify with him. The lieutenants called him pappy. He was just a plain tough tanker and only his commanders knew an intellectual was hiding behind the façade."

"Anytime his battalion attacked, he and his tank—which he named 'darling'—was up among the first five tanks in line. A hell of a lot closer to the point of the spear than doctrine advised."

"One of the best tank commanders I have ever seen."

LIEUTENANT COLONEL JOHN CHARLTON (1-15 INFANTRY)

"He had a natural talent for being right in the thick of a fight. His offensive spirit defined how his unit fought."

LIEUTENANT COLONEL WESLEY GILLMAN (1-30 INFANTRY)

"He was a seasoned warrior and a thinking fighter. Whenever I had a mission that was very complex and required deliberate, well-thought-out operational planning, I gave it to him. I knew his plan would be detailed and that he would not accept any risk that could be dispelled by preparation. I also knew that when told to move he would execute ruthlessly."

LIEUTENANT COLONEL ERIC SCHWARTZ (1-64 ARMOR)

"He was like a father figure to the battalion. He had a strong command presence and when he spoke everyone listened. On the battlefield he was very reassuring. No matter how hard things got he never lost his cool. He had a calming effect and let me and anyone he spoke with know everything was going to be okay."

"His ability to command in battle was his greatest single virtue."

"His steadiness and inability to be rattled saved a lot of lives."

"He was a very reluctant warrior and you could easily see how much every loss we suffered pained him."

"He was just an all-around nice guy who happened to be a great combat leader."

"He was a great commander who was always calm. He was almost impossible to spin up."

"He was well liked by his subordinates and seemed always conscious of what they were going through. There was a family-like atmosphere in his battalion."

"One of the two greatest Americans I ever met. He was always calm and absolutely fearless."

LIEUTENANT COLONEL STEPHEN TWITTY (3-15 INFANTRY)

"He was a commander's commander. At times he was very hard on his staff, but it was only to ensure they provided the troops with the plans and resources they needed to win."

"He was very direct, almost always calm, and incredibly tactically competent. If he raised his voice it meant someone had screwed up badly."

"A complex person, but a great trainer and very aggressive in combat. He was not a pretty boy for senior officers, but pushed his men hard because it was what they needed."

"There are a lot of kids alive today because of his tactical performance. When I had something hard to do I called Twitty. He often did not get the glamorous tasks. In fact, he got a lot of dirty ones, but he did them all superbly."

"I found him easy to get along with. He always valued our input as company commanders over that of his staff, which may have grated on them."

LIEUTENANT COLONEL ERNST MARCONE (3-69 ARMOR)

"He brought the battalion an attitude that we will always win. It gave the unit a certain swagger."

"He's good and he knows it. If anyone was born to do what we did it was him. I would serve with him again in a heartbeat and if there was combat he is the only guy I want to serve with."

"He possessed an aggressive instinct, which is critical to combat survival and getting the tough job done."

LIEUTENANT COLONEL SCOTT RUTTER (2-7 INFANTRY)

"Tough and experienced commander. He did not have a lot of polish, but in a bar fight he would stick with you until death."

"He had an approved retirement when we got a deployment order, but postponed it rather then leave his troops as they were getting ready for a fight. That says something about a man."

"He had been in constant combat for three days and I told him I would give him 48 hours to rest and refit. Twelve hours later I had to call him and tell him 2nd Brigade needed help. Forty-five minutes later his battalion was rolling back into combat."

These are the men who will make up a big part of the story of the 3rd Infantry Division in Iraq. Judging from what their peers and subordinates had to say about them, they shared some common characteristics: they were smart, aggressive, compassionate men; they were also absolutely merciless fighters.

2

The Breach

ALL DURING THE DAY AND NIGHT of 19 March 2003, the 3rd Infantry Division's three assault battalions moved forward to their attack positions, approximately five to seven miles from the Iraqi border. Kuwaiti contractors were already busy removing obstacles on their side of the border, while engineer battalions filled in the anti-tank ditch at selected breaching points.

The assault battalions, which expected to remain in their attack positions for twenty-four to forty-eight hours, were surprised to receive orders to push their breaching teams forward before they were even settled into their new positions. The initial plan called for a full day of air attacks (A-Day) before the ground attack (G-Day) was launched. The abortive attempt to kill Saddam and decapitate the regime on the night of the 19th made that plan obsolete. Because of the complexities inherent in the massive air-tasking-order, it was impossible for the Air Force to move up the completion of its prearranged sorties. However, the ground forces were ready to go and were ordered to launch. G-Day and A-Day were reversed, and for the first twenty-four hours of the invasion the 3rd ID would rush across the Iraqi desert as the soldiers often said, "alone, naked, and unafraid."

As the bulldozers cut a dozen lanes into the berm that ran the length of the border, several batteries of supporting artillery rained close to 450 rounds of 155mm shells on a dozen Iraqi observation posts just beyond the breaching points. Ten outposts were obliterated by the sudden hail of fire, while two that survived were rapidly destroyed by 4th Brigade's Apache attack helicopters, which were up en masse to support the breaching operation.

By 2:00 A.M. on the 20th, Colonel Grimsley's 1st Brigade Combat Team had cut several lanes through the berm and was spreading out into Iraq to make room for Colonel Allyn's 3rd Brigade Combat Team to push through to Tallil Air Base. To the southwest, Colonel Perkins's 2nd Brigade Combat Team was also punching through the berm to begin its race across the desert to Samarra, almost two hundred miles distant. In all, the 3rd ID was crossing the border with ten thousand vehicles. Many of them were not part of the division at all, but were sheltering behind the division's firepower in case of trouble. Normally when a unit joins with other units, a formal relationship such as OPCON (Operational Control) is established, which gives one unit the ability to control the actions of another. In combat, this clear line of authority measurably reduces confusion and saves lives. However, most of the units rolling up to cross the border with the 3rd ID did not come under its control at all. They were just "with" the 3rd ID for protection and would go their own way whenever they desired. Commanders in the 3rd ID called these units "WITHCOM."

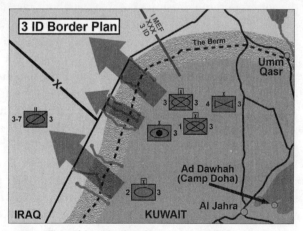

MAP 1. Breaching the border

One of them was the 507th Maintenance Battalion, which was soon to become famous when part of the unit got lost and several of its soldiers were killed or captured, including Private Jessica Lynch. Many 3rd ID soldiers dealt with this unit before it crossed the border, but its leadership structure was never clear to most. The battalion arrived at its assembly area late and seemingly somewhat disorganized. Visiting officers from the 3rd ID, noticing rusted and sand-filled weapons, wondered how equipped this battalion was for combat survival. Later they would hear that most of the soldiers who were with Lynch had been unable to defend themselves because their weapons were clogged with sand.

One 3rd ID company commander observed that an officer could not read a military map or work his GPS (global positioning satellite) device. The 3rd ID commander put in the waypoints on the GPS, but the unit nevertheless got lost. When Lynch and the others became POWs and other Americans were killed in the same ambush, widespread opinion in the 3rd ID was that leadership problems may have played a role.

It was the opposite that made possible the tremendous success of the 3rd ID over the next few trying weeks.

Only hours into the start of the invasion the breaching lanes were in near chaos. Hundreds of vehicles were bogging down in the sand, and many others already had failing engines. Lane control officers were screaming curses and doing their best to maintain order as ten thousand vehicles uncurled into Iraq. Unwilling to wait for all the chaos to be sorted out, the division's combat battalions raced towards their objectives with whatever combat power they could muster. This often meant leaving behind the wheeled supply vehicles along with other support, with orders to catch up as best they could. Forming up and advancing these units almost universally fell to the battalion executive officers (XOs), who became the unsung heroes of the advance.

For battalion and company XOs and the soldiers with them, the early stages of the advance were a nightmare. Some vehicles had to be dug out of the sand more than a dozen times before a road or track was found that could support them. Other vehicles lost rollers or broke axles on the rough terrain. Still others burnt up their engines. By the time the support columns caught up with the combat power, it was not unusual to find half the vehicles towing the other half. At every pause, maintenance teams leapt from their vehicles and began whatever emergency repairs were possible. Hundreds of other soldiers had to resort to pure muscle power to keep the advance going. The most technologically advanced invading force in history would have bogged down well short of Baghdad had not thousands of soldiers wielded shovels.

Colonel Perkins's 2nd Brigade Combat Team, split far to the west of the rest of the division, had to traverse the worst ground in the early stages of the advance. Prior to the invasion, he and his staff had given a lot of thought to terrain, and his solutions were innovative, to say the least. As Samawah, the brigade's first objective, was three hundred kilometers from the unit's starting point, and the brigade would have to make the trip over mostly open desert with only what it could take with it—no resupply was planned.

Perkins had the tremendous benefit of having been in the desert since September 2002. As the rest of the division rolled into Kuwait in the late fall and winter, he was told to "stay out of the way and go play in the sand." He took full advantage of the opportunity and in the process learned what it would take to move an armored brigade faster and farther then had ever been done before. For the next few months Perkins trained his brigade for war in ways that would have been impossible back in the States. He later said, "We were doing things that would cause a range control officer back in the States to have a heart attack and die."

Because his units had focused on gunnery before leaving Fort Stewart, Perkins spent very little time training on individual tank gunnery or other skills that are considered the bread and butter of peacetime training. As he said, "I had no worries about individual tank battles. When an M-1 meets a T-72 the result is preordained. What I wanted to train on was how to maneuver and control large formations in combat." To do this he organized massive exercises in which the entire brigade was on the move and firing weapons at the same time. All of these exercises were done with live ammo. As Perkins relates, "I had units maneuvering in front of other units that were firing over and around them. The only thing that kept us from killing each other was everyone staying alert and keeping total situational awareness. Even so, we made a lot of mistakes and learned from them. In order to do this, I had to make sure company commanders and others knew there would be no witch hunts if mistakes were made. That made them willing to take calculated risks in order to hone their units close to perfection. I wanted company commanders training to excel, not training to avoid screwing up."

In the process Perkins learned a lot about armored warfare that is not in the doctrine or taught in Army training courses. Doctrine says that the Tactical Operation Center (TOC) leap frogs as the unit advances. This is necessary because in order to be effective a TOC must be stationary and running on a continuous basis. During a leap frog, parts of each staff section jump forward while the rest remain in place to continue controlling operations. Because the Army gives each staff section only one vehicle, the part of the staff section left in place is stranded until their vehicle returns to pick them up. While training in the United States this is not a problem, because the distances involved are usually no obstacle. However, when the first leg of the advance was going to be three hundred kilometers, this method was clearly impractical. Perkins's solution was to put representatives of each staff section in each vehicle and create multiple TOCs, which would all move close behind the maneuver elements they were controlling.

To make sure he could control events even if the TOCs were down, Perkins replaced the enlisted .50-caliber gunner on his vehicle with an intelligence officer and made room in his track for a fire support coordinator and a communications specialist to handle all the radios he had added to his vehicle. Perkins and his fellow senior commanders also did something else in training that was not typical. They put commanders on the radios. As Perkins relates it, "In training, most of the status reports come from some staff officer. Even in the most realistic of training events you are much more likely to hear a staff officer on the radio than the commander. But, when people start getting killed, no one wants to hear from a staff officer. In training, we always focus on the staff process, and that puts staff officers on the net. In war, it's almost always commanders on the net. There were a lot of requests for immediate commander's assessments during the war. No one was much interested in green, amber, and red bubble charts."

The relationships formed by commanders in constant contact during training was reinforced by hundreds of post-training discussions usually orchestrated by senior commanders. This started with General Blount, who brought his senior commanders together on a regular basis to discuss and wargame various scenarios they might encounter. It continued all the way down the chain of command to the most

junior leadership levels. As one company commander said, "Lieutenant Colonel Schwartz ran a nightly university on tactics and warfighting for all of us. I learned more about how to fight in those sessions
then I had in any Army school." One major said that all that time in
the desert seemed to be one long professional discussion about war.
It was during one such discussion Perkins told his assembled subordinates, "We can end this war quickly if we put a tank on Saddam's palace grounds." It was to prove a prophetic statement.

The final result of all this preparation was trust. Commanders at
every level knew each other and trusted each other. As Perkins said, "I
knew my commanders and trusted them. When they said they could
do something, that's it. They can do it! I don't ask them if they have
enough fuel or otherwise second guess them. When Will Grimsley
got on the radio at the decisive moment of the war and said, 'I have
Objective Peach [the key bridge over the Euphrates]' I did not ask
division for a confirmation. He has Peach . . . no question. I launched
my tanks."

Perkins's time training in the desert paid other major dividends. In
particular, it told him what he did not know. He learned, for instance,
that the Army knows how much fuel an M-1 tank uses, but it did not
have a clue how much a larger formation of M-1 tanks would use. An
M-1 burns fifty-six gallons of fuel an hour, standing still or moving. But
there were no calculations for how much fuel an armored unit would
use in a long move, which would be filled with halts, detours, delays,
and possibly combat. To solve this riddle, Perkins sent his entire brigade on a one-hundred-mile road march in the Kuwaiti desert. His
first shock was discovering that the last vehicle in his huge brigade
would not cross the line of departure until seven hours after the first
vehicle moved out. In effect, the lead units would be halting to refuel
before the trailing elements even began moving. He also learned
that even though armored vehicles could move at a sustained speed
of 50 mph, the maximum speed for an armored formation was only
30 mph.

In the initial war plan Perkins's brigade was scheduled to attack
along Highway 1. His desert training maneuvers convinced him that
he could maneuver his brigade in the open desert and that his brigade
would be better employed on the left flank, to the west of the rest of
the division. There he would have plenty of maneuver space and avoid
the certain congestion that was sure to plague Highway 1, which would

be in use by most of the other division elements. He would also be out in the middle of nowhere without any support if he got in trouble. But Perkins did not care, "I am an armored brigade, what can the Iraqis do to me."

Perkins took his new scheme of maneuver to the assistant division commander, Brigadier General Louis Weber, who championed it. Soon after the new plan was approved, Perkins discovered a fatal flaw in it. He did not have enough fuel transport assets to get him to Samawah and refuel him for further combat operations. All attempts to get more fuel trucks failed, as they were critically short throughout the entire theater. In a radical move, Perkins planned to separate his tracked vehicles from their wheeled support. While the bulk of the brigade—with all of his supplies and fuel—would take a circuitous route along the only road in his sector; Perkins would take the tracked armored vehicles on a straight line march across open desert to Samawah. He named the wheeled vehicle convoy "Rock and Roll" and placed it under his executive officer, Lieutenant Colonel Eric Wesley. Perkins himself led the armored column, which he named "Heavy Metal."

As Perkins himself said, "This was not a plan that briefed well." In fact, both his own executive officer and his operations officer were against it. However, Perkins was resolved, and he took the plan to Brigadier General Lloyd Austin, the assistant division commander for maneuver, for approval. Perkins later said, "A lot of people at division headquarters were unsure. They kept asking, what about this and what about that. I did not have any sure answers for them. There were no perfect solutions. But war is about accepting certain risks. I told them I was sure of two things though; we could not carry enough fuel to get to our objective if we followed traditional doctrine, and the Iraqis had nothing that could stop an onrushing armored brigade in the open desert." In the end, General Austin signed off on the idea, and he sold it to those above him. Perkins later related that it was not an easy sell, even for Austin: "Everyone hated the idea, but they could not dispute the calculations. If we did it by the book we could not carry enough fuel to make it to our first objective. But, if we went to Samawah by sending the armor cross-country and shut down, it would save 200,000 gallons. At some point they stopped fighting the idea and said, 'You asked for it. Don't screw it up.'"

In the event, Perkins's advance to Samawah was uneventful. Lieutenant Colonel Wesley led the wheeled vehicles of Task Force Rock and Roll on the circuitous road that was often more fiction than fact, while Perkins took Task Force Heavy Metal in a straight line across the desert to his objective. At his final refueling stop, his driver was holding the hose above the tank to make sure he got every last drop. Still, it was barely enough to make it to the objective. Perkins told his brigade logistics officer that he "appreciated the finely tuned accuracy of his calculations, but to add a little extra to the margin next time."

In a swift move through the desert the 2nd Brigade had arrived outside of Samawah even before the division cavalry got there. Once there, they shut down their tanks and waited for fuel to arrive. As they waited, they watched Lieutenant Colonel Terry Ferrell's 3-7 CAV drive past them and into Samawah, where its lead elements ran head-on into a maelstrom of Iraqi fire.

3

First Clash: Tallil Air Base

(21 MARCH)

A S PERKINS RACED HIS BRIGADE across the desert, Colonel Allyn had his own travails trying to move his 3rd Brigade out of Kuwait. After struggling for two hours to move through the soft sand and mud around the border breaches, Allyn's brigade finally found room to spread out and maneuver in the open desert. Its first assault position (Barrows) was just outside of An Nasiriyah, approximately one hundred miles distant. Allyn's original plan aimed at establishing a security zone near An Nasiriyah with the brigade reconnaissance troop, which would give his commanders a chance to set eyes on the objective—Tallil Air Base. Then, sometime in the late afternoon or early evening, he would attack and seize the airbase, which was also the headquarters of the Iraqi 11th Division. In the same attack, Allyn planned to seize the bridge site over the Euphrates north of the city on Highway 1—this was part of the division's deception plan designed to convince the Iraqis that the 3rd ID was going to attack up the east side of the Euphrates River.

At 9:00 A.M., while still moving towards his assault position, Allyn received a call from General Austin telling him that, since they had not heard from their key CIA contact in Iraq—a mysterious man known only as "Bob"—the Division was slightly altering the plan. Instead of

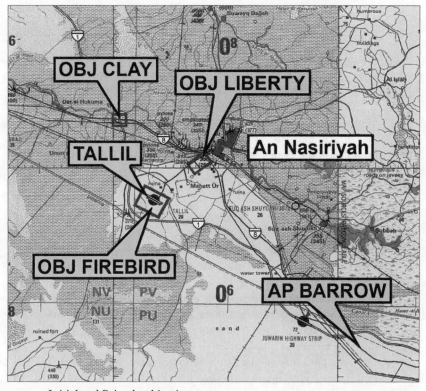

MAP 2. Initial 3rd Brigade objectives

building up combat power on the assault position, Austin wanted Allyn to attack as soon as he thought practicable—the earlier the better. While the 3rd Brigade slowly assembled within the assault position's perimeter, Allyn desperately attempted to ascertain the nature of Iraqi resistance his men would confront when they began their attack. Asked after the war about the level of intelligence received, Allyn replied, "About the same as it was the rest of the war, which was shitty." According to Allyn:

> The best picture I had was what was to my immediate front, because my recon team got out there and reported it to me. At Tallil my recon guys identified some trucks and some Iraqis that we thought were laying mines. They destroyed the trucks, and captured the Iraqis.

Previously, we got some reports that the Iraqi 11th Division was going to capitulate without a fight. We did not really believe that things would go that smoothly, but we did not anticipate the degree of resistance we encountered. As we were getting ready to go, we received a series of reports from 3rd Division headquarters in rapid succession. Each one changed the description of the situation radically.

The first report from Special Forces guys already on the ground said that the Highway 1 bridge was not defended and that the Iraqis had not prepared it for demolition. We were told that local tribes would seize the bridge without a fight and that we would walk onto the objective.

The second report that came in was that the bridge was heavily defended and that the Iraqis had rigged it for demolition and that as soon as we attacked they would blow it.

Report number three said that there was some defensive preparations in the vicinity of the bridge, and that it might be rigged for destruction. There was no information on status of the Special Forces team that had been sending these reports.

Multiple UAV flights prior to our arriving in the area near An Nasiriyah had indicated that there was not a significant defense in vicinity of Tallil Air Base. The Iraqi forces there had done no patrolling and had set up no obstacles.

Good hard intelligence on the situation at An Nasiriyah was slim, especially considering the multiple resources that the nation has at its disposal. On the ground, we did not get what we needed and we quickly found out that mass capitulation was not going to be the way things worked out.

Being pushed by division headquarters to attack as soon as possible, Allyn decided—based on what he could see of the enemy—that he could accept some risk. With only part of his force assembled on the assault position, he ordered the attack to commence. Later he said, "This was not something they would let you get away with at the National Training Center. In fact if I were facing an enemy who could maneuver competently, I would not have tried it."

The attack began late in the afternoon with Lieutenant Colonel Jeffrey Sanderson's 2-69 AR as the main effort. As the attack started, Lieutenant Colonel John Charlton's 1-15 IN was just closing on the assault position after a grueling all night and day march from the border. Allyn had also hoped to have three full artillery battalions firing in support of the attack, but the second of the three supporting artillery battalions was just arriving and the third was strung out well to the

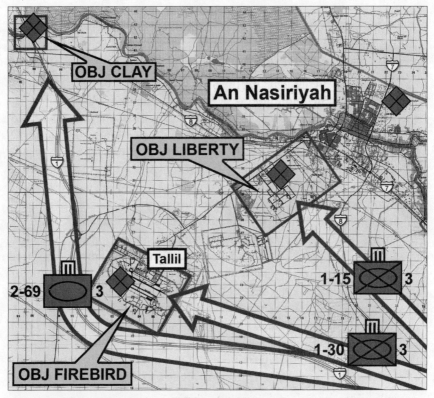

MAP 3. 3rd Brigade's assault on Tallil and vicinity

rear. Fully aware that this fragmentation was piecemealing his attack, Allyn felt he had sufficient combat power nearby so that more fire-power would be available as required.

The Highway 1 bridge (Objective Clay) was a key objective for the 3rd ID, and Sanderson hoped he could take it intact without a fight. To help him accomplish that task he had a few of what he called "special friends" (a euphemism for CIA operatives) traveling with him. One of these friends was supposedly in contact with local Iraqi dissidents, and he told Sanderson that he had bought the bridge and that Sanderson would find nothing but friendlies there. A bit later he reported that he was not sure; he continued to flip-flop on his answer. With only a few minutes left before Sanderson had to decide how 2-69 AR was going to make its final approach, he again asked his "special friend" if anyone he met on the bridge would be friendly or enemy. His special friend had no idea, and Sanderson later said that he regretted not taking a moment to do the country a service and kick the hell out of the CIA operative.

As his battalion made the final turn for the bridge, Sanderson reached for his radio and ordered his company commanders to go with the plan—see the enemy first and kill them. At the time, Sanderson was in contact with six Apache helicopters from the Division's 4th Brigade, which were helping clear the way and reporting on the enemy situation to his front. Sanderson made rapid progress as the Apaches, using Hellfire missiles, destroyed several Russian-made BMP armored vehicles just south of the bridge and dispatched an enemy infantry squad that was setting up an ambush for Sanderson's lead elements. Due to this superb aviation support, Sanderson's men made it to the bridge without meeting resistance. His tanks immediately seized the south end of the Highway 1 bridge, while his dismounted infantry busily cleared adjacent buildings. According to Sanderson: "When we got up there, we realized that the bridge was still in good shape. There was no significant contact on or around the bridge. It was dark now and I got up and walked across it and got the EOD [explosives experts] guys out to determine that it was not rigged for demolition. I also brought out some engineers to make sure the bridge had the classification necessary to cross heavy tanks."

Seeing that the bridge area appeared clear, Sanderson threw one of his companies across the Euphrates and kept it there unmolested through the night. After the war he said that he could never figure out why the Marines did not immediately jump on that bridge to continue their attack north, instead of using the one at Nasiriyah, which was secured only after a long bloody fight that left nineteen Marines dead.

As Sanderson was seizing the Highway 1 bridge, Lieutenant Colonel Gillman's 1-30 IN Battalion positioned itself to overrun Tallil Air Base, which it accomplished in short order. Capturing the bridge was vital, since V Corps planned to make the airbase a primary forward logistics base, but at the moment a more important objective stood almost directly between Gillman's battalion at the airport and Sanderson's at the bridge. The 3rd ID had named it Objective Liberty, and it was the headquarters for Iraq's 11th Infantry Division. Intelligence reported that there were between thirty-five and fifty old, but still serviceable, T-55 tanks at the objective. Since there had been no mass capitulation by the 11th Division, Allyn had to assume they were still in the fight. There was no way the 3rd ID could bypass that much combat power, which, if not destroyed, would remain a continuous threat to the division's supply lines as it closed on Baghdad. Fifth Corps had planned to launch two battalions of the 11th Attack Helicopter Regiment at the objective, but poor weather had grounded the heavy lift helicopters needed to establish a refueling point for the Apaches. Unable to ensure he could refuel his Apache attack helicopters, the mission commander had cancelled the mission.

Allyn then ordered Lieutenant Colonel Charlton to move his 1-15 IN Battalion around Tallil Air Base and occupy positions north of Sanderson's and Gillman's battalions. The dual missions were to ensure that none of the Iraqi 11th Division escaped north towards Baghdad and to destroy any unit inclined to come to their aid. Allyn planned to launch both battalions in the morning in a combined assault on Objective Liberty as well as on the hapless 11th Division. Before that, though, he wanted to make sure the Iraqis had a wretched night that would leave them drained of the will to fight. He therefore ordered his artillery support to concentrate its fires on Liberty throughout the night.

In the early phases of the 3rd Brigade's assault, the artillery had focused primarily on counterbattery fire. The plentiful Iraqi artillery in the area had already made its presence known. Though their fire was often heavy, the Iraqis demonstrated little ability to shift fire to follow the 3rd ID's maneuver units as they moved. Still, the Iraqi guns were a threat to the brigade and the follow-on units, and they needed to be destroyed. Using Q-36 and Q-37 countfire radars, the 3rd ID artillery battalions located all of the Iraqi firing positions and systematically eliminated them. Lieutenant Colonel Doug Harding, who commanded one of the artillery battalions, relates:

> We are able to mass our artillery, while the Iraqis were unable to mass theirs. They would fire a few rounds falling on what was in my estimation preplanned targets. They had very little mobility to adjust his targets. Using our much better acquisition systems and the ability to mass a huge volume of fire on a single point, we overwhelmed their guns in what was our first artillery-to-artillery duel. When we were set, we could mass three battalions on a single spot. His artillery consisted of towed guns and was not mobile. I envisioned Iraqi cannoneers would run up, pull the lanyard and then run away, because they knew we would be acquiring.

In an hour the artillery duel was over and the Iraqi guns were silenced. The 3rd ID artillery battalions turned their sights on Liberty to begin their new mission. An infantry officer describes what he saw from a position just outside of Objective Liberty:

> They pounded the crap out of Liberty. The good thing about it was the enemy was inside an enclosed area and was really feeling each shell that went off. We just pounded the snot out of them, with indirect fires, and anything that came out we shot with direct fire. It was not a good day to be inside Objective Liberty, if you were in the Iraqi army or Fedayeen forces. Early in the morning the close air support was brought in on Liberty, and it was the best I've ever seen. It was low and lethal. For a long while we had our own direct fires going in simultaneously with close air support. The Air Force dropped a bomb on a building from which we were receiving enemy fire and the building just went away. It seemed as if we were firing everything in the inventory and it was phenomenal. We went through a lot of mortar ammo and I know the artillery elements expended huge amounts of Class V [ammo] in suppressing this objective, they were the real winning edge in this battle.

While the artillery was suppressing Objective Liberty, Lieutenant Colonel Charlton prepared his 1-15 IN to attack:

> Captain Dave Waldron's tank team began moving towards Objective Liberty, trying to get in position to either accept the Iraqi's surrender or destroy them if they fought. What the tankers found gave me the first shock of the night. As soon as Waldron had line-of-sight to Objective Liberty, he discovered that the Iraqis had moved an armored force into prepared fighting positions around the perimeter. These tanks were hot spots in the thermal sights, which proved that their engines were running and they were combat ready. Waldron sent a message that was both short and sweet. It didn't need to be any longer, since everyone who heard it knew what it meant. "Dragon 6, Knight 6. Tanks! Out."[1]

With that, the fighting kicked into high gear. Charlton continues his account:

> The Iraqis in the tanks dug in around Objective Liberty never had a chance, not that B Company was planning on giving them one. As

---

1. "Dragon 6" was Charlton's call-sign; "Knight 6" was Waldron's; "Tanks" notified Charlton what was in front of him; "Out" ended the message.

soon as he sent me his short contact report, Waldron issued a platoon fire command to this lead platoon and added his firepower to the four others in his lead platoon. Less than thirty seconds after the radio call, the massive 120mm cannons on five tanks roared in unison. Firing continued for two minutes as the gunners and tank commanders traversed left and right, seeking out and destroying other vehicles dug into supporting positions around the perimeter. In less time than it takes to tell, B company had destroyed half a dozen T-62 tanks and several other armored vehicles, mostly BMP1s, as well as some trucks that were moving behind the bunkers.

As Waldron engaged Iraqi armor on the perimeter Charlton ordered the rest of his battalion to move closer to the objective. This move brought an immediate reaction as Iraqi infantry with small arms, machine guns and light mortars began engaging Charlton's advancing force. Every weapon the Iraqis possessed, including heavy anti-aircraft guns, lashed out against the Americans. Charlton picks up the action:

> At this point, every one of my companies was engaged. B Company was shooting to the northeast [towards An Nasiriyah] and to the east at forces coming out of Objective Liberty. The tank company team was shooting to the east and southeast against forces inside the 11th Division compound and on the perimeter. A Company was shooting both direct and indirect fire against the Iraqis in and around the airbase. The task force mortars were firing in support of A Company, and the scouts were hanging on the fringes of the fights, identifying targets deep inside both objectives and reporting them to me.
>
> It was during this heavy fighting in the dark of night that one of the scouts identified what he was sure was a T-55 tank. He lased the tank and determined an accurate grid. The coordinates were quickly passed to the 1-10th Field Artillery, and that unit fired the first SADARM mission of the war.[2] When the mission had fired I asked, "Did we kill it?" The scouts replied excitedly, "Damn right! Awesome!"
>
> The fighting around all three companies of 1-15 Infantry Battalion slowed occasionally during the evening, but never stopped completely. By early morning on 21 March, things had quieted down significantly,

---

2. The SADARM (Search and Destroy Armor) is a special anti-armor munition that is fired from the Paladin howitzer. It is programmed to deploy a special sub-munition that has a sensor to find enemy armor. Once the sensor identifies an armored vehicle, it directs an explosive device to send a powerful slug against the target that penetrates the vulnerable upper surfaces of the luckless tank.

but the infantrymen and tankers continued scanning their sectors nervously. The quiet did not last. As Charlton put it, "At sun up, the mice began to come out of the woodwork."

Iraqi attacks intensified as the sun rose higher. A significant amount of Iraqi Fedayeen in light armed pick-up trucks attacked out of An Nasiriyah towards our blocking positions. Just as we seen the day before, these attackers were intermingled with small groups of Iraqis, mostly from the conventional army and air force, wishing to surrender. This situation presented difficult challenges to my small-unit leaders. It was difficult to keep the two groups apart, and to differentiate between them in time to kill the attackers but not harm those surrendering.

By midmorning my task force trains had closed into the area and we were able to shuttle platoons in and out of position during the short lulls in the fighting so that they could refuel and replenish ammunition. The Fedayeen continued to attack all day and seemed most determined, often making what amounted to suicide attacks against the Bradleys and tanks of the task force.

During the fighting we sustained our first combat casualty. A scout was wounded and his HMMWV damaged by an RPG. Unable to move the vehicle to a more protected position, his fellow scouts were attempting to give him emergency treatment and extract him from the smashed vehicle while under close and accurate enemy small arms fire. Without orders, two M-113s from 317th Engineers moved into exposed position to block the enemy fire, allowing the scouts to get their wounded man back to safety.

As the fighting rose to a crescendo, Colonel Allyn called for Air Force close air support. Several A-10 Warthogs arrived and started to attack the exposed Iraqi infantry, who continued pressing forward regardless of casualties. The A-10s formed a protective umbrella over the task force. They made multiple attacks, dropping two 500-pound bombs right on target but closer than my soldiers had ever seen them drop before. The shockwaves rippled past the heavy armored vehicles and almost deafened all of us. The A-10s returned time after time, firing Maverick missiles and making low-level strafing runs with their powerful 30mm cannons.

My men were yelling support at each pass, and right before our eyes the Iraqi attack just dissolved. After the A-10s struck, the Iraqi attacks slackened noticeably. As night settled in, more and more Iraqis came forward waving scraps of white clothing, offering to surrender.

At daylight Allyn's combat battalions began to close on Liberty to finish off what remained of the enemy. Lieutenant Colonel Charlton remembers the moment:

> A lot of soldiers just stood up and surrendered, including officers. It wasn't the capitulation we had been led to expect two days before, but they were very cooperative and actually helped us find weapons caches on the objective. It was as close to an organized surrender as one can expect from a unit that had gotten crap beat out of them for two days. We even captured an Air Force general, the commander of Tallil airfield, who had valuable information for the interrogators.

As the 3rd Brigade was launching its final attack on Objective Liberty, things were heating up at Samawah—fifty miles farther up the Euphrates.

4

The Ba'ath Armies

PRIOR TO THE INVASION the 3rd ID expected to sweep aside the Regular Army forces at the border, race unopposed across the Shi'a dominated southern regions, and then crush the Republican Guard outside of Baghdad. They never expected the fanatical resistance they encountered all along the line of advance by new political armies raised since 1991 by the Saddam regime. This was a new type of threat, and it forced the 3rd ID to adapt rapidly while in combat. Before continuing with the invasion narrative, we should pause briefly to examine the origins, organization, training, and effectiveness of this new threat.

Origins

It is hard to overestimate the effects that the Shi'a and Kurd uprisings in 1991 had on Saddam's outlook; the threat of another uprising always remained his top security concern. One of the precautions he took to prevent and, if necessary, crush a future rebellion was to create private armies made up of politically reliable troops: the *Saddam Fedayeen,* the *Al-Quds* army, and the Ba'ath militia. Before the Coalition invasion Western analysts mostly argued that Saddam created these organizations to defend Iraq from external attack. Later, this did become one of their missions, as Saddam became fascinated with the success of the Palestinian *intifadas* and the American experience in Somalia. However, new discoveries indicate that the original and primary purpose of these paramilitary forces had little to do with defending Iraq from invasion. In fact, because these organizations had a dramatic effect on army recruiting and stripped the military of needed equipment, they actually had a negative impact on conventional elements of Iraqi national security. Worse still, when they eventually were committed to battle against the onrushing Coalition forces, they were obliterated in relatively short order.

The Al-Quds Army

The Al-Quds army was a regional militia created to control specific areas and, after the experience of 1991, to crush as rapidly as possible any disturbance that did occur. Its actual size could not be determined at the time of this writing, but it was likely an order-of-magnitude less than the seven million strong Saddam's advisors claimed it to be. The best estimate is that close to half a million joined the Al-Quds, but they came with widely varying degrees of commitment. They focused exclusively on defending specific Iraqi locales listed in various Ba'ath "emergency" plans. For example, the August 2002 emergency plan for the city of Kirkuk, located fifty miles north of Baghdad, described the friendly forces as including the various Governate and local Ba'ath militia commands as well as the Al-Quds force. This detailed planning document described the mission of Al-Quds "fighters" as follows:

> The Ba'ath Governate Forces Command—Al Quds, supported by subordinate troops, shall fight the enemy rebels boldly. With deep belief in the Mighty God, our forces shall achieve an earth shaking triumph on that enemy, and will prevent that enemy from achieving any despised goals. We shall keep stability and security.

The specified tasks that flowed from this less-than-specific mission statement provide a glimpse of the national security utility of various Ba'ath military capabilities:

- Defend the sector of responsibility from Al-Hurriyyah playground east to the Laylan Bridge south and prevent the enemy rebels from occupying it, no matter what it may cost.

- Protect vital establishments within responsibility limits by assigning a proper force and identifying the commandant and the assistant.
- Prevent rebels from infiltrating the town to achieve their goals.
- Maintain security and stability in town.
- Keep all possible village routes and roads under surveillance to prevent saboteurs from infiltrating the town.

One finds the same tone in contingency planning for the Al-Quds in southern Iraq, where the Shi'a represented the main threat. The commander of the Al-Quds Karbala division issued a detailed plan on 9 March 2003 for dealing with internal and external threats. His plan took the form of protecting against what he termed "agent-inspired spontaneous disorder against vital targets in order to destroy the infrastructure of Iraq and create pressures against the nation." This commander also worried that this time the Coalition might assist the rebels with "a media and psychological war meant to affect morale" and possibly "a push towards vital targets with the use of infantry supported by air force and helicopters." In response to the anticipated threats, the order spelled out the following tasks:

- Prepare alternative methods to deal with the possibility of an interruption in communication.
- Combat rumors and hostile propaganda.
- Keep the main roads open at all times and adopt flexible and effective measures if bridges are destroyed.
- Move, camouflage, and hide all weapons, equipment, and vehicles to their assigned holes. Disperse and evacuate. Move to alternative headquarters.
- Avoid using the entire force in the early stages until after the most serious threat has been identified.

As to their value as a military force in time of war, the Minister of Defense best expressed the conventional military evaluation of their capabilities: "The Quds Force was a headache, they had no equipment for a serious war, and their creation was a bad idea. The Ministry of Defense was required to give them weapons that were taken from the real Army. But the Army had no control of them. Their instructions came only from the President's office and not from normal military channels." According to another senior Iraqi general, the Al-Quds was not a serious combat force: "It never had anything to do with the liberation of Jerusalem or fighting the Zionists, and was merely another organ of regime protection."

During the war, the information system crafted by Saddam continued to pass a stream of boasts, half-truths, and lies about the abilities and performance of the Al-Quds. Because Saddam fully expected its members to fight like lions and bleed the Americans dry, no one was courageous enough to tell him the truth. A typical report from early in the war was captured by a public release from the Iraqi army general command: "A hostile force backed by jet fighters and helicopters attempted to approach the outskirts of the Al-Muthanna Governate. Our unrivaled men of the Al-Quds Army confronted it and forced it to stop and then retreat. They inflicted on it huge human and equipment losses. This included the destruction of seven vehicles of various types. Congratulations to the Al-Quds Army on its absolute victory over the allies of the wicked Zionists." That the event never happened as described was immaterial to the Ba'ath command. The report closely mirrored the stream of Al-Quds reporting throughout late March 2003. For the military high command, reality was whatever Saddam expected it to be.

However, the military advisor to the commander of the central Euphrates region presented a more realistic assessment of the Al-Quds martial spirit on the same day as the report above:

> According to the leadership, the Ba'ath party members were to fight inside the city and had built some sandbagged positions, while the Al-Quds Force was to remain outside. During my inspection I could not find even 10 percent of the 30,000 Al-Quds that they assured me were ready. When I asked where they were, I was told they were all locals and at that moment they were either at home or changing shifts—but I was assured that they would be right back. In the Al-Quds fighting positions, where I should have should have found approximately 200 soldiers, there were not even 50 present.

The reality that Saddam's inner circle refused to tell him was that the Al-Quds started dissolving as American tanks approached. By the time Coalition tanks arrived at many Al-Quds defensive positions, Saddam's vaunted warriors had vanished. As another military advisor to the central Euphrates region noted after the war: "The Quds Force numbers were not fixed. Before the war (in normal times) each regiment had 300 fighters. These numbers started dropping to zero during the war. Some were wounded in action, but most deserted." This same advisor went on to state that virtually every professional military officer in the field knew what the Ba'athists chose to ignore: "All of these Al-Quds were not prepared to fight because their commanders were civilians who had no military experience. . . . The military advisors to the Al-Quds had no role, because the Ba'ath commanders made the decisions and wouldn't listen to the advisor. But Ba'ath commanders, especially Saddam Hussein, lived an illusion. Commanders told him that we have seen millions in the Quds Army and Saddam Hussein would depend on them."

The Fedayeen Saddam

The Fedayeen Saddam is an even more interesting example than the Al-Quds of Saddam's growing infatuation with popular forces. If the Al-Quds was viewed as a part-time territorial defense force to be used in times of crisis, the Fedayeen Saddam was a permanent force tasked with a number of state security missions. Before the war, Coalition planners believed the Fedayeen Saddam was a paramilitary group with wide-ranging missions—counterinsurgency, domestic direct action, and surveillance operations. They also understood that the Fedayeen Saddam served as a backup to the Regular Army and Al-Quds in case of a local uprising. Such assessments were generally correct, but the real significance of the Fedayeen Saddam and its sometimes bizarre evolution became clear only after the war.

Saddam formed the Fedayeen Saddam in October 1994 in reaction to the Shiite and Kurdish uprisings of March 1991. As previously mentioned, these uprisings, which Saddam called the "Page of Treason and Treachery," seared the soul of the regime. Together the Shi'a in the south and the Kurds in the north revealed to Saddam the potentially fatal flaws in his internal security concepts.

- First, without external support the local Ba'ath organs were not capable of crushing an uprising by local populations.
- Second, the Iraqi army, and to a lesser extent the Republican Guard, were unable to act with sufficient speed and ruthlessness to suppress any rebellion.

- And finally, the tribes of Iraq still represented a significant threat even after more than twenty-five years of Ba'athist pan-Arabic, socialist indoctrination.

As with the creation of the Al-Quds, Saddam moved rapidly to create other military capabilities to prevent a recurrence of the 1991 rebellion—even at the risk of further weakening Iraq's military capabilities to defend against an external attack. The fanatically loyal Fedayeen Saddam was the perfect tool to ensure that any future revolt would be rapidly crushed. A growing challenge that drove Saddam to expand the powers of the Fedayeen Saddam was maintaining civil order as the effects of the United Nations sanctions began to unravel the social fabric of the nation. While many in the West may find it difficult to understand how criminal groups could function effectively in a police state, the tribal culture of Iraq made the formation of secret criminal gangs an easy and often lucrative enterprise. After 1991, criminal gangs became involved in a burgeoning black market. The gangs were growing steadily in power, influence, and, above all, riches. It is ironic that while the Fedayeen Saddam was charged with controlling a growing lawlessness, its members were also heavily involved in large-scale criminal activity.

It would be easy to view the Fedayeen Saddam as a particularly ruthless state police force, but that would be a mistake. According to Fedayeen Saddam planning documents captured by the Coalition, the mission of the Fedayeen Saddam was to protect Iraq "from any threats inside and outside." To accomplish this mission, the Fedayeen Saddam was to defeat any enemy, defined as whoever sought to sabotage, destroy, or threaten the safety, security, and sovereignty of Iraq, whether from inside or outside, including those involved in the following activities:

- The destruction of Iraq's economic environment.
- Smuggling and forging.
- Spying and being agents.
- Corruption in the armed forces.
- Spreading negative rumors.

Meticulous Fedayeen Saddam records listed numerous operations conducted in the decade after the creation of the Fedayeen Saddam:

- "Extermination operations" against saboteurs in Al-Muthana.
- An operation to "ambush and arrest" car thieves in Al-Anbar.
- The monitoring of Shi'ite civilians at the holy places of Karbala.
- A plan to bomb a humanitarian outpost in Irbil, which the Iraqi secret police suspected of being a Western intelligence operation.

The Fedayeen Saddam also took part in the regime's terrorism operations, which they conducted inside Iraq, and it at least planned for attacks in major Western cities. In a document dated May 1999, Saddam's son and Fedayeen commander, Uday Hussein, ordered preparations for "special operations, assassinations, and bombings, for the centers and traitor symbols in London, Iran, and the self-ruled areas [Kurdistan]."

In the final months before Operation Iraqi Freedom, the Fedayeen Saddam began actively planning operations against the Coalition, including suicide missions aimed at crossing into Kuwait to "explode volcanoes under the feet of the invaders," if Coalition forces were to reach Baghdad. While it appears that they never crossed into Kuwait, a number of Fedayeen Saddam suicide attacks did take place during the war.

Equipping and training the Fedayeen Saddam was a priority mission for the regular Iraqi Army and for the fast-growing bureaucracy of the Fedayeen Saddam. The organization also became a hobby for Uday Hussein when he was not running Iraq's Olympic Committee or the Iraqi Youth Union. Saddam's support and Uday's involvement ensured that the Fedayeen Saddam remained near the top of the priority list for men and materiel. Thus, it became just one more organization sapping the strength and morale of the regular Iraqi army and focusing the security energy at the internal threat.

Fedayeen Saddam's training focused primarily on small arms, small-unit tactics, sabotage techniques, and military surveillance and reconnaissance tasks. The Fedayeen Saddam also became a primary consumer for many of the "niche" military capabilities that proliferated throughout the regime. One such project was the Iraqi Intelligence Service's "Division 27," which supplied the Fedayeen Saddam with silencers, equipment for booby-trapping vehicles, special training in the use of certain explosive devices, special molds for explosives, and a variety of explosive timers.

An M-1 tank crushes insurgent suicide vehicle south of Baghdad.

The only apparent use for all of this Division 27 equipment was to conduct commando or terrorist operations. The Military Industrial Commission also got into the business of supplying—or at least promising to supply—the Fedayeen Saddam with a surprising array of special capabilities. According to a December 2000 memorandum, these capabilities included specially armed helicopters, unmanned aerial vehicles, and specially modified fishing boats capable of firing rockets with a range of ten to twenty kilometers and torpedoes in international waters.

Beginning in 1994, the Fedayeen Saddam opened its own paramilitary training camps for volunteers, graduating more than 7,200 "good men racing full with courage and enthusiasm" in the first year. Beginning in 1998, these camps began hosting "Arab volunteers from Egypt, Palestine, Jordan, 'the Gulf,' and Syria." It is not clear from available evidence where all of these non-Iraqi volunteers who were "sacrificing for the cause" went to ply their newfound skills. Before the summer of 2002, most volunteers went home upon the completion of training. But these training camps were humming with frenzied activity in the months immediately prior to the war. As late as January 2003, the volunteers participated in a special training event called the "Heroes Attack." This training event was designed in part to prepare regional Fedayeen Saddam commands to "obstruct the enemy from achieving his goal and to support keeping peace and stability in the province."

Less than a month before the start of the war, the Directorate of General Military Intelligence's Special Mission Unit took charge of the training of a group of Fedayeen Saddam volunteers. They were to form "small kamikaze combat groups, equipped with weapons, and munitions suitable for use behind enemy lines and on the flanks, . . . causing additional damage in the enemy's armor and helicopters." The volunteers attended a condensed thirty-day course, which included physical training, weapons training, planning, map reading, recognizing enemy weapons, using communications devices, military engineering, combat in rough conditions, and swimming. The course was topped off with a practical exercise. Assuming this group started training in the first week of March 2003, some of them were undoubtedly available to test their new skills against the U.S. 3rd Infantry Division during its "Thunder Runs" into the heart of Baghdad.

Not atypically, corruption soon worked its way into the Fedayeen Saddam. Despite regular showers of cash, on-the-spot bonuses for successful missions, educational benefits, military privileges if injured, martyr privileges if killed, and free land just for volunteering, a number of Fedayeen Saddam still joined the growing underground economy. In 2001, reports surfaced that members of the organization were smuggling weapons to the Saudi border for cash and establishing roadblocks in order to shake down travelers unlucky enough to be caught on the roads.

These failures of discipline elicited a strong response from the regime. After all, the Fedayeen Saddam was the regime's private army —therefore Saddam expected it to possess the highest standards of personal honor and virtue. Beginning in 1996, harsh penalties, in some cases resembling the harshest examples of Sharia (Islamic) law, became the norm for the Fedayeen Saddam. These punishments included amputating hands for theft, being tossed off towers for sodomy, being whipped one hundred times for sexual harassment, stoning for various infractions, and cutting out tongues for lying. Given the mixed missions, it was only a matter of time until military failure also became punishable as a criminal offense. In typical Iraqi bureaucratic fashion, a table of specific failures and the punishment to be meted out was created and approved. In 1998 the Secretariat of the Fedayeen Saddam issued the following "regulations for . . . an execution order against the commanders of the various Fedayeen":

- Any section commander will be executed if his section is defeated.
- Any platoon commander will be executed if two of his sections are defeated.
- Any company commander will be executed if two of his platoons are defeated.
- Any regiment commander will be executed if two of his companies are defeated.
- Any area commander will be executed if his Governate is defeated.
- Any Fedayeen Saddam fighter, including commanders, will be executed if he hesitates in completing his duties, cooperates with the enemy, gives up his weapons, or hides any information concerning the security of the state.

It is no wonder that the Fedayeen Saddam often proved the most fanatical fighters among the various Iraqi forces the 3rd ID faced during its march to Baghdad. On numerous occasions, Fedayeen forces hurled themselves against the division's armored formations rushing past the southern cities of Samawah, Najaf, and Karbala; they finally even tried to bar entry into Baghdad itself, long after the Republican Guard had mostly quit the field. In the years preceding the Coalition invasion, their leaders became imbued with the belief that the spirit of the Fedayeen "Arab warriors" could overcome rapid maneuver and precision fires that were the major attributes of American military doctrine.

In the event, they were wrong, and the Fedayeen proved totally unprepared for the kind of war they were asked to fight. The 3rd ID killed them by the hundreds and then thousands. As one officer in Perkins's 2nd Brigade stated, "They were curiously tenacious. At times they just kept coming, seemingly from all directions. They were like gnats, only to be swatted by an armored brigade."

5

Samawah: We Planned a Parade

AS COLONEL ALLYN'S 3RD BRIGADE began its fight at Tallil, Lieutenant Colonel Terry Ferrell led his powerful 3-7 CAV Squadron on an end run around the airbase and through the desert to Samawah. The 3-7 CAV, which traced its lineage back to Custer and the Battle of the Little Big Horn, was a unique squadron. It was not part of any the 3rd ID's maneuver brigades and instead was part of Colonel Potts's 4th Brigade (aviation). The unit was designed to operate on its own, whether forward of the rest of the division or as a screening force on one of its flanks. Since such missions often meant that the 3-7 CAV would be on its own, it possessed considerably more organic firepower than the average combat battalion. It was a mix of M-1 tanks and Bradleys. It also had its own dedicated artillery battery and a troop of armed Kiowa helicopters. However, because the unit was never intended to fight in cities, it lacked infantry who could dismount and clear buildings.

Ferrell's immediate mission was to seize two bridges over the Euphrates River about two miles west of Samawah (Objective Saber) and a canal bridge approximately three miles north of the river (Objective Pistol). After securing these, Ferrell planned to send forces into the city and secure two more bridges over the Euphrates that were within the city (Objective Gatlin). The corps and division plan

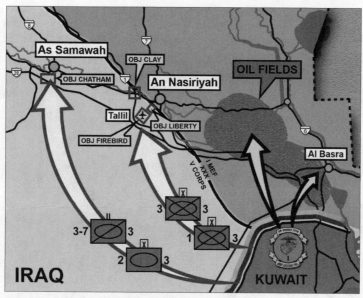

MAP 4. Overview of initial 3rd ID plan

then called for 3-7 CAV to cross the Euphrates and continue its attack
up the east side of the river until it reached Objective Saints, just south
of Baghdad. From there, Colonel Perkins would eventually launch the
thunder run that brought down Saddam's regime. It was a bold plan
designed to convince the Iraqis that 3rd ID's main effort was coming
up the east side of the Euphrates, whereas in fact most of the division's
striking power rushed through the open desert on the west side of the
river until north of Karbala.

     In effect, Ferrell would be alone on the east side of the Euphrates
in hopes of attracting the Medina Division and the rest of the Republican Guard to him, so that General Blount, with the 3rd ID's main
combat power, could drive uncontested into the Republican Guard's
rear. For an indefinite period, his single squadron would be the only
Army unit on the ground actually locking horns with the Republican
Guard. To even the odds, General Blount planned to give Ferrell first
priority on Multiple Launch Rocket Systems (MLRS) and more air
support stacked overhead than he could use.

     That was in the future. First, Ferrell had to accept the surrender
of Samawah, greet the local officials, and perhaps organize a quick
parade to impress the locals. At least that was what he had been told

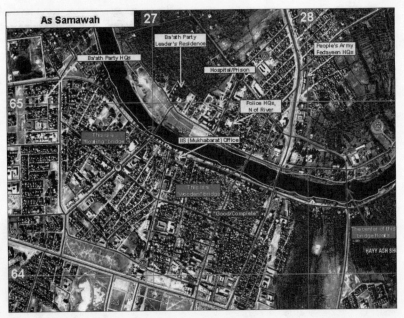

Aerial view of As Samawah

to expect. Before the war Ferrell had been told that all he would find in Samawah was an untrained brigade of militia with small arms and maybe some RPGs. They were not expected to put up much of a fight. It was much more likely, he was told, that the local Shi'as would revolt and kill or expel regime loyalists from the city. Ferrell was informed that he could expect to find thousands of Iraqis along his route waving small American flags, courteously supplied to them by OGA personnel (OGA stood for Other Government Agencies and was a thinly disguised term applied to CIA agents, whom Lieutenant Colonel Sanderson had termed his "special friends"). As he approached Samawah, Ferrell found the information that his own "special friends" supplied him with as worthless as had Sanderson found it.

The first thing Ferrell's soldiers saw as they reached the outskirts of Samawah was Lieutenant Colonel Schwartz's 1-64 AR Battalion parked in a large depression. The 1-64 AR was the first part of Perkins's 2nd Brigade to reach Samawah after their 160-mile race across open desert. They had paused, waiting for their logistics to arrive with fuel so they could continue on to Objective Rams, 70 miles to the north. As the 3-7 CAV soldiers passed the parked 1-64 AR tanks, they noted that many of the soldiers were sleeping or conducting maintenance. They appeared totally unconcerned about an enemy threat in Samawah. For the 3-7 CAV troopers this was a good sign: how bad could the resistance be in Samawah if the 2nd Brigade could bed down just a few miles away and remain unmolested. Just maybe there would be handshakes and a parade after all. By the time 3-7 CAV found itself locked in a life-and-death struggle in Samawah, Perkins and the awesome power of his armored brigade had finished refueling and was heading north. The 3-7 CAV was on its own.

The introduction of this book covered in some detail 3-7 CAV's first contact with the enemy at Samawah. That first bloody engagement will not be recounted here, except to say that Sergeant Johnson's and Sergeant Broadhead's ferocious fight woke Ferrell and the rest of 3-7 CAV to the reality that they were in for a hard fight in Samawah. Plans for a parade would have to be cancelled.

As 3-7 CAV rolled up to its objectives, it had no trouble seizing the bridges, but it then immediately came under heavy Fedayeen attack. Fights similar to those Johnson and Broadhead fought were occurring throughout the 3-7 CAV's sector. Moreover, the Iraqis had begun to engage with heavy artillery and mortar fire. Without counterfire radars, 3-7 CAV could not engage in an artillery duel like the one that silenced Iraqi artillery around Tallil. Instead, they counted on the squadron's Kiowas to find and engage enemy artillery with rockets.

The small helicopters flying at altitudes anywhere from ten to thirty feet off the ground did their best to engage targets invisible to troopers on the ground. Besides fighting in a city, for which they had not trained, the 3-7 CAV pilots had to adjust to an enemy who did not fight according to the rules. As Captain Kara Bates, Commander, E Troop, relates:

> We came up and started providing early warning for C Troop. That was our mission, to cover them so they could go and seize the bridges. We were continuously engaged by RPG fire, AK-47s, and sometimes they would even shoot at us with mortars. With our maneuverability though, only one aircraft sustained damage, and it was able to make it home and got back in the fight within an hour. Despite the heavy fire, we were able to provide continuous coverage to the guys on the ground.

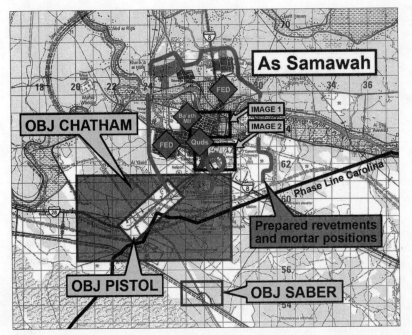

MAP 5. Samawah objective locations

We were able to destroy some Iraqi elements, but our biggest contribution was providing suppressive fires that kept the Iraqi's heads down so the ground elements could move in and destroy whatever was shooting at them.

The Fedayeen were using civilians to protect themselves, and we quickly understood that our enemy did not look like soldiers. They were dressed like civilians, and they intermingled with the civilians, especially women and children. We had to adjust to that. Multiple times we saw the enemy actually holding a person in front of them as they shot at C Troop. Another thing we saw constantly was civilians waving white flags, acting like they were going to surrender. But when they got close to any of our positions, someone behind them would pull out an AK-47 and start shooting. We saw this in every area of the city. Consistently we'd see people that looked like they were surrendering and we'd go in for a closer look, we would see a major weapon system, ammo caches, and well-armed personnel behind them. The armed guys would engage from behind the guys still waving white flags.

I don't know. There were probably people who were genuinely trying to surrender. Some of them were not. We would engage and destroy the fighters and what caches we could without engaging the guys waving white flags. They were probably Fedayeen, but we did not engage them, because we could not be certain. We did destroy the weapons.

As his troopers engaged hundreds of fanatical Fedayeen, Ferrell tried calling General Blount to let him know the true situation. When he finally reached division headquarters on his satellite TacSat, Ferrell told them, "There is not a goddamn flag anywhere in sight, but there are artillery rounds and small arms going off all around us." Blount called Ferrell a little bit later, and Ferrell filled him in on his situation. For the first time Blount learned that the biggest threat 3rd ID would face between Kuwait and Baghdad was not the conventional threat the division was superbly prepared to take on. "There's no tanks, there's no BMPs, there's no one in uniform," Ferrell told him. "This is nothing like we planned to fight. I mean, there are a lot of guys running around in pajamas, using women and children as shields to move from building to building." Blount took it all in, but for the moment he had nothing to offer in the way of help.

After considering what to do next, Ferrell decided to push farther into Samawah in order to conduct his primary mission of crossing the Euphrates and attacking up the east side of the river. He was just about to order the squadron to move forward when the Iraqis launched a SCUD missile from the center of the city, which streaked off to the south. He reported the missile launch, and Vth Corps in return informed him it was going to destroy the enemy missile site with an ATACMS (surface-to-surface missile). Ferrell had no interest in keeping his men anywhere near where an ATACMS, with it massive warhead of thousands of smaller munitions, was about to impact. He ordered most of his forces to pull back from positions they had seized inside the city but to keep them under observation.

Three hours later Vth Corps informed Ferrell that they had cancelled the ATACMS. Corps had decided that it did not want to fire such powerful munitions into the heart of a densely populated city. It was a humane and probably correct decision, but it did allow the Iraqis three hours to retake and then fortify their lost positions. Throughout the wait for the ATACMS strike that never came, the Iraqis continued to engage with mortars and rockets. In one galling move, they repeatedly reinforced their positions by using ambulances, which brought up fresh Fedayeen by the dozens. This continued all day long, and there were heated arguments among some of the junior troopers

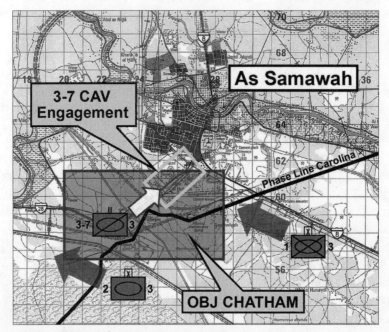

MAP 6. 3-7 CAV attacks Samawah

about whether they should destroy these ambulances. Sergeant Broad-head ended the debate by telling them that as long as a vehicle had a Red Crescent on it, they could not fire on it. But he also told them to "feel free to kill anyone who left the vehicles carrying a weapon."

Late that night, CIA operatives working in the city linked up with Ferrell's troopers and provided the location of the Fedayeen head-quarters. They ordered Ferrell to destroy the building immediately, but at this point in the war Ferrell was not about to blow up a building in the middle of the city without checking with Division. A small argu-ment broke out between the head of the CIA team and Ferrell about who was in charge at Samawah. The CIA operative told Ferrell that he was told by his leadership that he was in charge, that he had been in the area longer, and that he still had the contacts in the city. Ferrell reminded his new "special friend" that he was the one with the tanks, and then he ignored him. As Ferrell waited for instructions on what to do about the Fedayeen headquarters, he ordered his aviation ele-ment to put eyes on the building and confirm that it really was a mili-tary headquarters. After a five-hour wait, Ferrell received permission to destroy the building. A combination of hellfire missiles fired by his helicopters and three JDAM's dropped by circling F-15s then obliterated the building.

As Ferrell pressed the fight at Samawah, Colonel Grimsley's 1st Brigade was already passing through Allyn's positions near Tallil. Grimsley planned to use Highways 8 and 28 as his brigade rushed north towards Baghdad. He was not expecting any delays enroute. Like other 3rd ID units, the brigade expected to conduct a tactical road march from Kuwait to its first contact with the Republican Guard. Two small engagements along the way, in which his scouts suffered light causalities, caused some concern, but Grimsley saw no reason to alter his original assumptions or plans. At the small town of Al Kindr, south of Samawah, townspeople had even emerged from their homes and frantically tried to warn one of his leading elements that there was a Fedayeen ambush ahead as the CIA had promised. However, with no translators available to tell them what the locals were saying, the soldiers just waved back, smiled, and walked right into the ambush. Luckily, the first RPG missed the leading Humvee, and the American reaction to being shot at was overwhelming. The battalion history relates: "Heavy machine gun fire broke the silence as every gun in the lead unit opened fire on the Iraqi positions, and did not stop until someone shouted over the radio, 'They're dead.'"

Because Kindr was a major choke point along Highway 8—the key logistics route for the division's further advance—Grimsley ordered the 2-7 IN Battalion commander, Scott Rutter, to leave a company there to secure the town. Captain Robert Smith's Alpha Company remained behind, while the remainder of the brigade headed north to Samawah. By the time the company received orders to rejoin the brigade, it had killed nearly a dozen Fedayeen and captured more than fifty. It was also two hundred miles away from its parent unit and out of radio contact. Smith led his company across the desert alone, borrowing gas from other units along the way; he rejoined the brigade just before its final assault towards Baghdad.

While Captain Smith dealt with the Fedayeen in Kindr, the rest of his parent battalion continued north to Samawah. Grimsley had been listening sporadically to Ferrell's battle reports, but he was uncertain how heavily Ferrell was engaged. Since he had heard nothing from Division about Highway 8, which ran through Samawah, Grimsley continued moving half his units in that direction. The remainder, led by Lieutenant Colonel Marcone's 3-69 AR, moved along Highway 28 and bypassed the Samawah fight. From the beginning, Grimsley had planned to stop at Samawah to refuel and possibly give his soldiers a short rest. He aimed to use that halt to develop the situation and change plans if required. Sticking with his original plans, Grimsley ordered Lieutenant Colonel Rutter to seize the southern edge of Samawah and begin refueling operations. Things went wrong almost immediately.

Captain James Lee, commanding 2-7 IN's Bravo Tank Company, missed a turn and headed straight into the middle of Samawah. Both Grimsley and Rutter watched their Blue Force Trackers in horror as the company headed straight into the city. Visions of another "Blackhawk Down"[1] scenario raced through everyone's mind. Tanks unsupported by infantry in the narrow streets of an ancient city rated high on the list of every commander's nightmares. According to the 2-7 IN's unofficial history:

> The enormous M-1 tanks found themselves wedged into narrow avenues and side streets. Lieutenant Colonel Rutter frantically ordered Captain Lee to turn his unit around, which was easier said than done. Lee was reporting that the streets were filling up with men in uniform armed with small arms, RPGs, and machine guns. RPGs slammed into the sides of the company's armored vehicles with deafening explosions, but left only small black marks on the armor, while the small arms rounds made no impression whatsoever.
>
> Unsure of the rules of engagement, Captain Lee asked for instructions. After checking to make sure there were no 3-7 CAV units in the area, Rutter ordered Lee to engage the crowds swarming around his vehicles. The armed mass of men had grown bold because the tanks had not engaged so far, so the ensuing machine gun fire caught most of them in the open and slammed into them with terrible impact. Those not killed in the initial bursts of fire scrambled to find shelter from the now overwhelming American fire. With the armed Iraqis momentarily suppressed, Captain Lee managed to maneuver his element through the narrow alleyways and streets back to the missed turn.

When Division decided that Highway 8 was still too dangerous to be used as a movement route north, Rutter and other 1st Brigade

---

1. "Blackhawk Down" refers to the now-famous 1993 battle in Mogadishu in which eighteen Rangers were killed and eighty-four were wounded.

elements were ordered to skirt the southern edge of the city and continue north.

General Blount was not happy. Reports that 3rd ID units on Highway 8 were being fired on surprised him. He had interpreted Ferrell's report that he had secured his objectives to mean that resistance had ended. His call to Ferrell to discover what was going on was so angry that Ferrell believed the general was on the verge of relieving him of his command. But after a two-day fight without rest, Ferrell's emotions were also close to the surface. "I told him," Ferrell noted later, "I never reported the route was secure. All day I have been reporting that I am in heavy contact, but not once have I said the route is secure. I own an intact bridge and I can cross it at will, but I will cross it under fire."

The unexpectedly heavy resistance at Samawah forced Blount to change his plans. Calling Allyn, he ordered him to leave a battalion to secure Tallil until relieved by the Marines and to take the rest of his 3rd Brigade north to isolate Samawah.

Colonel Allyn moved almost immediately with the 1-15 IN and 2-70 AR Battalions. By the time they arrived, the bulk of the 3rd ID combat units had skirted the city and were heading for Objective Rams. Allyn, who had expected to be heading north with them, was ordered by Blount to contain all of the bad guys in their towns and cities in order to secure the division's several-hundred-mile line-of-communication (LOC). It was a thankless but critical mission, as without secure LOCs the division advance would grind to a halt well short of Baghdad. Soon after receiving his mission, Allyn found himself stripped of a significant portion of his combat power, when Division ordered 3-7 CAV to continue its advance north and the 2-70 AR to move to secure Objective Rams. Having already giving up Lieutenant Colonel Sanderson's 2-69 AR to the 1st Brigade, Allyn now had the task of securing 250 miles of front from Fedayeen attack with one under-strength brigade. In a similar situation, most commanders would have opted to dig in around key points and await enemy developments. Allyn was not like most commanders. Determining that the only way to secure such a large area was to keep the Iraqis off balance, he launched a continuous series of attacks at targets the Iraqis were sure to defend. The "Battle of the LOCs" was about to start. For the 3rd Brigade it would rage without letup until the 82nd and 101st Airborne Divisions relieved Allyn's troops almost a week later.

6

Battle of the LOCs

(22–30 MARCH)

ON THE MORNING OF 23 March, Lieutenant Colonel John Charlton, Commander, 1-15 IN, had just completed his mission at Tallil and was en route to join Perkins's 2nd Brigade for the assault on Baghdad when he received a call from Allyn with a change of orders. He was a bit chagrined to be told that instead of participating in the great assault on the Republican Guard, he was to head for Samawah to relieve 3-7 CAV. Because the entire division was now detouring around Samawah, the going was slow as Charlton's column wove in and out of halted units and often had to move cross country or use narrow canal roads. Charlton used the military shorthand "cluster-fuck" to describe the situation on the roads.

Going ahead of the column, Charlton was able to link up with Ferrell on the outskirts of Samawah, where Allyn soon joined them. After a quick situation briefing, Allyn decided on a plan that was to have momentous consequences for the 3-7 CAV. Calling General Austin, he advised Austin to cancel 3-7 CAV's feint up the east side of the Euphrates. The original plan rested on the assumption that the 3rd ID would not meet any serious resistance along the way. The fight at Samawah had disabused everyone of that notion. At this point, Allyn was also worried about 3-7 CAV being able to carry sufficient fuel and ammo to sustain itself if it got into another big fight, because resupplying them on the other side of the river, with hostile forces along the route, was problematical at best. Later that day, after checking with Blount, Austin ordered the 3-7 CAV out of the line in order to rearm and refuel. Once its resupply was completed, the unit was to move up the west side of the river with the rest of the division.

From Charlton's point of view the conference was disappointing. All he really learned was that Ferrell's squadron had run into large numbers of Fedayeen armed with small arms, mortars, and RPGs. He did not learn where they were or in what numbers. As the meeting ended Charlton knew only that there were a lot of bad guys in the city and he was to make sure they did not get out. By this time his executive officer was arriving with the rest of the battalion, which was strung out in a long column behind him. Charlton asked Ferrell if he had anything else to say, to which Ferrell replied, "Well, at least we have not been hit with artillery."

At that moment, what Ferrell called the most accurate artillery barrage the Iraqis fired during the war ranged up and down the entire

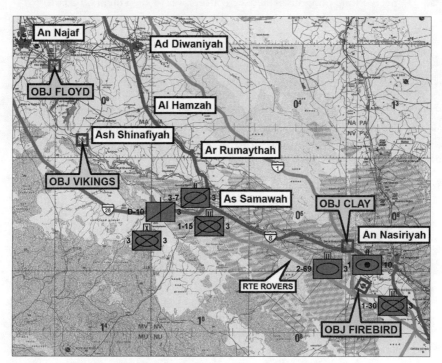

MAP 7. The line of communications (LOC) from Najaf southward

1-15 IN column, inflicting several casualties in an ambulance. Charlton considered it an inauspicious beginning for his new mission.

As Charlton's companies moved into positions that would provide a good view of the city, they noted something interesting. Every
time they moved into a new position, the Iraqis would mass substantial combat power and attack them. Unfortunately for the Iraqis, the
battalion's three-day fight at Tallil had made them experts in this kind
of fighting, and the massed firepower of the battalion's Bradleys and
M-1s broke each successive Iraqi attack. However, the Iraqi reaction
to Charlton's movements allowed him to develop a plan to contain
the Iraqis in Samawah and away from the hundreds of fuel and ammo
trucks sweeping past the city. As Charlton commented after the war:

> After noting that, if we went anywhere, the Iraqis would come and
> attack, we split the city into eight zones and designated attack by fire
> positions within those zones. My plan was to put combat forces into a
> zone and establish an attack by fire. The enemy would either come to
> us and be destroyed or we would use the zone to launch attack on sus-
> pected Iraqi positions. The basic concept was to keep them off-guard
> by being in one zone part of the day and shift to another zone later.
> We were showing them a lot of different threats and making them
> react. They seemed certain we were trying to find a way into the city
> and were determined to keep us out. I wanted them so busy doing
> that they had no time to think about coming out themselves.

Learning from a captured Iraqi officer that there were a number
of Fedayeen, including their leaders, gathered in northeast Samawah,
Charlton planned to move into the nearest of his designated zones
and destroy them.

> My scheme of maneuver was to use the city's rail line to move into
> position and find out if there was any enemy in the area. Once we con-
> firmed that the enemy was where we were told they were, we would
> destroy them.
>   The rail line usually served as a good means of moving, but on
> this day the sandstorm from hell struck. Visibility went to zero and
> it became tremendously hard to move. There were a lot of buildings
> and rail cars we had to maneuver around in the middle of a sand-
> storm. The sandstorm was so blinding that we had to use Blue Force
> Tracker to identify the location of buildings along the way. The rail
> line helped keep us oriented, but we were moving almost blind.

After waiting two hours in position there was no let-up in the storm and no enemy contact. Since there was no activity and we could not see anything, I decided to bring everyone back to the assembly area. As we moved back, the sandstorm grew worse. It became difficult to move even along the rail line, and we were forced to move up to the highway, which we habitually avoided so as not to telegraph our movements to Iraqi observers. The enemy must have gotten word we were moving down by the train station, and, true to form, they were coming to attack us.

Two technical vehicles came straight by us on the highway. They obviously were not expecting us to be there, and in the limited visibility they could not, at first, tell we were Americans. They were moving at a high rate of speed down the road, and the first one went by so fast I couldn't really tell what it was. The second one came by and I got a better look at it. I could recognize guys in the back with RPGs. What made it interesting though was that, as the vehicle went by, one of the guys in the back waved to me. It was a nice friendly wave, but I still radioed the Bravo 2-69 commander and told him he had two enemy vehicles coming at him fast and to engage. No sooner had I said this than all hell broke loose as tanks and Bradleys opened fire. They managed to destroy the two vehicles and all the personnel, but it was a pretty unnerving moment because you couldn't see anything.

Such fighting typified the 3rd Brigade's war until 29 March, when elements of the 82nd Airborne relieved them of responsibility for Samawah and most of Iraq south of Najaf, which was soon to be transitioned over to the 101st Airborne Division. The brigade had fought an enemy fundamentally different from the one they had expected, but they had made the necessary adjustments and destroyed every Fedayeen unit that had the temerity to try their luck against them. Under almost impossible conditions the 3rd Brigade had kept the Fedayeen away from the division's lifeline and thousands of tons of fuel, food, and ammo went forward unmolested. By the time the 3rd Brigade was relieved, the 1st and 2nd Brigades were 150 miles to the north, rearming and refueling as they waited out the sandstorm and prepared for the final lunge.

Blount and Austin now ordered the 3rd Brigade to move as rapidly as possible to join the division in the attack. In the middle of the sandstorm, Colonel Allyn loaded his tanks on transports and took his brigade north.

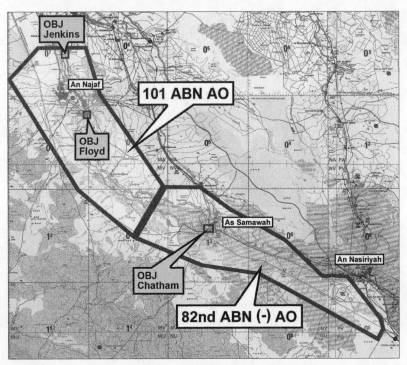

MAP 8. Airborne troops assume the battle of the LOCs

As they left their positions near Samawah, neither Allyn nor Charlton had any idea of the impact their operations had had on the enemy, particularly the Iraqi high command. Their policy of not taking the cities, but rather launching a series of feint attacks, paid a massive unexpected dividend. As a result of this tactical approach, Saddam became convinced he was winning the war.

Thus even as Allyn began his move north, and Perkins and Grimsley prepared their respective Brigades for the final assault, Saddam had his diplomats deliver quite a remarkable message to the French and the Russians: he asked them to cease their efforts to secure a ceasefire. He was winning the war, and he wanted more time to humiliate the Americans. A remarkable conclusion, but one totally justified when one understands Saddam's image of the battlefield situation.

7

Objective Rams

(22–23 MARCH)

AFTER GETTING HIS HEAVY METAL task force across the desert to the outskirts of Samawah, Perkins had ordered the tanks to shut down; then they settled in to await his fuel trucks. As he waited, he watched Ferrell's 3-7 CAV enter Samawah and heard the initial reports of the fighting within the city. However, that fight was not Perkins's mission. He was focused on his next objective far to the north—securing Objective Rams.

Lieutenant Colonel Schwartz's 1-64 Armored Battalion was the first of Perkins's units to finish refueling; Perkins immediately ordered it to begin its seventy-mile move to Objective Rams. Rams itself was just a massive piece of desert real estate southwest of Najaf. Because of its hard surface and easy accessibility, the Vth Corps had selected it to be the main logistical base for supporting the final push to Baghdad. The corps also planned to place its headquarters there as soon as it became practical. In the immediate future, though, the corps leadership desired Rams as a secure position to fuel and arm the Apache attack helicopters of the 11th Attack Helicopter Regiment, which was planning to conduct a deep attack and to begin attriting the Republican Guard's Medina Division before the 3rd ID barreled into it.

Intelligence had confirmed to both Schwartz and Perkins that they would find Rams unoccupied except for some civilian workers and

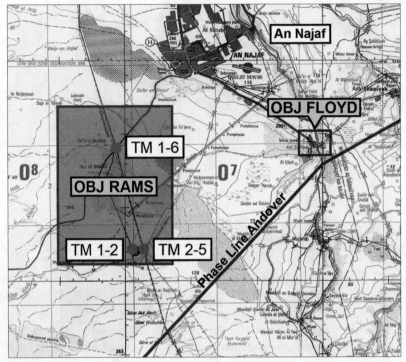

MAP 9. Objective Rams (showing company objectives)

local Bedouin herdsmen. Accepting that the intelligence was accurate, Schwartz approached Rams in a single column. Moreover, many of his tanks were towing other tanks, which had broken down during the march. Knowing he would need as much combat power as possible when his unit confronted the Medina Division outside of Baghdad, he was loath to leave behind any vehicle in the surely vain hope that it would catch up later. He was expecting at least a full day of rest at Rams to refuel and conduct maintenance on broken-down vehicles before the final push to Baghdad.

Up to this point 1-64 AR had traveled several hundred miles without engaging any enemy forces. That was about to change. Like 3rd ID units fighting at Samawah, the 1-64 AR was to discover that the Iraqis were prepared to offer fanatical, and often suicidal, resistance.

Schwartz wanted to arrive at Rams while there was still daylight. So, as his column moved down Highway 28, he ordered his combat elements to increase speed from 25 mph to 45 mph. With Captain Scott

Woodward's brigade recon troop leading the way, Schwartz expected to roar on to an undefended Objective Rams with an hour or two of daylight left for establishing his positions and preparing for possible Iraqi counterattacks. According to Colonel Perkins,

> The significance of Rams is that this is where my brigade was going to come in, occupy it, and then pass the 1st Brigade through. The 1st Brigade would continue on up to Objective Raiders, and we would follow behind. So, this is really the first time since the division crossed the line of departure that the brigades would be coming together. We were not planning to have a major fight at Rams. This was a tactical assembly area where we would refuel, re-task, organize, and continue on up to Objectives Spartan and Raiders. From there, we would eventually launch the attack through the Karbala Gap, across the Euphrates, and into Baghdad.

Instead, Rams turned out to be what Perkins called "a pretty substantial fight." Unknown to his intelligence briefers, the Iraqis had built a small airfield on Rams and the local Ba'ath officials and Fedayeen commanders were convinced it was a prime target for an air assault by helicopters or paratroopers. To fend off this expected attack, they had positioned a significant number of dismounted troops throughout the area. After the war Perkins commented, "We were not expecting to find any defenders, but on the other hand they were not expecting to face tanks."

The brigade reconnaissance troop, commanded by Captain Woodward, was the first unit to approach Rams, and it immediately made contact with four Iraqis guarding a communications tower. In matter-of-fact terms Woodward related, "It was our first contact. We engaged those guys and continued to move." As the recon troop continued on to the objective, Woodward's lead platoon reported that they had stumbled on a roadblock consisting of a couple of trucks parked on the road with dismounts around them. Because there were civilians in the area, and the persons at the roadblock were wearing civilian clothes, Woodward didn't think anything of it. But as his platoon moved closer to the roadblock, they started taking fire from a half-dozen Iraqis behind the trucks. Woodward's men returned fire and noted a white pickup truck heading towards them from the east. To the recon troopers it looked like just another civilian truck, so they remained cautious about firing on it. Unmolested, the truck drove up to the road block and dropped off more Iraqi soldiers, who immediately joined the fight. Woodward later related this version of the rapidly developing fight:

> We were getting fired on from two directions by people dressed in civilian clothes, which we learned later were Fedayeen militia. We engaged them as well. We needed to take out the roadblock and continue to move, because our mission was to clear Objective Rams of any enemy. But I could not see what was behind the roadblock, because of the way we were situated on the approach. So I made the decision to stop where we were, continue to observe, and call the brigade for help. They sent 1-64 up here. It's a good thing they did that, because once 1-64 went over the high ground, they made contact with a lot of bad guys.

Schwartz was listening to the reports of the initial contacts, and when he heard they had engaged a white pick-up truck he was sure his recon soldiers had made a terrible mistake. One of his missions on Rams was to link up with a Special Forces (SOF), or Long Range Recon, team inserted into the vicinity days before. This unit was also supposed to have white trucks. Fearing a blue-on-blue engagement, Schwartz worked his staff to make contact with the SOF team or at least find someone who knew their present location. Eventually, he learned the SOF team was dug deep into a hole and out of the way.

In the meantime, Schwartz began receiving better intelligence from Captain Woodward about what his troop was facing on Rams. That convinced him that a real fight was developing. Mentally forming a battle plan as his armored battalion continued to advance in column, Schwartz reached for the radio. "Guidons, guidons, battle orders to follow."

Every company in the army has a small pennant-like flag or "guidon" that it brings out for unit formations, and it is usually carried by a soldier standing directly behind the company commander. By calling for guidons, Schwartz was using shorthand to make clear he wanted his company commanders to listen closely. When each company commander had responded in sequence, Schwartz gave a brief update of the situation and his immediate orders, using company nicknames, "Guidons, this is Rogue 6. Wildbunch, your task is to destroy in order to prevent displacement of the enemy. Rock, tie into Wildbunch to destroy with a secondary task to exploit. Cobra, your task is to secure the long range recon element and destroy dismounts in the vicinity of the engagement area, then tie into Wildbunch's west flank. Dawg, you're the task force reserve with a task to exploit."

As one company commander said long afterwards, "We all understood our mission on Rams. It was simple—destroy. We did not hesitate. We did not slow down. We went right on into Objective Rams and started to execute our combat mission."

For most of the soldiers in the 1-64 AR this was their first combat experience. Not surprisingly, in the initial moment of contact there was sporadic hesitation, as caught in this telling exchange when a young lieutenant called Schwartz.

> LIEUTENANT: People are shooting at me . . . instructions?
> SCHWARTZ: Kill them.
> LT.: They are dressed in civilian clothes.
> SCHWARTZ: Are they shooting at you?
> LT.: Yes.
> SCHWARTZ: Kill them.

Schwartz later noted that his soldiers needed only a bit of direction. "As soon as I said kill them, they unleashed on the enemy force that was there. Then I think everyone else understood the seriousness of what was going on." (In an interesting aside, Army psychologists two decades earlier had interviewed large numbers of combat veterans and asked them what was the most important factor in their being able to engage and kill the enemy. Overwhelming, they replied, "Being told by a superior authority to shoot and to kill.")

C Company was the first 1-64 AR company on the objective. Its commander, Captain Larry Burris, relates the next phase of the action:

Upon reaching Ram, we identified a couple guys in civilian clothes to the east. We definitely pursued those guys and I dismounted one infantry platoon, to clear three buildings in the vicinity of the pump house. They didn't find any troops in there, but they did find a pretty good-sized weapons cache.

While that was going on, Cobra Company moved farther north toward the processing plant and were met with some RPG and small arms fire. We were directed to move further north to assist in that fight. I left the platoon that was still clearing buildings where they were and took my tank platoon and a mech platoon north. When we got to the plant, I kept the tank platoon in overwatch, while I took the mech infantry platoon into the plant and began clearing it. As my infantry was dismounting, most of the Iraqis present took the opportunity to surrender.

While we cleared the plant, Cobra continued farther north about 2 kilometers and came into contact with numerous RPG teams firing from a bunker and berm complex, and I took my tank platoon further to the north to assist Cobra. When we got there, Cobra's commander told me that we needed to go around the right-hand side of him and come up on their flank. As we did so, we ran into some canals and came under RPG fire. We finally found a crossing site and maneuvered the tank platoon into an L-shape adjacent to Cobra.

It was just starting to get dusk, but we could identify the guys in the light and see the technicals [Toyota pickups] dropping guys off. We attacked the trucks with the 25mm high explosive rounds and I don't think any of us realized exactly how devastating they were until we actually saw them hit individuals and they'd basically disappear.

Approximately an hour or an hour and a half after it got dark, these guys continued to drive up with their headlights off, thinking we couldn't see them. They would dismount in groups of eight to ten folks and they would just walk around, standing straight up. Lieutenant Colonel Schwartz said we would wait until they were in our range and then absolutely just mow them down. It was a little bit like a turkey shoot with the technological advantage we had over these guys.

First Lieutenant Ed Panetta, a platoon leader in C Company, describes other aspects of the same scene:

They were all oriented west towards Cobra right in front of my platoon, so we started firing at them. We were shooting .50-caliber and main gun rounds. It was a turkey shoot. These guys had absolutely no idea what was going on. They were in a total panic. It was total chaos for them, especially once the sun went down. We could identify guys in our thermal sites with their hands on each other's shoulders trying to reposition themselves on the battlefield; mostly they were just walking around in circles. It was hell on earth for those guys and I felt that they couldn't possibly want to fight any more. I said, "Let's give them a chance to surrender." We gave them about five minutes without firing on them to see if they would give up. They didn't surrender. Instead they kept firing and trying to do buddy rushes as they tried to maneuver on us. After about five minutes of taking fire, I was like, "Okay, let's finish them off." After that, it was open season on these guys. We just tore them apart.

Two thousand years ago Josephus wrote about the wearying but incredibly realistic training the Roman legions endured: "Their exercises were bloodless battles and their battles were bloody exercise." Like thousands of others in the 3rd ID, the 1-64 AR soldiers were rediscovering the ancient truism that units really do fight as they trained.

For the 1-64 soldiers, the battle so resembled previous training exercises that the killing almost became methodical. A sampling of comments from postwar interviews suffices to show a pattern that appeared not only at Rams but in virtually every other major engagement the 3rd ID fought:

> These guys were like stick-looking targets. We'd just gun them down. With the trucks, it was the same thing. For us, it was a really good feeling knowing all our training started to pay dividends.
>
> It was a very weird feeling to get up here and come on line. As I looked around, everyone was down in the hatches. Everyone was engaging. It looked like a Table 12 scenario.[1] I talked to a platoon leader afterwards and he said it was like a training event, as if we were at a gunnery range and shooting targets. But every time an RPG round would hit the tank or rounds would skip off it, you would get knocked back into reality—you were being shot at.

The Iraqis also fought exactly as they had trained and had been ordered to fight. From prisoners Schwartz later learned that an Iraqi general had marched them out onto Objective Rams and swept his hand around the area he told them they would fight on. After he left, junior officers took many of the men to their assigned positions and painted a circle around them. Each soldier was told that he was expected to fight to the death from his assigned circle. Once this was done, the officers left for Najaf, and only the sergeants remained to keep the men in place. Against hopeless odds and deserted by their officers, many of these soldiers fought as ordered. In the morning, 1-64 AR soldiers found dozens of Iraqis dead inside their circles.

At Rams the Fedayeen proved as fanatical and brave as they had at Samawah and were to prove in future engagements. Though they possessed no conception of U.S. technological capabilities and were woefully unprepared for their assigned tasks, the Iraqis continued their attacks on the 1-64 positions throughout the night. In doing so they died by the hundreds and maybe thousands. These suicidal attacks at times unnerved the 1-64 soldiers, who could not fathom their purpose. According to A Company's commander, Captain Himes:

> The thing that was really the weirdest through the night was that the enemy did not seem to understand that we had night vision scopes.

---

1. "Table 12" or "TT XII" designates the standard scenario for platoon gunnery exercise, usually accomplished at the unit's home station.

We would engage these guys, and hit our intended target and the guy that was just next to him would drop down and hide for a couple minutes. Then he'd get right back up and keep walking at you. They just didn't seem to understand our night vision capabilities.

That made you feel a little bit unnerved. It seemed as if they must have had a plan. We kept checking our rear and our flanks, thinking maybe these guys were trying to distract us. We spent all night trying to figure out what they were trying to accomplish by moving toward us.

They kept walking toward us. They knew where we were, because we were firing at them, but they didn't understand that we could see them clearly every time they got out from behind a berm or out of a ditch.

Some of the junior officers began to pity them, and wondered why they did not just give up.

It seemed as if they didn't realize how good our night sight was because they just stood up and started walking toward you and stuff. They were acting like they couldn't be seen. Since they couldn't see us, they figured we couldn't see them. They kept bringing more and more troops and dropping them off. The trucks came, we identified them and we destroyed them.

They really had no clue what was going on. I can imagine the kind of havoc that we created for those guys by destroying all their trucks and killing them the way we did. There were mortar rounds dropping all over them. The 25s on the Bradleys were all over them. It was pretty terrible for those guys. I'm sure they had no clue what was going on. No way in hell.

I got the mortar platoon on the radio and did a call for fire. About a minute and half later, eight mortar rounds came crashing in. We found out later there were about twenty to thirty Iraqis there, and when the rounds hit I saw a bunch of white spots and specks flying all over the place. These guys were literally just standing around waiting to get shot. I could see caches blowing up. I could see guys running around. Some were crawling across the ground trying to get in a position to attack us.

Twenty minutes later, there were two more Iraqi platoons in the exact same spot. We called for a repeat of the mortar mission. The new bunch of Iraqis had moved right in on top of their own dead and died in the same place. The discipline of these guys was amazing.

So it went throughout the night. The Iraqi's never let up in their determination to close with and kill as many Americans as possible.

For the brigade commander, Colonel Perkins, the fanatical resistance his lead battalion confronted at Rams was somewhat of a shock. Like Schwartz, he initially thought that his troops were accidentally engaging civilians. But as battle reports streamed in, Perkins realized there was a determined enemy ahead with whom his forces had to deal. His first action was to order most of the brigade off the road to make way for the artillery, which was moving up to positions from which it could range Rams with supporting fires. After that "interesting exercise," he informed Division headquarters that, until further notice, U.S. forces could not use Rams as an assembly point or logistical base.

Until daybreak, Perkins remained busy coordinating close air support and artillery strikes that often had to be fired within danger-close range of his own men. He could not help being proud of his men. They had stumbled into an unexpected fight and, although for almost all of them it was their first taste of combat, they were behaving like seasoned veterans. As he listened to various radio nets, he found himself awed by how fast his troops went up the combat learning curve for this kind of fight: "They would watch the Iraqi's move forward and begin to congregate—thinking they were invisible to us in the dark. When enough of them had gathered, a gunner would fire an MPAT [multipurpose anti-tank] round and get them all with one shot. Gunners learned this on their own, and it spread like wildfire. For a few minutes all you could hear on the radio was 'Let them gather.'"

By dawn, Perkins had also managed to move more of the brigade's maneuver combat power up onto Rams, and he was able to secure Highway 28 with two battalions—one on each side of the road. Although his battalions were still fighting on both sides of the road, Perkins considered the corridor secure enough to allow 1st Brigade to pass through. He called Colonel Grimsley to tell him to come on through.

As soon as Colonel Grimsley's 1st Brigade had passed through Rams and headed on to the great escarpment and their next objective (Raiders), Perkins followed with two battalions. He left Schwartz and 1-64 AR in place to secure Rams and isolate the city of Najaf.

8

The Escarpment

(23–24 MARCH)

PERKINS'S 2ND BRIGADE WAS STILL fighting off repeated Fedayeen attacks as the lead elements of Grimsley's 1st Brigade began to close on his positions. The 3rd ID plan called for Grimsley's brigade to pass through Perkins on the way to Objective Raiders, northwest of Najaf. There he would rearm and refit in preparation for the rush to Baghdad. As Grimsley moved up to Rams, however, he found himself listening to reports of heavy fighting ahead, and he became unsure whether the original plan was still workable. He was also troubled by how spread out his brigade had become, due to traffic jams and intermittent engagements with Fedayeen forces, particularly around Samawah. Some of his logistics units were still trying to fight their way through traffic as far back as Tallil Air Base. Grimsley knew that if he ran into a hard fight, he would have only Lieutenant Colonel Marcone's 3-69 AR Battalion with which to fight it.

As he approached Rams, Grimsley received word that Perkins's battalions were holding open a corridor for him. Grimsley had hoped to pause at Rams long enough to refuel, but with fighting still going on throughout the area, he wanted to take advantage of the corridor while it was still secure. With Marcone's soldiers in the lead, the 1st Brigade barreled through Rams and on to the first significant geographic obstacle the division faced—the escarpment.

The Najaf escarpment is a 100-meter tall, sheer cliff face that extends for several hundred miles, offering no way around it and precious few ways through it. During planning exercises the engineers had considered the escarpment more formidable than the Euphrates and spent countless hours analyzing its makeup and potential routes through it. The only roads going through the escarpment climbed at a slope of 14 percent. To put this in context, interstate highways in the United States have warning signs posted whenever the slope exceeds less than half of what the 3rd ID would have to ascend. Route selection was critical, because the route chosen would serve the combat brigades and would also become the division's main service route (MSR), over which every ounce of supplies would travel. The final engineer assessment of the problem concluded, "The choke point created by the escarpment was severe, limiting maneuver to a one-vehicle defile, and was a perfect place for the enemy to ambush the division's combat power and trains."

In his prewar analysis of the problem, Grimsley had concluded that there were only two practical alternatives: go through Najaf or follow a narrow defile about a mile north of the city. He ruled out Najaf because no one wanted to offend Shi'a sensitivities by attacking one of their holy cities. (Later Fedayeen attacks would make such an assault unavoidable.) By selecting the second route, Grimsley avoided Najaf's urban sprawl but placed the brigade perilously close to one of the holiest Shi'a cemeteries.

Initial intelligence estimates, which 3rd ID commanders were learning to discount, suggested that Grimsley would not face significant resistance at his chosen point. "We really thought the only enemy up there was an air defense unit placed to defend a giant ammo plant just north of the escarpment. That was all we planned for up there, and we assumed Iraqi positions were riveted on the escarpment ridge line itself. We did know that Najaf was filled with Al-Quds and Fedayeen. But because Najaf was a hotbed of Shi'a insurrectionism, we had assumed that they were there to enforce internal stability and not to fight us."

As Grimsley pushed through the 2nd Brigade, an alarming report came across the division radio net. Air Force pilots reported Iraqi armor moving south, towards the exact point the brigade planned to move up the escarpment. Grimsley now had a dilemma.

Perkins's boys have fought through Rams, fought off a Fedayeen battalion, and now had established position on the north side of Rams,
close to the escarpment. I am getting ready to move into contact, but
until now I had no reports of anything up on the escarpment itself,
except possibly the air defense unit we always expected. Now all of
a sudden I am hearing the Iraqis are getting armor reinforcements.
For a few minutes Dave [Perkins] and I debate back and forth, if he
should just continue on with his lead battalion, or whether I should
go ahead as planned.

Ultimately he [Perkins] pressed Schwartz's 1-64 AR battalion out
a little further along the northern edge of Rams so they could give
me some direct fire coverage as my guys climbed the escarpment.

By "my guys" Grimsley meant Lieutenant Colonel Rock Marcone's
3-69 AR Battalion, which almost immediately began ascending the
steep road. Ahead of him 1-41 Artillery's guns were laying a heavy
smoke screen, while Coalition air power pounded the plateau. During the course of the day, Air Force, Marine, Navy, and Royal Air Force
pilots all took turns destroying Iraqi positions and forcing the Iraqis
to keep their heads down while Marcone's soldiers closed for the kill.
As Grimsley relates: "We flew the CAS [close air support] up there in
designated kill boxes along the escarpment and they start providing
reports. At first they are all A-10s. These guys fly along the road and
as they get close to the escarpment they start reacting to Iraqi contacts
on the left and right all the way down the ridgeline picking target up
and killing stuff for us. They were literally opening a breach for us.
They essentially opened the shoulders at the top of the escarpment
and gave us a hole to bolt through."

Racing at top speed, Marcone's first armored vehicles broke over
the top of the ridge and began splitting into small combat teams of
two tanks, two Bradleys, and some engineers. Fanning out like the
spokes of a wheel, each of these teams moved forward to expand the
safe distance around their penetration.

At the top, Grimsley learned that the reality behind most of the
reports of Iraqi tanks he had been receiving was "a whole host of these
truck-mounted air defense systems and other stuff on the back of flat-
beds." According to Grimsley, "Everything the Air Force saw moving
with a gun tube on it became a tank." Still, both Grimsley and Marcone found themselves startled by how much firepower they were facing, and the Iraqis were being reinforced by the minute. Grimsley
knew there was a major ammo depot at the top of the escarpment,

but not that it also served as a Fedayeen training center. The Fedayeen had used the ammo bunkers and local caves to fortify their positions. Now, with Grimsley's soldiers pushing over the top of the escarpment, the Iraqi hornets' nest stirred. The 3rd ID soldiers found themselves on the receiving end of small arms, mortars, RPGs, and even heavy artillery fire.

Spotting the Iraqi mortar positions, Marcone dispatched a company to silence them. "Dave Benton's guys rolled down to the east and knock out all the mortar positions that were trained on the road. His tanks pretty much raced up to our assigned limit of advance, killing everything in sight. They destroyed the mortars, but also killed a lot of trucks pulling anti-aircraft guns, artillery pieces, and all kinds of other stuff."

To silence the Iraqis firing from caves and revetments throughout the area, Captain Todd Kelly dismounted his infantry and began clearing the rough terrain along the edge of the escarpment. Under the cover of artillery and close air support, Kelly started clearing out the dug-in Iraqi positions on both sides of the breach. According to Grimsley:

> Kelly started knocking out entire Iraqi squads hiding in revetment positions and bunkers. He was using the 25mm HE on his Bradleys for suppression as his infantry moved position by position. He told his other guys to just recon by fire on suspected and likely positions. He had guys trolling with 25mm while he brought in artillery on the far side of the Iraqi position, to keep them isolated from help. We used the CAS guys, who were hitting unbelievably close to our forward elements. As the infantry maneuvered, Kelly pounded the Iraqis with his vehicle's main guns and advanced his armored vehicles almost on top of the Iraqi positions, in order to draw fire away from his infantry. As the armor advanced they made contact with the remainder of the Iraqi air defense vehicles and killed them.

For First Lieutenant Michael Flynn, the executive officer of A Company, 3-69 AR, the battle at the top of the escarpment was up close and personal.

> At that time, my tank and 3-2 tank set up positions and began to engage the enemy right away. Because of the heavy Iraqi fire I ordered the company trains out of the area. A Hemmet fueler got stuck in the soft sand, where the crew abandoned it and got out of dodge. Because we needed that fuel the first sergeant took some

soldiers, moved forward, secured the area and got the fueler. He got it out of the sand and drove it away while under fire from an enemy ambush.

We continued to fight there for approximately an hour. At the time, we were a good distance from the rest of the company and out of radio contact. Eventually, a platoon from our company moved south of us with the company commander. They helped us stabilize the situation off the road. The company commander moved with the mech platoon toward Najaf and ran into twenty-five to thirty enemy soldiers. The mech guys destroyed them and continued to move south.

By the time we linked up with the rest of the company, the tanks were critically low on fuel. We backed out of there, refueled and went to link up with the rest of the battalion, already approximately 15 kilometers to our north. On the way we ran into Iraqis, who immediately opened up on us. They were trying to destroy the tank and seemed to be going after the loader. A lot of RPGs hit the tank at the same time and there were a lot of crew-served weapons firing at us. The top of my tank was all messed up, and then they actually hit my loader in the chest with an AK round. He was hit just to the left of his heart, but fortunately he was wearing his vest with the plates. It knocked him back in the hatch, but all it did was throb at the time.

I continued to have my gunner engage the enemy while I checked him out. At the same time, we had mortars falling all around us within about 25 meters. The other tank was also being shot up, but I was about 200 meters in front of him, so I was the focus of their fire at that time. Once my loader was hit, I decided we needed to back up so I could do a better check on him. We backed up 200 to 300 meters—out of effective small arms range for them—and I checked out my loader. It turned out he was unhurt. He just had a bad bruise the next day, but it wasn't as bad as I had feared. After I checked him out, a crew-served weapon began firing on us. I had to load a tank round in order to take out the bunker he was hiding in. Immediately after that, my loader was back in his hatch, returning fire with his machine gun.

Everything just went crazy up there. When they first opened fire, I thought, "I can't believe these guys are shooting at me." But we returned fire immediately, just like we'd been taught to. After we pulled back 300 meters, we were out of the effective range for them, but from that range we could pick them off. What really surprised me was they were light infantry and they were trying to maneuver on tanks. They were using people's houses, farms, ditches, and large berms—anything they could find to let them get closer to us. One group actually snuck up within 100 meters of us, but my loader spotted and took care of them.

They continued to move toward us for quite a while. They were very determined, but not very competent. I found I could engage them without getting anywhere near them. As soon as they'd move closer with their crew-served weapons, I would back off to where they couldn't use them any more, but I'd still be able to engage them with coax, and .50-caliber.

By this time, Grimsley's major concern was the Iraqi heavy artillery that continued to shell the top of the escarpment. Because it was so erratic, Grimsley assumed the Iraqis were firing blind and had not pre-registered their targets. However, with the rest of the division setting up to crowd in behind his lead elements on the top of the escarpment, they had to be silenced. Unfortunately, the brigade's counterfire radar was broken, so Grimsley had to count on the Air Force to spot the muzzle flashes as the guns fired—an almost impossible task.

To help them, Grimsley's artillery men went out and did things the old-fashioned way. "The artillery guys went out and did crater analysis to figure caliber and direction, and then we did a little templating and figured out where they were and established kill boxes. Giving the Air Force a box to look in made it possible for them to find many of the Iraqi guns and destroy them. The others were wiped out when we sent tanks into the kill boxes."

After two hours of hard fighting, most of the fight had gone out of the Iraqis. Except for the odd pickup truck filled with fanatics rushing headlong to their deaths from inside Najaf, all that remained were what more and more of the 3rd ID soldiers were beginning to call "the knuckleheads." "After a while all we are running into are all types of knuckleheads. They will fight or shoot a couple of rounds up to the 100-meter mark. But as soon as our infantry get within 100 meters of them, and they start feeling very effective fire, they just quit and start surrendering."

As the fighting died down, Grimsley brought forward his next battalion and sent it on to Objective Raiders, where he planned to assemble the remainder of the brigade and give it time to rest and refit before the final hard push. Marcone's 2-69 AR stayed behind to secure the objective as the division's combat power and logistical support rolled through. As darkness fell, he faced a new kind of enemy, an enemy with which other 3rd ID forces in Samawah and southern Najaf were also becoming intimately familiar. Grimsley relates:

> While I have some elements consolidating on Raiders, Marcone stayed on the escarpment fighting probes from every direction. It was amazing how many ways they came up with to come at him. First, it's a mounted reconnaissance, then it's dismounted reconnaissance, then it's these guys driving out of Najaf in pickup trucks. Most of the time they headed directly for some nearby quarries where the ground is all chopped up by mining gravel. They had a lot of mortars and ammo cached out there. So a pickup truck of knuckleheads, or ten taxis full of them, drive full speed out of Najaf and disappear out there in the desert. Eventually, they scurry into the quarries, hook up with some mortars, lob a few rounds, and scurry back. Other times they'll form little ambush parties and go attack something.

Even as Marcone's men were engaging and killing as many of these infiltrators as they could, he had to call Grimsley for instructions on how to deal with one contact for which his training had not prepared him.

> Marcone calls me and says, "Hey I've got all these women out here all along the marshes along the Euphrates. They want to police up the dead bodies. What should we do boss?" I said, "Well, I think we should let them," and I said, "Question them. Use your linguist," and it turns out that the men they are policing up are not their husbands or loved ones. They kept saying, "We don't know who they are, but the Fedayeen are holding our families." They were told to pick up the Fedayeen dead, and their families were being held hostage until it was done.

Even as the Iraqi women retrieved fallen Iraqis, the battle raged along the escarpment. As the 3rd ID armored forces moved about on the plateau they came under heavy fire: they began to realize that the Iraqis had devised some ingenious low-tech methods to overcome their inability to see in the dark. As one company commander explains:

> One of the things we learned was they'd use women to build huge fires. We first saw them building them at dusk. From a distance you could tell they were women from the long hair, and there were children around. When we were dealing with the men, there were no children around. When we hit these certain areas, the bonfires would be lit and as soon as that happened, we started receiving fire.

One of my platoons was moving up and when they hit a certain point the bonfires went up. About two minutes later, we'd start taking mortar and RPG fire from the village. They were shooting from quite a distance without effect. Since one of my rules of engagement at the time was not to engage unless we were threatened, we did not return fire.

By dawn the battle of the escarpment was over, except for random mortar fire coming out of Najaf. Even as the fight was raging, huge amounts of the division's combat power had filed through the escarpment to consolidate at Objectives Spartan and Raiders. Marcone's weary soldiers were preparing to join them when word arrived that significant Iraqi reinforcements were heading for Najaf and would cross the Euphrates at a place called Al Kifl.

9

Ambush Alley

(24–25 MARCH)

LIEUTENANT COLONEL TERRY FERRELL pulled his 3-7 CAV out of Samawah early on 24 March, and after consolidating on the town's outskirts he was ready to move north by noon. Since he was out of radio range, the division G-3 (operations officer), Lieutenant Colonel Pete Beyer, sent him his new objective coordinates by text message on Blue Force Tracker. Beyer apparently intended to have Ferrell move to his new objective along the same route the rest of the division had followed, which was now known to be clear of the enemy. However, with only a grid coordinate to his supposed destination, Ferrell assumed he was supposed to take the most direct route, which ran along the Euphrates. This route made sense to him for another reason, as he still had the mission of deceiving the enemy as to the division's true intent. By moving along a route far removed from the rest of the division, he would continue to confuse the Iraqis about where the main attack was coming from.

As far as Ferrell knew, his mission upon reaching his new objective would be to position his squadron for an attack to the east of Najaf. To do so, he planned to establish a screen east of Najaf to block reinforcements into or evacuations out of the city, while the division's main body prepared their attack into the Karbala Gap. In effect he would be mimicking the operations Allyn's 3rd Brigade was conducting to the south. Division planners still hoped that, by maintaining continuous pressure on Najaf, Ferrell's operation would continue to serve as part of the corps deception plan, by portraying the main attack as still coming along Highways 1 and 8.

After a hasty analysis of the mission and route, Ferrell gave verbal orders to reorganize the squadron and to move out. He would be moving along a single road with his A Troop (Apache) leading, B Troop (Bonecrusher) following, and then the squadron artillery battery. His trains, which took longer to prepare, would follow later, escorted by C Troop (Crazyhorse). Ferrell wanted to get on the road with as many daylight hours left as possible and close on his new position before midnight. Once there, his exhausted troopers could rest before beginning combat operations in the morning. Many of them had been awake for four days and in contact almost continuously for the past two days.

By 3:00 P.M. the squadron was on the move. Despite the fanatical willingness to fight that the Iraqis had demonstrated in Samawah, Ferrell still expected an uneventful road march. But as he said, "The enemy got a vote on that issue." For the first six hours Ferrell got what he expected—no contact or delays. His soldiers were alert but becoming more relaxed as each hour went by without contact. As they approached a small town, Apache Troop's lead platoon leader, First Lieutenant Matt Garrett, commented that the Iraqi landscape was beginning to look like Florida. As they passed a mosque that looked like a popular restaurant in Orlando he commented on the radio, "Hey look, we really are in Florida, it's Middle Eastern Times," which was immediately followed by, "Oh, shit!" as small arms fire slammed into his vehicle from both sides of the road.

As Ferrell later noted, "We had walked directly into a textbook-perfect ambush. They were hitting us from the front and both sides of the road all along the two-and-a-half-mile length of my column." The Apache Troop commander, Captain Clay Lyle, reported he was in the middle of a "doctrinally sound" ambush and was fighting in all directions. He was not telling Ferrell anything the latter did know. Every vehicle in his column was fighting with alternating turrets to the right or left of the road. There was so much tracer coming in and ricocheting off the squadron vehicles that one lieutenant said it "looked like a Star Wars movie." Besides the small arms fire, swarms of RPGs pelted the squadron as mortar rounds ranged up and down the length of the

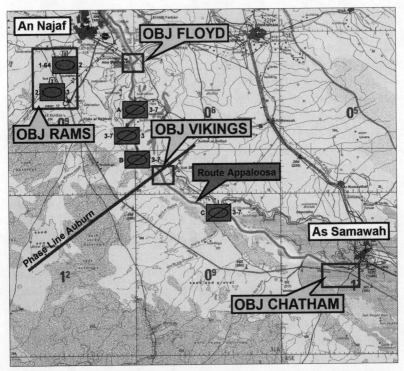

MAP 10. 3-7 CAV moves to Objective Floyd

column. The Iraqis were fighting from prepared positions in the tree lines, which were hard to pinpoint, and they were using civilian trucks to move forces and supplies to their fighting positions.

Ferrell's troopers were engaging targets at distances from 300 meters to point-blank range. At times the Iraqis were so close that troopers fought with their individual weapons in lieu of the 120mm on the M-1 or the 25mm on the M-3. Ferrell also had his artillery battery firing furiously, and although its fire was devastating where it hit, the battery could not engage throughout the entire enemy position. Desperate for more firepower, Ferrell called his forward air controller, Technical Sergeant Mike Keehan, to see if there was any close air support available. After being told that there were A-10s on station above them, Ferrell gave Keehan map grids on both sides of the road and told him to bring in the planes. A few seconds later Keehan informed

Ferrell that the grid coordinates were so close to his squadron's position that there was a significant chance of a friendly fire incident. A staff officer was saying the Air Force would not come to Ferrell's aid unless he assumed full responsibility. He wanted Ferrell's full name, rank, and social security number for the record. Flabbergasted that some bureaucrat sitting safely in Kuwait was thinking about how best to cover his ass, while his soldiers were fighting for their lives, Ferrell tersely provided the requested information. Still upset, he ordered Keehan to tell whoever was on the other end of the radio to keep the information on file, as they might want to reuse it in the future.

Only a moment later the A-10s swept in, flying so low that even in the dark, Ferrell commented, "I thought I could see the rivets." On the first pass they fired flares to mark the target area. On the second they fired rockets. On the third they strafed with their 30mm cannon, firing hundreds of high explosive rounds a minute. On the fourth they dropped 500-lb. bombs, which fell so close to the squadron that the concussion rocked the column. An Apache Troop lieutenant later reported, "The A-10 made the most delightful sound." With both tree lines in flames the Iraqi fire ceased. Keehan said it looked like the Apocalypse. Another soldier commented, "One moment everything looked like you were driving through the Bible, and in the next it looked like you were moving through hell."

As Ferrell's lead elements cleared the ambush zone, he attempted to call his trains and Crazyhorse Troop, now twenty-five miles behind, to tell them to follow a different route. They were too far away for the radios, so he sent them a text message on Blue Force Tracker. The message went unnoticed, and the vulnerable trains continued up the road blissfully unaware they would soon be entering the same "kill sack" the combat troops were now leaving.

As they fought through the ambush, 3-7 CAV, with Apache Troop still leading, came on the small town of Al-Faysaliyah. As Apache entered the town, they discovered that the planned route was nothing more than a series of back alleys and narrow streets. After talking with Ferrell, the lead platoon leader, Lieutenant Garrett, was told to find a new route, which he did by map. Following the new route, the squadron soon found itself on dirt trails sitting on top of elevated dikes. The slightest misstep would send a tank or Bradley plunging into the water and mud of adjacent canals. In many areas vehicle tracks hung halfway off both sides of the dikes. It was impossible for the squadron's vehicles to maneuver off the dikes even when the canal disappeared, because the soil was too wet to support seventy-ton vehicles.

After an hour of perilous driving, Apache Troop came upon two small bridges over deep canals; the first was a solid concrete bridge that it crossed without incident. The second, however, consisted of two I beams packed with dirt and light gravel. After some discussion over whether the bridge could hold tanks, an engineer sapper squad went forward to make the final determination. The sappers reported back with a definitive, "Maybe." Ferrell decided to risk it and with the sappers watching, vehicles began inching across one at a time. Lieutenant Garrett crossed with his Bradley, followed by two more Bradleys and one Abrams. As Second Lieutenant Luke Devlon crossed with his Abrams he began to feel the bridge give way, and his driver gunned the engine to cross quickly. Devlon noticed that this was causing the bridge to collapse more quickly and it would fall right on the sappers, who were watching from below. He ordered the driver to let off the gas as the sappers scrambled out of the way. With a jolt, the bridge gave way and Devlon's tank plunged twenty feet into the canal below. Miraculously, no one was hurt, but the tank was hopelessly stuck.

Lieutenant Garrett, on the far side of the ravine, was ordered to leave the stricken Abrams behind and proceed with the two Bradleys to the final checkpoint before Objective Floyd. The other tank that had made it successfully would remain behind to provide protection for the stuck tank. As Apache Troop tried to recover the Abrams, Ferrell was in a bind. His squadron could no longer go forward, and the only other route was the one he had rejected. Doubt that his vehicles could even turn around on the narrow dikes compounded his problem. In actuality there was no decision to make: Ferrell ordered the squadron to turn around. Cautiously, the massive armored vehicles began to pivot steer in position, while ground guides tried to direct several fuel trucks on how best to maneuver themselves. Most of them made it, but two tanks and one truck slipped into the mud and had to be left behind. In order to save the truck driver, his comrades cut the top of his cab and winched him out of the mud.

It was 3:00 A.M. before the column was turned around. By now the more than 200 vehicles of the squadron trains were entering the original ambush area. Even though the Iraqis had suffered severely in their prior engagement with the squadron and from the A-10 strikes, they had managed to reorganize their remnants and were waiting for the convoy. For the second time that night, squadron vehicles had to run a gauntlet of fire, but this time most of the vehicles were thin-skinned supply and headquarters vehicles. Captain Jeff McCoy interspersed Crazyhorse's combat vehicles throughout the vulnerable column, and once again turrets were alternated to the left and right sides of the road. Without artillery or air support McCoy's troop escorted the convoy through with remarkably light losses.

While the squadron's trains were fighting their way clear of the ambush, Ferrell's troops had negotiated the maze of streets of Al-Faysaliyah and were again barreling towards Objective Floyd. As they neared the objective, they ran into another well-prepared Fedayeen ambush, later named by the unit "Machine Gun Alley." It was a repeat of the earlier ambush. For the second time in six hours, mortars, RPGs, and automatic weapons fire raked the column. Again, the column was engaging fanatical Fedayeen at point-blank range. Several times tanks had to use their machine guns to sweep Fedayeen off tanks to their front. On at least one occasion, a tank commander emptied his pistol into an Iraqi who was climbing onto his turret. After the lead troop had passed, Ferrell noted that the Iraqi positions were being reinforced in the lull as his next troop approached. He had no way of knowing how many Fedayeen there were, but he was near his objective and could not leave such a strong position in his rear to attack his rapidly closing trains. This time 3-7 CAV would not barrel through. It would stand and fight until they had destroyed the enemy.

By now Ferrell could talk to division headquarters, but they had nothing to offer. The weather had grounded the Apache helicopters, and he was out of range of the artillery and MLRS battalions. The A-10s were back overhead, though, and he called on them. This time they came in even closer then before, and soldiers who were manning their vehicles' exposed weapons felt the heat blasts wash over them. Again the A-10 strikes annihilated the Iraqi positions. This time, however, the Iraqis did not pull off to lick their wounds. Truck after truck drove up loaded with Fedayeen intent on continuing the assault. Dawn was only two hours away, a long two hours.

As 3rd ID soldiers discovered in fight after fight, the Iraqis appeared to have no conception of the squadron's ability to see at night. Each truck drove up and began to unload, as if it were invisible in the pitch black night. The enemy finally gave up at dawn, two hours after the fight had begun.

Just after 6:00 A.M., Ferrell was able to talk to General Austin. He was behind schedule and still not on Objective Floyd. Austin asked three questions in rapid succession: "Where are you? Where are you supposed to be? Why are you on that road?" It was apparent that Austin had no idea that the squadron had taken the wrong road and had been in a vicious, all-night fight. Ferrell, who was exhausted beyond measure, filled him in on the night's activities. After considering what the squadron had been through, Austin told Ferrel to rest, refuel, and rearm his weary troops. They could move on to Objective Rams the next day. Ferrell sighed in relief—it seemed the ordeal was over. An hour later, Austin called back. Najaf had become a hornets' nest, and he needed it sealed off. To do that, he needed the 3-7 CAV on Objective Floyd. Ferrell waited for the order he knew was coming: "As soon as you are able I need you to execute. I need you to execute as soon as possible."

Ferrell's trains closed up. His exhausted soldiers drew ammo, refueled their vehicles, and lined up. Two hours after receiving the mission the 3-7 CAV was again on the attack.

10

"Tell Saddam We're Winning"

A S THE 3RD ID CONTINUED its advance, bypassing Nasiriyah, Samawah, and Najaf to gain a position from which it
could drive through the Karbala Gap and attack Bagh-
dad, it came under increasingly heavy attack from Ba'ath militia and
Fedayeen. To the 3rd ID soldiers, these attacks appeared fanatical and
beyond reason. In fact, they were suicidal. In the 3rd Infantry Division,
unit after unit reported going "black" on ammunition (almost empty)
as they dealt with Fedayeen who charged tanks in small groups or in
the back of Toyota pick-ups (Technicals). However, the picture of the
war forming in the Iraqi high command was entirely different from
what was actually happening. All Iraqi prewar planning assumed that
Coalition forces would attack each of the cities along the Euphrates so
as not to leave their supply lines open to attack by Iraqi forces operating from these cities. The reports reaching Baghdad of heavy fighting
around the outskirts of the southern cities reinforced this preconcep-
tion. As Iraqi units attacked out from the cities, their commanders
reported exactly the message that Baghdad expected to hear: everything was going wonderfully and Iraqi forces were slaughtering the
invaders in surprisingly large numbers.

Throughout the war, the quality of the reporting from the military and security channels to the regime leadership was mixed; reporting through political channels, which was the channel Saddam most

trusted, was uniformly bad. These reports indicate the Fedayeen were fiercely resisting American efforts to conquer the southern cities. From the Iraqi perspective, the fact that they still controlled the major cities, despite incessant American assaults, meant that their overall strategy was working. The minister of defense announced in a news conference on 27 March:

> The enemy encircled the town of Samawah from the direction of the desert and is now in the back of the town. The tribes of Al-Muthanna, the Ba'ath Party, Saddam Fedayeen, and military units are now implementing special operations aimed at these American units. . . . Now, as to the situation in the mid-Euphrates sector; in the past three days, the enemy's losses were very heavy, as they are losing tanks and personnel carriers; they are firing at civilians in more than one place and in more than one sector. The performance of our units is very good and there is very good cooperation in the mid-Euphrates sector between the Saddam Fedayeen, the Ba'ath Party fighters, and the tribesmen. Before I came to the news conference, I talked to Staff Lieutenant General Salah Abbud, deputy commander of the region. He told me that the enemy had withdrawn because they sustained heavy losses.

Since this optimistic assessment was being presented at the same time the 3rd Infantry Division was rapidly destroying all Iraqi units that challenged them, it would be easy to believe that the minister of defense was simply parroting regime-generated propaganda. But a close study of captured documentary evidence indicates that many of the regime elites truly believed this assessment. Ba'ath Party commanders were reporting accurately that they were still holding the cities, though their reports of inflicting heavy losses on the Coalition forces were false. No one in Baghdad had any reason or desire to doubt them. Typical of the reporting reaching Baghdad was this 21 March report from the southern region command's control center: "The enemy is advancing toward the airport in An-Nasiriyah . . . a counterattack force of the 11th Infantry Division made contact with the enemy and [was able to] destroy six enemy tanks . . . one Iraqi tank has been destroyed." This report reflects a small sampling of what Baghdad was being told about the fight around Tallil, where Colonel Allyn's 3rd Brigade was in the middle of eviscerating the 11th Infantry Division. However, the fact that most of the 11th Infantry Division had effectively evaporated under the impact of the 3rd ID assault was something that neither Saddam nor those around him had any way of knowing. They were receiving similarly optimistic reports from the militia forces to complement those from trusted party officials. For instance, the security officer of one Fedayeen unit based in a southern city enthusiastically reported on 24 March, "The latest attack . . . by the Fedayeen and the heroic men of the Party on the remnants of the enemy . . . on the Az-Zubayr Bridge fired up two tanks with their crews and the enemy was routed to the rear. . . . The routed force of the enemy is estimated to be more than fifty tanks." A week into the campaign, perhaps sensing that he was receiving inflated reports, the minister of defense, displaying a rare flash of military professionalism, established a committee to explore exactly how American ground forces were fighting the campaign. On 27 March, this committee forwarded its report titled "The Methods of the U.S. Enemy During the Aggression Against Our Steadfast, Fighting Country." It was a mixture of already well-understood generalizations of American capabilities and some fanciful conjecture to explain events that were not making sense in Baghdad. This report stated that the Americans were avoiding entering the cities, "while capturing important communications nodes to control entry and exit points for towns and cities, with the objective of preventing the arrival of reinforcements."

The committee also warned that U.S. forces were attacking at a number of places at the same time, "in order to dilute our effort and confuse our troops, coupled with a propensity to withdraw in case of casualties and to hold onto land in case of any success." Both of these items might have provided the regime hints as to what was actually happening, but it appears the report either was not widely circulated or was ignored. Possibly the minister of defense failed to take it seriously because of the report's more bizarre elements. One of its explanations for how the Americans could appear at so many different places was that Chinook helicopters were capable of air-landing heavy battle tanks—which Chinooks are not.

Since the Iraqi high command's vision of the war's progress largely reflected reports it was receiving from the battlefront, it is worth taking a close look at what local officials were actually dealing with, as opposed to what they were reporting. The best source on what local Ba'athists were seeing in one region was Lieutenant General Yahya Taha Huwaysh-Fadani Al-Ani, the assistant military advisor to the Ba'ath commander in the central Euphrates region. In his previous career, General Yahya had reached the pinnacle of commander of the Naval and Coastal Defense Force, from which position he had retired from military service. However, in January 2003 he had been pressed back into service. By his own admission, General Yahya had no experience in coordinating a land battle, but he did have a front row seat to events as they occurred. Yahya had a particularly good view of the 3rd ID's advance and its effect on local Ba'ath officials. On 28 March, General Yahya first came into contact with American forces. According to his account:

> On the 28th, after the Coalition had rested and resupplied some distance away, the Bradley armored personnel carriers arrived at the outskirts of Samawah, but did not enter the city. They covered and penned us in the city while their supply columns moved to the north behind a screen of tanks. Some Fedayeen patrols attacked with RPG-7s, while the Al-Quds force fired 20mm mortars. I went to the roof of the As Samawah hospital to see what I could outside the city. I saw tanks and armored personnel carriers approaching, covered by eight helicopters.
>
> Around 29 or 30 March, we learned that the fighting in Najaf had started. I lost communications with my boss, regional governor Mizban. I contacted Ad-Diwaniyah and Najaf and asked them to contact the governor, but they said they had not heard from him for two days. We then heard that regional governor Mizban had been dismissed and sent back to Baghdad, but we did not know who his replacement was.

Clearly, he was able to see that the Americans were making no effort to enter Samawah, and since he could see the supply columns heading north, it would be easy to deduce that most of the 3rd ID's combat power must be proceeding ahead of it. Had he needed further confirmation that Coalition forces were bypassing the area, then the fighting around Najaf (one hundred miles north of his position) the next day should have done the trick. There is no evidence that any such reasoned analysis traveled up the chain of command. Rather, local Ba'athists continued to report to Baghdad that they were fighting gloriously and inflicting heavy losses on every American attempt to occupy the southern cities.

By the time Saddam received any accurate reports on the situation, it was already too late to take effective action. Iraq's former trade minister records Saddam's anger in the following terms:

Saddam appeared upset with the events in Najaf, telling the ministers that the situation in An-Najaf was "difficult," that it appeared the city was about to fall to Coalition forces, and that "even the Ba'ath Party was facing difficulty in Najaf." After a brief discussion, Saddam ordered Mahmoud Dhiab Al-Ahmad [minister of interior] to leave the meeting and contact Mizban Khuthair al-Hadi [who had been placed back in charge three days after his dismissal], the central Euphrates regional commander, and direct him to order Iraqi forces to withdraw from An-Najaf. Al-Ahmad returned shortly thereafter and reported that he was not successful in contacting Mizban.

By now, the 3rd ID had already moved north of Najaf in preparation for its final lunge to Baghdad; Allyn's 3rd Brigade had already turned over its duties in the south to the 82nd Airborne, which, along with the 101st Airborne, was preparing to enter the cities. For Samawah's defenders the situation was becoming increasingly desperate. General Yahya continues his account of events: "On 31 March I noticed that there were only approximately 200 fighters left in Samawah. The Al-Quds fighters complained that they no longer had any soldiers. The Ba'ath Party said they no longer had any men." By this time, communications with Baghdad were all but cut off. On April 3, the local Ba'ath leadership of Samawah decamped. As General Yahya indicated, "No one knew where they had gone. Their guards didn't even know where they had gone." At this point, Yahya and his staff decided that discretion was the better part of valor, and they left the city. With the departure of the Ba'ath officials, civic order quickly disintegrated. General Yahya recalled, "In the morning . . . when we started out, the mobs started looting everything. They came to steal our cars, but my guards scared them off." When General Yahya finally reached Baghdad, he was told to resume his former duties as head of the Iraqi Military Academy.

Putting aside the bizarre fact that the Ministry of Defense was worried about staffing its military academies just as 3rd ID tanks entered Baghdad's suburbs, General Yahya's account suggests a complete breakdown of military-political cooperation in the Euphrates region. The authorities in Baghdad had little sense of what Iraqi forces were confronting near the cities; for their part, local authorities clearly had lost all control of their subordinates. While local Ba'ath leaders dithered, fought amongst themselves, and then finally ran off, thousands of Fedayeen Saddam continued to sacrifice themselves to maintain the regime. Their attacks caused 3rd ID soldiers some local difficulties as they sped towards Baghdad, but their operational impact on the course of the conventional war was next to nothing.

In summary, the final result of Allyn's and Charlton's strategy for securing the LOCs was something neither they nor other 3rd ID commander's foresaw. By not trying to seize the cities, but at the same time feinting attacks into them: they had allowed the local political leaders to claim to Saddam that they were defeating the Americans. Their inflated reports of victory after victory fed Saddam and the Iraqi high command's perception that the Coalition attack was faltering. Although the Iraqis defending the southern cities could easily see the 3rd ID's massed combat power, and that followed by tens of thousands of tons of supplies slipping along the outskirts of their cities, it does not appear that any reports of these movements made their way to Baghdad.

Americans got used to laughing at the pronouncements of "Baghdad Bob" as he went into great detail about how the Americans were being destroyed against the invincible Iraqi bulwarks. It is now clear, though, that Saddam and his senior officials believed every word of it, since "Baghdad Bob" was only repeating the battlefield reports that were coming to them from the southern cities. As far as they were concerned, they were winning, and they were looking forward to humiliating the United States—as long as the French and Russians did not interfere with a pesky ceasefire resolution.

11

Najaf: The Hornets' Nest

(25–27 MARCH)

A S PERKINS'S 2ND BRIGADE finished clearing Objective
Rams, the 3rd Infantry division headquarters received intelligence that the Iraqis were heavily reinforcing Najaf; hundreds, perhaps thousands, of Fedayeen were moving into the city.
This information presented General Blount with a unique challenge,
because, in contrast to the Fedayeen in Nasiriyah and Samawah, those
in Najaf had demonstrated a willingness to attack U.S. forces outside
of the city. Rams was only a few miles outside the city limits, and it
was already filling up with thousands of tons of supplies as Vth Corps
turned it into a major logistics base. Furthermore, every road the division planned to move supplies along was within easy striking distance
of Najaf.

Najaf itself presented major tactical problems. First, it was a massive city—easily three times the size of Samawah—and could not be
contained by a single battalion. Moreover, it was one of the holiest
cities in Islam and "the holiest" for the Shi'a sect, on whose overall
friendliness 3rd ID was still counting. Inside the city were some of the
holiest sites of the Shi'a faith and its grandest mosque. The massive
mosque complex was also the home of the Shi'a's religious leader, the
Grand Ayatollah Sistani. It was obvious that if the 3rd ID was going
to enter Najaf, it would have to tread lightly. Not that any of its com-

manders were eager to enter the city with armor: Najaf was an ancient city with narrow and twisting streets. It was just the kind of terrain that every doctrinal textbook said not to put unsupported armor into, as it was a deathtrap for tanks.

Blount and his commanders did not have the time or inclination to take the city by storm, but it was certainly too dangerous to bypass. They would have to isolate Najaf until the 101st Airborne Division could make its way up the clogged roads and take control of the city. To do the job, General Blount ordered Colonel Grimsley's 1st Brigade to seize the bridge at Al Kifl, thereby isolating he city from the north (see next chapter). He ordered Colonel Perkins to move most of his brigade to Objective Spartans, north of Rams, but to leave Lieutenant Colonel Schwartz's 1-64 AR to secure Rams and isolate Najaf on the west. Ferrell's 3-7 CAV would then seize the two bridges south of Najaf (Objective Floyd) and close the ring on the south and east.

The 3-7 CAV troopers had been in contact with the enemy almost continuously for the past four days. As a result, Ferrell was becoming concerned about his soldiers' ability to continue at this pace. Few if any of his troopers had actually slept, except while riding or standing in a hatch, since leaving Kuwait. Ferrell knew that he himself was operating on pure adrenaline and figured that was what was animating his soldiers also. General Austin said, "When I talked to Ferrell, he no longer sounded human, but his assessments were still spot on." After visiting around the squadron and looking each of his key leaders in the eye, Ferrell talked it over with Command Sergeant Major Berhane. Both agreed—the 3-7 CAV was good for another fight.

After receiving General Austin's order to continue to Objective Floyd, Ferrell made a new plan and briefed his troop commanders. Bonecrusher Troop would lead and was ordered to seize the initial crossing site the squadron would need in order to pass east of An Najaf. Then, Apache Troop would pass through Bonecrusher and continue the attack to the northern bridge, up Najaf's northeast side. Finally, Bonecrusher Troop would conduct battle handover with Crazyhorse Troop before moving to the center of the zone to block exits out of the city.

Ferrell planned to move full tilt to the objective, but just as his advance began, the sandstorm from hell hit, depriving him of helicopter support. With no eyes in the sky and visibility—even with thermals—down to fifty yards, the squadron moved cautiously. However, before noon, Bonecrusher Troop had made the unimpeded four-mile

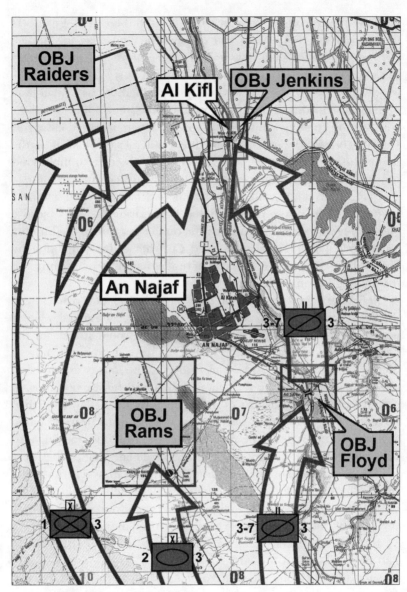

MAP 11. Initial plan to isolate Najaf

move to the first bridge site and seized it without incident. Engineers found close to 100 pounds of explosives on and near the bridge, but the Iraqis had failed to wire it for demolition. As Apache Troop closed on the crossing site, they were assaulted by small bands of RPG-wielding Fedayeen; these were quickly dispatched. It was a small taste of what the squadron would face over the next twenty-four hours.

With the crossing site secured, Apache Troop, followed closely by Ferrell's command tracks, assaulted the southeast side of Najaf. As the hours passed, the weather worsened. Winds exceeded 50 mph, sand reduced visibility to nearly zero, and the sky turned an eerie orange that convinced some soldiers that someone had "popped a nuke." Eventually, Crazyhorse Troop relieved Bonecrusher at the Objective Floyd bridge sites and then pushed out on the east side of the Euphrates. Ferrell had intentionally placed Crazyhorse Troop in what he assumed was his rear to give it a bit of rest, as it had borne the brunt of the fighting in Samawah.

At first, Apache's progress was uneventful, but about two miles from the bridge at Floyd, the lead element encountered Iraqi Fedayeen. It was the first in a long series of ambushes that would stretch for the next twenty miles that Apache still had to travel before reaching its objective. For three hours, Apache Troop and the squadron command tracks fought through a series of well-prepared defensive positions. In a repeat of their performances the day before, the Fedayeen rushed the column with technical vehicles, fired small arms from prepared fighting positions along the road and on the rooftops, and engaged with a mix of RPGs and mortar rounds. Ferrell later said, "They were making sure they kept our attention." As Apache moved through the Iraqi defensive zone, its now-veteran troopers methodically handed off targets from one vehicle to the next and then from one platoon to the next, until each Iraqi position was destroyed in succession.

By the time Apache closed on its final position, Bonecrusher Troop had been relieved at the bridge by Crazyhorse Troop, and the latter was now moving along the same route Apache had just followed. Ferrell assumed that Bonecrusher would have to engage only whatever remnants Apache had left in its wake; they should have little trouble getting to their assigned position in the center of his extended defensive line.

Bonecrusher's first contact report stunned Ferrell. Enemy fire had catastrophically destroyed an M-1 tank. A moment later reports

came in of a second M-1 destroyed, along with a Bradley severely damaged by RPG fire. Never before had an M-1 tank been catastrophically destroyed by enemy fire, and the news took everyone aback. If
the enemy could take out two Abrams, then Bonecrusher faced more
than remnants.

Bonecrusher's commander was at a loss as to what to do. He was
under attack from all sides and already had two tanks on fire. Using
the sandstorm for cover, Fedayeen were swarming in, their blood
up from the smell of success. Ferrell calmed the troop commander
and assured him support was on its way. He wanted him to pull back
approximately a mile, so he could call in an MLRS strike on the position. But first the crews of the stricken tanks had to be saved. Both
tanks were burning, but the crews, with the exception of one driver,
had managed to escape without injury. However, the hatch of one
tank had stuck shut, and the driver could not evacuate. Sergeant First
Class Javier Camocho, in a following tank, could see the crew of the
burning tank moving towards him with tracers flying over their heads.
He dismounted his own tank to help them.

> We brought them to the low ground and Sergeant Median [the com-
> mander of the crippled tank] asked if we could get his driver out, as
> he was in the tank alive. I told my gunner, Sergeant Geijgos, "Let's
> go." We stayed on the low ground as low as we could. When we got
> to the tank we thought the driver was dead because it looked like fire
> was coming out of his compartment. He managed to pop his hatch
> open and closed a couple of times to let us know he was still alive.
> There was propellant on fire and we needed fire extinguishers, which
> we grabbed off the tank. I crawled on top of the tank and I knew we
> are still getting shot at because I could hear the shots pinging off
> the pavement and the zinging of the bullets overhead. I sprayed the
> extinguisher but the fire kept burning. We got two more fire extin-
> guishers from another tank about 60 meters away. There was a lot of
> machine gun firing going on as we made our way back to the tank.
> By the time we got there a Bradley had arrived and was keeping the
> enemy down with a lot of 25mm fire. My own tank was helping with
> its coax. The Bradley's ramp was down so I went in and grabbed two
> more fire extinguishers. By now, the enemy had stopped firing at us,
> but the bustle rack on the burning tank had a bunch of .50-caliber
> and 240 rounds on it and they were cooking off. We ran back there
> and sprayed it until the fire was reduced to just a red glow.

Black smoke was pouring out of the tank, so we knew something inside was burning and could explode. The only way to get the driver out was through his hatch, which we had to open with a grappling. We pulled the driver out, half asphyxiated, and put him in the Bradley. When I got back to my tank we were hit by an RPG, which we shook off. We were turning around to leave the area, but could see Iraqis swarming over the destroyed tanks. We fired them up.

When Bonecrusher Troop had moved a safe distance away, Ferrell called for the MLRS strike. The coordinates used was the location of his crippled Bradley. Later, when he went back through the area he found the Bradley was unrecognizable. The tanks "still looked like tanks," Ferrell said, "but they had taken a lot of damage from the MLRS." Though the Fedayeen continued their attacks throughout the night, the MLRS strike broke their backs in this sector, and Bonecrusher had little problem containing the threat.[1]

The main part of 3-7 CAV's battle now switched to Crazyhorse, which remained in the south on the Objective Floyd bridges. It was assumed that this would be a relatively quiet sector, but that assumption was wrong. The Fedayeen wanted the bridge back, and they were willing to sacrifice heavily to regain it.

Ferrell, whose focus had been first on the close fight he had engaged in as he drove north with Apache and then on the near disaster in Bonecrusher's sector, now realized he had neglected Crazyhorse Troop. Since he had not heard from the troop commander, Captain McCoy, he assumed that "everything was still under control nearly 30 kilometers to my rear." As the fighting in the other two troop sectors diminished, Ferrell discovered that once again he was out of communications range with Crazyhorse. Attempts to contact McCoy through the late afternoon and early evening hours failed. At approximately 9:30 P.M., almost twelve hours since his last contact with McCoy, Staff Sergeant Keehan, the squadron's Air Force controller, notified Ferrell that McCoy was calling on the Air Force TacSat net. Ferrell immediately knew something was seriously wrong.

---

1. A postwar investigation determined that the two tanks were destroyed by friendly 25mm from a following Bradley, which had fired several rounds into the rear engine compartment of each vehicle. Both tanks had just turned a corner where the Bradley had recently engaged an Iraqi anti-aircraft gun in direct fire mode. In the poor visibility the Bradley commander misidentified the M-1 tanks as Iraqi tanks coming to reinforce the destroyed gun position.

Talking to Captain McCoy confirmed my worst thoughts. His troop had been engaged with waves of dismounts, suicide vehicles, and two armored vehicles over the past six hours. McCoy estimated they had already fought approximately five hundred dismounts, numerous wheeled-vehicle attacks, and armored personnel carriers all coming out of Najaf. I could tell from his voice that McCoy had everything under control and that he just needed to hear it from me. His force was being attacked from all directions and the severe weather had given the enemy the advantage. The weather was unbelievable, with winds so strong the blowing sand felt like rocks hitting your skin. When the winds finally decreased, the flying sand mixed with rain, and mud began falling from the sky. Because of the weather conditions and the enemy's willingness to attack in human waves, McCoy had directed his few dismounted troops to dig individual fighting positions—a task not commonly practiced in a cavalry organization.

As fate would have it, while I was on the Air Force radio with Crazyhorse Troop the next day, we received a report from the division headquarters that JSTARS[2] had identified a large force massing in the city, a few kilometers away from Crazyhorse Troop. I knew immediately that the enemy was planning one final counterattack against Crazyhorse Troop, and I did not have any squadron assets in a position to assist. I explained the situation to Brigadier General Austin, and after a brief discussion with him and General Blount, they once again gave me release authority for MLRS and any available Air Force assets in the area. Continuing to use the Air Force TACSAT net, McCoy and I coordinated the engagement. We were over 30 kilometers apart; but I had total confidence in him, as he was one of the best in the squadron. I fully trusted his decisions, and, once he reported that all his troops were set, we fired MLRS dangerously close to friendly forces. Normally we want two kilometers between friendly troops and the target, but in both engagements to date, the rockets were landing within 1,000 meters of the friendly location. The MLRS fires were effective, but did not destroy all the vehicles in the counterattack.

At this point we were able to direct a B1 bomber onto the target, who dropped a series of JDAMS to complete the destruction of the attacking force.

---

2. JSTARS (Joint Surveillance Target Attack Radar System) is a Boeing 707-300 designed to track enemy ground movements.

Captain Jeff McCoy's calmness while talking on the radio and his matter of fact retelling of the events at Objective Floyd failed at the time and later to convey how desperate a fight the troop was engaged in as it held its positions against determined attacks for two days. To get a full picture of the troop's fight, it is worth examining the viewpoint of just one soldier, remembering that his fight is being repeated by every vehicle and soldier in the troop's sector.

When we saw Staff Sergeant Dillard Johnson in the introduction he was making a heroic fight in Samawah. We pick up his story at Objective Floyd:

> Myself [Johnson], one other Bradley and an M-1 were moving forward, but as soon as I got on top of the bridge [Objective Floyd] and started to cross it, I took several RPG hits on my vehicle. Luckily the enemy was so close that the rounds didn't have enough time to arm themselves before they came into contact with us. I immediately called up a contact report and began returning fire. Unfortunately I was now on the eastern side of the bridge and my other two elements were still on the western side. Since there was a large volume of fire on the bridge itself, it seemed like it would keep us apart for awhile.
>
> I called up to the company commander and told him I was being engaged by RPGs and small arms fire and that I was east of the bridge. He said "Roger, go ahead and collapse it back." We turned around and started heading back and that's when the vehicle got caught on some obstruction on the bridge, leaving us in the enemy kill zone for a few minutes.
>
> I was putting out a large amount of fire now and when Red 4 found out I was stuck he came up to help cover us. He put a huge volume of HE [high explosive] fire on top of the guys shooting at us and we eventually cleared the obstruction and got back to the west side of the bridge.
>
> As we backed up, we kept taking dismounted fire and volleys of RPG fire at our vehicles. I told the tank to shift back behind us a little bit to engage a palm grove from where we were taking small arms fire. There were also some bunker positions on our flank which were delivering a lot of accurate fire on us, so I told my White 4 element to move over there and start engaging them. The Red 1 element and I continued to engage the area where we made our initial contact. After fifteen or twenty minutes of a high rate of fire from all three of the vehicles, the enemy had enough pounding and broke off contact.

At that point we shifted back to the left wing of the company position, and the commander gave us the order to hold our position and to stop all traffic from coming through. When the first vehicle approached we fired warning shot after warning shot, but it kept coming. It actually swerved around me and crashed into the front of the Red 1 vehicle. It was a taxicab with some civilians in it. They jumped out and ran away.

Another vehicle came in and I was up on top of my turret waving them back, which they did. Visibility at this point was anywhere between ten and maybe fifty meters depending on the wind. We were really concerned about civilian casualties or fratricide due to the fact that there were other squadron units mixed through the area, so we were holding our fire and making sure we confirmed everything. I saw two trucks take off from the compound that we were firing at on the other side of the bridge, and head up the road. Red 1 said he saw a crew-served weapon in the back of it but we couldn't identify it for sure, so we didn't engage that vehicle.

Just before night started to fall, we had a bus come up toward us. It was moving fairly fast. Visibility at this time was probably 150 to 200 meters. We picked him up as soon as he crossed the bridge and we fired tracers in front of the vehicle. He just stayed on the gas. We fired more tracers in front of him, but he just kept coming and rammed the taxicab and started pushing it towards the Red 1. That's when my gunner engaged the driver of the vehicle, killing him, but not before the bus crashed into Red 1, knocking the crew senseless for a few moments. We then pushed the bus sideways and used it for a blocking position, which would hopefully close that route to anymore suicidal vehicles. It did not really deter them and several more vehicles tried to come through us.

It was starting to get dark by the time we had the bus in position. After we moved it we saw what appeared to be a tan pickup truck, a little Toyota with a crew cab, racing up to our position. He stopped, turned around and then turned back. He did this several times before hitting the gas and whipping around the bus. I could tell that he knew where my position was because I was waving him around. He almost ran into Red 1 and a bunch of personnel started jumping out. I believe they were Fedayeen. I can't say for sure, but they were well armed. They jumped out of the back of the truck with RPGs, AK-47s and positioned themselves between myself and Red 1, so we couldn't engage them with our main guns without engaging each other. Fortunately my dismount was up in the back. He had mounted a 240 in the side of the track and engaged and destroyed all eight personnel and their vehicle. They thought that they were going to drive around the bus and drive around me in the sandstorm with their lights out and didn't realize there was a tank behind me. So I think they just had some really bad luck.

A few minutes after that event, we spotted another truck coming. It was a large truck. We couldn't tell exactly what it was. We thought it was a water truck to begin with. It drove up into the side of the bus and pushed it a little bit. We were firing warning shots at it, but it backed up again and came up and hit the bus. These guys were just really determined. They just kept ramming the bus and backing up and ramming it again, trying to get through to us. My gunner's looking at it through the sight; he says, 'These guys got weapons, they got uniforms.' That is when I told them to engage with everything we had and the truck exploded and we discovered it was a fuel tanker and not a water truck. When the bus also caught on fire from the spreading tanker flames, there was a pretty good explosion on the bus. It was much larger then you would see from a diesel vehicle blowing up, so we believe that it was rigged to blow and possibly my gunner had killed him before he could set off the charge when he hit the Bradley. I don't have any proof of that. That's just from what we were seeing.

The rest of the night we had several vehicles coming up and through that area. A lot of them turned around. Those that didn't were destroyed. Visibility lifted to where we had probably 400 or 500 meters.

I called up and told the commander that I had visibility of the bridge to the far side and requested permission for myself and White 4 to go up and secure the far side of the bridge. After getting permission we moved up, but due to the narrowness of the road and an embankment that was there we had to sit side by side. If the enemy wanted to get at us they had to come around a curve with little space for maneuver. They would have to come right at us.

As we sat there, side by side, we shot up several more vehicles with a lot of armed personnel on them, which continued until almost daylight. Daylight came, the volume of fire had ceased. We weren't seeing any more traffic coming down. Just a lot of civilians were moving around.

Later on that morning, I called up our status as far as ammunition went and was told to come back to the trains for more. We came back and got our ammo and gas back up and then moved back to our positions. During the daytime, civilians come around, peaceful and talking to us, moving around our vehicles and everything else. Soon as nighttime got there though, it started all over again.

When the first truck came at us, it was just myself and one other Bradley up there at that time. The trucks started coming at us and they looked a lot like the Bedouin trucks, so we held our fire. We weren't sure what they were until they were about seventy-five meters away from us. That's when we could tell that there were a lot of personnel jumping out of the back of the vehicles, and my dismount on the ground could see them with the new thermal sight. It was working better in the sandstorm than the thermals on the Bradley. He said that they had weapons and were running towards the bridge.

We started engaging those trucks and destroying them. More trucks were driving around those trucks. It was sort of the fish in a barrel thing, where they just kept driving into us and piling out of the back of the trucks while we shot them. We put a large volume of fire on them and finally stopped two trucks in the middle of the road. They were burning, which forced the dismounts to file around the side into my guns. Any that did manage to escape into the nearby field were engaged by Red 1.

I called for our mortar support, but they were firing for someone else so I called up and asked for artillery support. They were working the issue trying to get us some artillery in there when the commander ordered me back to the south side of the bridge. He was calling in some B-1 bombers with JDAMs, which busted up the road pretty good and took the fight out of the enemy. After that it was quiet for the rest of the night.

In the morning, soldiers discovered that there were 314 enemy KIAs in Staff Sergeant Johnson's sector alone. During this single evening's engagement, Johnson's M-3 Bradley had fired 2,800 rounds of 25mm HE, 7,200 rounds of 7.62 coax, and 305 rounds of 25mm DU (depleted uranium). The rest of the troop counted thousands of bodies littering a 360-degree circle around their unit the next day. Many of the Iraqi dead were within feet of the Crazyhorse's vehicles, where they had died as they swarmed into the troop's position. In this close fighting, the main guns of the Bradleys and Abrams were useless and the soldiers were often engaging at point-blank range with their personal weapons. When they ran out of ammo, they dismounted their vehicles and picked up the AK-47s off dead Iraqis and continued to engage. Along with the dead, Captain McCoy discovered the next morning that his soldiers had used up over a hundred AK-47s in the desperate all-night fight.

The troop did not lose a man. This lopsided victory was not due to a technology mismatch. The sandstorm had blinded the squadron to a degree that the fight was as close to even as it would ever be, with the Iraqis holding a decided advantage in numbers. They simply had been outfought by disciplined troopers who refused to panic in the midst of deadly chaos.

For now, the fight was over for Ferrell's 3-7 CAV Squadron, but there was no telling when the Fedayeen would elect to resume it. The squadron was almost out of 25mm HE, about which Staff Sergeant Johnson later said, "It's the one piece of ammo you never want to leave home without." It was dangerously short of all other types of ammunition. If the Fedayeen came again, the squadron would have little left with which to defend itself. But by now General Blount was fully aware of the 3-7 CAV's predicament, and help was on the way. Colonel Grimsley was sending units from Al Kifl south to link up with Apache Troop, while Perkins was ordering the 1-64 AR to move west from Objective Rams and link up with Apache Troop.

12

Al Kifl

THE NAJAF HORNETS' NEST caught the division's leadership by surprise. Intelligence had forecast Objective Rams, just to the west of Najaf, to be a safe location in which to establish a logistics base for the entire corps. Instead, it was under constant attack by fanatical Fedayeen charging out of Najaf. At the same time, the division's cavalry squadron was running out of ammo as it fended off suicidal attacks during its approach march south of Najaf. What was quickly becoming Fortress Najaf was just too dangerous to isolate and bypass, and intelligence poured in that it was becoming more dangerous by the moment, as large vehicle convoys headed south to reinforce Najaf.

Najaf needed to be sealed off.

On the night of 25 March, General Austin visited Colonel Grimsley's operations center, located in an expanse of desert approximately halfway between Najaf and the Karbala Gap. There he briefed Grimsley on the big picture and gave him his marching orders. As Grimsley recalls it, Austin pointed to the town of Al Kifl on the map and said: "Hey, here's what you need to do. Attack through there, seize this river crossing, and establish a block on Highway 8/80, which comes down from Baghdad into An Najaf. What you're going to do is isolate Najaf as best you can. But at a minimum make sure no more guys go into Najaf, and also try and kill as many as possible that 3-7 CAV pushes out of the city."

With no indication of much enemy activity in the area, Grimsley assigned the task of establishing the blocking position to his air defense unit (ADA) reinforced with elements of the brigade reconnaissance company. The Bradleys and Avenger air defense systems the unit possessed were ideal for blocking access across the Al Kifl bridge. Since there was no air threat, Grimsley saw the air defense unit as ideally suited to the mission. By sending the air defenders, he was also giving his heavy task forces more time to rest, rearm, and refit prior to their assault through the Karbala Gap.

Captain Branson, commanding the ADA company, received the mission at ten that night. By midnight he was rolling towards Al Kifl. Lieutenant Colonel Rock Marcone's 3-69 Armor Battalion was told to have a company team ready as a quick reaction force in case Branson ran into more then he could handle. At 3:00 A.M. he did.

For two hours Branson's air defenders tried to battle their way into Al Kifl, but without infantry to clear buildings they were incapable of making progress against waves of Iraqis wielding RPGs and intense small arms fire. At 5:00 A.M. Colonel Grimsley ordered Marcone to send in the quick reaction force. Within the hour, Captain Dave Benton was leading Bravo Company, originally from the 3-7 Infantry, but now attached to Marcone's armored battalion, towards Al Kifl. He linked up with the ADA near dawn and, after a quick assessment of the situation, he put his column onto a four-lane highway and headed into town.

Bravo Company walked into a maelstrom of fire. Captain Benton reported that his leading tanks were taking hits from all sides by RPGs. Overwhelmed by the intensity of the fire, Benton ordered a withdrawal to a position where he could use long-range fire to suppress the enemy before making another attempt to seize the bridge. Just as he was giving the order, though, accurate mortar fire ranged throughout the depth of his company column. With restrictive terrain on both sides of the road and Iraqi mortars able to engage any suitable location to which he could retreat, Benton ordered the lead tanks to fight their way to the bridge.

For the next three hours, the tanks of the lead platoon slowly ground down the Iraqi resistance as they pushed forward. It was past

10:00 A.M. when his lead element reached the bridge. Major Oliver, Marcone's operations officer, had appeared on the scene to coordinate the activities of the various groups now engaged around the town. Oliver ordered the ADA units to cover the south, in case anything came out of Najaf. While Bravo Company reduced the last enemy strong points on the west side of the bridge, he also ordered the reconnaissance detachment to move forward to take a close look at the bridge.

Within minutes the recon element reported they were at the bridge and had found only five defenders, whom they had dispatched. Hearing that the bridge was lightly defended, Oliver ordered Benton to use his tank platoon to seize the far side of the bridge quickly. Lieutenant Rowland, the tank platoon leader, immediately lunged for the bridge with his four tanks. The first two crossed without incident and took up overwatch positions facing north and south. As the third tank crossed, the Iraqis blew the bridge. The driver gunned his engine and rushed across unscathed, while the fourth tank halted just short of the bridge. Lieutenant Rowland spotted an Iraqi officer working the firing device for another set of explosives and immediately killed him.

By this time, both Grimsley and Marcone realized they had stumbled on a bigger fight at Al Kifl then they had expected, and both were rushing to the site. Grimsley recalled that all he knew at this point was that he had most of a tank platoon on the far side of the Euphrates, and they were now trapped. With the bridge destroyed, Grimsley was another commander reliving the nightmare "Blackhawk Down" scenario in his mind as drove across the desert to Al Kifl.

Marcone, rushing to the area, was having many of the same thoughts. He had his air liaison officer (ALO) in tow and, as he approached the town, he kept the Air Force officer busy spinning up all the close air support available; simultaneously he alerted all the artillery in range that one of his companies needed help. As far as he knew, he had a platoon on the wrong side of a destroyed bridge, and it was being set upon by waves of fanatical attackers. He knew that Grimsley was sending engineers to put in an assault bridge, but until that was done he was going to surround the trapped tanks with a curtain of steel.

By the time Marcone arrived at the bridge, the sandstorm from hell, which had begun that morning, had reduced visibility to only a few yards. Even the magnificent thermal sights could barely detect targets much past 200 meters. He approached the bridge, but in the sandstorm could not see the far side. He turned to a recon team scout and asked if the bridge had been blown on the far side. The scout told him, "No sir, they blew it right here." Marcone was incredulous. Looking at the spot he exclaimed, "You've got to be kidding me—this little indentation? That's the bridge we have blown?" He ran down the stairs beside the bridge to examine the underside, and returning announced, "This will hold a tank."

As Lieutenant Rowland and his three tanks repelled repeated assaults, Marcone called his tank forward to prove the bridge was sturdy. With enemy fire buzzing past his head and pinging off nearby girders, he walked ahead of the tank to guide it over the damaged structure. On the far side, Marcone walked to Rowland's tank. On the way he passed a wounded Iraqi sitting against a wall with hands up and his weapon lying beside him. Marcone paused to kick the weapon away and spotted another Iraqi using the wall for cover. Both Marcone and the Iraqi were momentarily startled, but Marcone recovered faster and snatched the AK-47 from the Iraqi and hit him over the head with it. Later he had the Iraqi evacuated to an aide station, where he was treated for what Marcone said was a "very ugly gash on his head."

Noting that the area had only limited fields of fire, Marcone ordered Captain Benton to take his tanks back across the river and replace them with his two infantry platoons. Before heading back across the bridge, he ordered a second infantry company to reinforce Benton's Bravo Company.

By 1:00 P.M. Colonel Grimsley had arrived. He brought along Lieutenant Colonel Tom Smith, who commanded 1st Brigade's combat engineers. Within minutes the engineers swarmed over the bridge, trying to estimate whether it was safe. Not willing to trust Marcone's judgment—proven by driving a tank across the span—as the final word, the engineers took pictures of the entire bridge and sent them digitally to bridge experts in the United States. Less then an hour later, stateside experts confirmed the bridge was safe for heavy armored traffic.

While the leaders waited for the bridge assessment, Captain Dan Hibner led elements of his engineer company onto the bridge to search for any more explosive charges. They found what they were looking. Hibner figured the Iraqis had been waiting to set them off when there were more Americans on the bridge. Not knowing that Rowland's tanks had killed the officer with the detonation device, Hibner assumed the initial assault had cut the wires to the charges. He and his engineers busied themselves cutting every wire in sight and then removing the more dangerously placed explosives.

In the meantime, Grimsley sought out Marcone and planned the next steps. Since Marcone had already replaced the tanks on the far side of the bridge with infantry the situation seemed to be in hand. Having ensured that Marcone had access to those assets he needed to continue the fight, Grimsley returned to his brigade headquarters to begin preparations for the assault through the Karbala Gap. Marcone's battalion still had a long twenty-four hours of fighting left at Al Kifl.

Ten minutes after Grimsley departed, a mortar round injured Marcone while he was out checking positions. He was evacuated to a local aid station, treated for his wounds, and returned to the fight before most of his subordinates knew he was gone. Marcone then stayed for another hour, supervising the preparation of platoon strongpoints, before returning to his headquarters.

Captain Benton and the soldiers of Bravo Company were left to defend the bridge. He was told that he would be relieved in a couple of hours by elements of Lieutenant Colonel Jeff Sanderson's 2-69 Armored Battalion. However, close to dusk, Benton received the news that the sandstorm would delay relief until the next morning. Short of ammo, fuel, and water, and having made only limited defensive preparations, Benton realized his company had a lot of work to do and not much time to do it.

Supplies were brought forward from his company trains, and soldiers began laying barbed wire in the alleyways in order to limit access to their positions. Benton then pulled some of his men and vehicles into a tighter perimeter where they could better support each other. And then he waited. He did not have to wait long.

For the Iraqi high command, the capture of the Al Kifl Bridge came as a shock. The Republican Guard commander for the area, Lieutenant General Hamdani, did not learn that the bridge was under attack until the 3rd ID had already captured it. The unit assigned to hold the bridge was a combination of Al-Quds and Fedayeen mixed into what was optimistically referred to as the Jerusalem Division (so named to remind its members that their ultimate objective was the liberation of Jerusalem). This division was under the command of the local Ba'ath leadership, who had no military experience. Despite being nominally in charge of the geographic area, General Hamdani had no authority over the Jerusalem Division or any of the units in the area. Sensing a potential crisis, Hamdani asked for an immediate meeting with Qusay Hussein, Republican Guard commander and Saddam's younger son.

They met early in the afternoon of 26 March in what Hamdani described as the most violent sandstorm Iraq had seen in fifty years. The meeting, which took place in the rich Mansour neighborhood of Baghdad, turned out to be not only a planning session for what to do now, but also a confidence test of Hamdani's ability to continue to command. As he describes the meeting:

> After exchanging greetings and asking him [Qusay] about the situation, we stood next to a map hanging on the wall. Everything in the hall was shaking due to the force of the bombs and missiles coming down on targets near our location at that time. He asked me what opinions he should give to President Saddam Hussein about what to do about the situation in al Kifl. He wanted to know if we could defend the city successfully without getting into a pitched battle. He was concerned that we preserve the capabilities of the Republican Guard for the battle of Baghdad. I assured him that such a mission could be completed if God wills, and that we could get a high payoff with few losses, because the enemy's airplanes and helicopters were grounded because of the storm. At this point, I explained several of the things I had done already: sending out combat patrols, harassing the enemy with artillery, moving several units outside the control of the high command for field expedience. Qusay blessed my actions and expressed confidence in my command and in my forces. He looked over at General Sayf al-Rawi and said, "My confidence in Major General Raad al-Hamdani is great, despite those who want to shake it.
>
> From Qusay's office, I contacted my Corps' Chief of Staff, Staff Major General Fayiq Abdullah and I asked him to alert the duty unit from the Special Forces Brigade. This unit should gather in al-Muhawwil (28 km north of al-Kifl), and that the Brigade Commander should also be waiting for me at the same place before 1600 that afternoon. I also ordered the Corps Artillery Commander to exploit the storm conditions, to move a number of artillery batteries from the Medina Division and from the Corps' artillery to support the operation.
>
> After leaving Qusay it took a little effort to find the secret location for the regional command; it had been set up in a girls' school in order to avoid the infallible air strikes. My meeting with the Special Forces brigade commander and all others concerned took place at the appointed time. We had to use handheld flashlights to see our wristwatches due to the extreme darkness caused by this storm, which had changed the light day to deep, dark night.

I was appalled by the situation that I discovered. The chief of this command was a member of the political leadership, Mahmoud Gharib, along with the mayor of Babylon and a number of party officials, and the military consultant, Retired Staff Major General Juwad Kazim. None of those people had a grasp on the situation and I eventually walked out to search for specific information about the situation in order to develop a plan of attack. After a huge ordeal, I found the commander of the Jerusalem Division that had lost the battle of al-Kifl. He got on my nerves; time was slipping away to do anything because of his extreme stupidity and his ignorance of his own situation. However, I left him alone, and cursed the one who made the decision to place politicians in the posts of military commanders.

After wasting three hours of valuable time, I stopped at one of the military barracks north of al-Kifl. There I met one of my friends, a retired major general who was working as a consultant with the party members. He was an area resident, so he was able to explain to me in detail what the situation was, as well as the layout of the land. He offered some good advice and I thanked him.

I conducted the necessary reconnaissance with a lot of difficulty because of the low visibility. The brigade commander and the regiment commander who were with me for the reconnaissance almost hit an enemy armored vehicle, which was parked at the entrance of the occupied city.

The time we wasted because of the poor visibility made us late, and there were many things that forced me to postpone the beginning of this attack until after midnight, with the main attack scheduled for dawn. The sandstorm got more violent and, despite all of the plans I had made concerning engaging target at ranges of no less than 300 meters, the poor visibility sometimes forced the range down to a few meters. With heavy fire support, we launched the violent raid with the Special Forces' light weapons with huge success. The explosions of the armored vehicles which had been hit were easy to hear, and the attack force withdrew with twelve injured and three martyrs, who had been left on the battlefield despite all attempts to extract their bodies, because of the intensity of the enemy response with various types of firepower.

For Captain Benton the Iraqi attack was the beginning of what he later referred to as "one of the hairiest nights of my life," as his small command fended off attack after attack. As Benton remembers the fight:

Darkness and the sandstorm combined to make the night pitch black. All through the night they probed and the battle was usually very close. They were able to get in right next to us, because our thermals were very limited by the storm. They were using alleyways and the homes to move in close, deliver some pot shots and back off. Several times during the night one of my Bradleys would receive a direct hit. I had to put infantry on the ground to put an end to these attacks. I had dismounted infantry throwing grenades over walls and down alleyways, which stopped the Iraqis from daring to get too close for awhile. Those that did dare it were eliminated. We went through this throughout the night. Visibility was so bad I had to turn off the Bradley's engines repeatedly so we could hear the enemy.

The next morning the Iraqis had pulled themselves together enough to make their first major counterattack. Twenty vehicles of assorted types, but including some armored vehicles, were spotted coming from the north. Captain Benton still had priority of artillery fires and close air support, and he called for them now. A few minutes later a storm of steel annihilated the Iraqi column. Benton said he could see some remnants of them form up as light infantry and make their way into town with RPGs. However, the sudden catastrophic barrage they just endured sapped their will to fight, and they soon evaporated away.

For the next couple of hours Benton's biggest worry was the number of civilians who were trying to enter his positions. Even though he was still under sporadic fire, civilians were approaching and trying to cross the bridge. The continuing sandstorm was still affecting visibility, and the soldiers of Bravo Company were having a hard time trying to determine who was a civilian and who they needed to kill. Often during the day the determination could not be made until a supposed civilian whipped out a hidden weapon and opened, or tried to open, fire. Benton kept the Arabic speakers in his attached PSYOPS (psychological operations) team busy on their loudspeakers, warning civilians to stay clear of his forces.

Before noon, Benton was told that another twenty-vehicle convoy was heading his way and that an even larger force was on the road only fifteen minutes behind them. Despite the still limited visibility, Benton prepared to repel a strong armored counterattack. The Air Force, though, was now up in force. Initial runs on the Iraq convoys were made by F-15s and F-18s on gun runs. This was followed by the long range rocket fires of the MLRS batteries and capped off by B-52 bombers dropping precision JDAMs on what remained. Thirty minutes after being warned to prepare for a heavy counterattack, Benton was told that the Iraqi force had been obliterated before any of his men made contact with it.

This was not the last time close air support was going to save American ground forces. The praise the officers and soldiers of the 3rd Infantry Division have for the pilots who often flew lower than the treetops to give them fire support is often effusive. Despite the renowned peacetime rivalries between the services, when the going got tough there was no ground soldier who did not look up and thank God when he saw an Air Force jet rolling in to help him. After the war Lieutenant Colonel Jeffrey Sanderson said, "As long as that A-10 is flying, moving, turning you can do anything you want to do because the bad guys are hugging the ground. I can say without shame that I would bend over and kiss the ass of any A-10 pilot who flew in Iraq and give you ten minutes to draw a crowd before I did it."

Around 7:00 that evening the lead company of Sanderson's 2-69 AR rolled into Al Kifl to relieve Captain Benton's exhausted force, after thirty-six hours of almost continuous fighting. Before midnight Benton's force was back in the battalion assembly area to get a few hours sleep before preparing for the assault on the Karbala Gap.

The battle at Al Kifl was far from over. Sanderson was ordered to move across the Euphrates, seize Al Kifl, and penetrate to a depth of ten kilometers. This was just the kind of battle the Iraqis were hoping for. By luring the Americans into an urban environment they hoped to replay the U.S. Rangers' experience in Somalia. What they did not factor into their plan, according to Sanderson, "was the combat power of the Abrams main battle tank. When they went through town, it was decisive."

Sanderson sent his tanks right through the town. When they came out on the other side, they encountered a large enemy unit in traveling formation. According to Sanderson, "The Iraqis appeared surprised to find us in front of them, and we did not give them any time to recover from that surprise." For the next seventy hours, Sanderson's battalion held off attack after attack, as the Iraqis made every effort to retake the bridge. Sanderson was not much intimidated by the enemy's tactical ability ("If they had well-trained, disciplined infantry they could have forced me out of the town"), but he could not help but be impressed by the ferocity and suicidal courage of the Fedayeen. "I saw guys that showed a great willingness to die, by attacking tanks with pick-up trucks mounting .50-caliber machine guns. We were forced to assist many of them in their goal." Regular army and even some Republican Guard soldiers were not as impressive. In fact, Sanderson's troopers captured many, both army and Guard, in the process of changing out of their uniforms into civilian clothes. He was absolutely astounded by the hundreds of POWs who were wearing civilian clothes under their uniforms.

There was, however, one thing Sanderson encountered for the first time, which infuriated him. As he relates it: "At Al Kifl it was the first time my unit truly began to see violations of the laws of land warfare. Iraqis would approach under a white flag and as my men came forward to accept the surrender, they would open fire. Even now, I am still shocked at the number of violations I witnessed."

Sanderson had been in his new position around Al Kifl for only a few hours when he got a call that JSTARS (which could spot virtually any vehicle moving in Iraq) had spotted a convoy of more than one thousand vehicles bearing down on his positions. Sanderson had a lot of faith in his battalion, but he doubted they could defeat a force that big. Though JSTARS was becoming notorious for alarming and incorrect reports, Sanderson could not afford to take any chances. He ordered his engineers to use shape charges to destroy the roads leading into Al Kifl. At the same time he brought as much of his armored combat power forward as possible; he laid them in with interlocking fields of fire, making a giant kill-sack to his front. To keep RPG-armed infiltrators at bay, Sanderson dismounted his infantry and ordered them to occupy buildings in the vicinity of his tanks and Bradleys. Finally, he asked for and was very appreciative of Air Force support, which soon began pummeling the advancing column.

By the time the leading units of the Iraqi counterattack began arriving, the great sandstorm was letting up. Sanderson's soldiers could see the approaching enemy at more than one thousand meters away, with predictable results. Any Iraqis who had managed to survive constant air bombardment and strafing were now trying to unload right in the center of Sanderson's prepared kill-zones. The Iraqi's attack collapsed under a storm of fire, which left the area quiet until relief arrived.

After almost three days of continuous fighting Sanderson's battalion was relieved by units of the 101st Airborne and he returned to his parent 3rd Brigade. After rearming and conducting hasty maintenance, the exhausted unit was ordered to move to and seize the Karbala Gap.

So what did the 3rd ID and the Coalition effort gain from the fight at Al Kifl? First and foremost, it cut off aid that was flowing south into Najaf, where the 3-7 CAV was fighting for its life. That aid would have been a major threat to the logistical buildup going on at Rams. Furthermore, according to Colonel Grimsley, "We found out later from maps captured at Objective Peach that they had Kifl circled in red as the place they thought we were going to cross on the way to Baghdad. So if nothing else, in addition to killing a whole lot of the enemy who we would now not have to face in Baghdad and allowing us to isolate Najaf from outside help, what it really did for us was add to part of the grand deception that we were only after ways to cross the Euphrates and we were still going to use what they thought was our major lane of approach, Highway 8, up to Baghdad."

The 3rd ID could not have cared less about Highway 8, but the Iraqis kept nearly all of their Republican Guard combat power on the east side of the Euphrates to guard that approach. The fight at Al Kifl went a long way towards convincing the Iraqi supreme command that they had correctly guessed American intentions. As the 3rd ID prepared to push through the Karbala Gap, west of the Euphrates, this Iraqi error in judgment would doom the Saddam regime.

13

Riding to the Cavalry's Rescue

(27–29 MARCH)

LIEUTENANT COLONEL ERIC SCHWARTZ's 1-64 Armor
had conducted an active defense of Objective Rams since their
arrival three days before; meanwhile the rest of the 2nd Brigade
was resting, rearming, and refueling on Objective Spartans, approximately thirty miles to the north. Moreover, most of the 1st Brigade,
except those units fighting at Al Kifl, were in position, adjacent to the
2nd brigade, on Objective Raiders. Schwartz was operating alone; in
order to keep the Fedayeen off balance, he adopted the same methods
of attack and withdrawal Charlton was using at Samawah. In the midst
of these operations he got word from Brigadier General Louis Weber
that the 3-7 CAV was heavily engaged and almost out of ammunition.
Weber wanted Schwartz to ride to the rescue of the cavalry as soon as
possible, leaving the recently arrived 2-70 AR to secure Rams.

Schwartz did a hasty mission analysis and decided that the best bet
was to drive straight through the southern portion of Najaf and seize
three bridges over the Euphrates. He hoped his soldiers could make
contact with the CAV at one of them. It was a big mission. By itself,
seizing three bridgeheads was going to strain the resources of the battalion, but Schwartz's troops would also have to maintain route security along their entire path through the city. As Schwartz later noted:

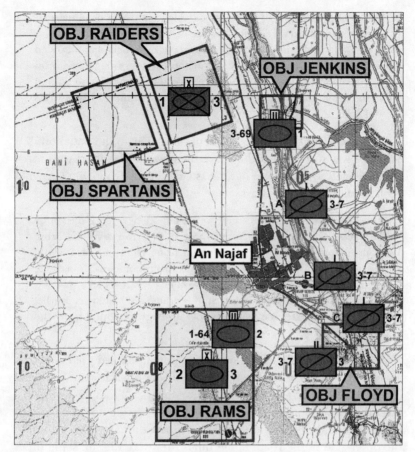

MAP 12. 3-7 CAV just before rescue mission was launched

We determined that it was gong to be tight and we were going to probably face something similar to the fight we had on Rams with militia and Fedayeen. We also knew that there were some regulars in Najaf who would provide more of a mechanized, anti-tank look. We put a package together, where we were going to attack deliberately and quickly into Najaf.

The main obstacle at the time was the weather. I don't know where the term came from, but we call it negative illumination. The conditions were absolutely horrible. The Martian sandstorm was that day. Everybody's faces were green from the raining mud. It was terrible, but we also knew that, if it was unbearable weather for us, it must be worse for them. So we decided to seize that opportunity to attack.

We attacked swiftly. We put a combat package together and rolled right up the road, right to Najaf, in the early morning. We got in there, and within four or five minutes from our start point, we started taking some pretty substantial dismounted fire. Initially, it was RPGs and AKs.

The small arms and RPGs were nothing new to the battalion, but Schwartz was surprised at the more unconventional attacks his force was subjected to—the kind of attacks Crazyhorse Troop, 3-7 CAV had been fending off for two days.

As we drove deeper into the city, we started seeing a lot of the tricks. The Fedayeen were firing from private homes. You saw them firing from behind families. You'd see them firing from mosques. You'd see them firing from rooftops with anti-aircraft guns. You'd see them trying to ram us with trucks or other civilian vehicles. It was a bit shocking to see that kind of stuff, because we hadn't seen it before. We would later see quite a bit of it in Baghdad. But this was the first time.

Captain Andy Hilmes, A Company commander, led the battalion's attack into Najaf. He credited the fight through Najaf with preparing him and his soldiers for the remainder of the war. "From this point on," he said, "the war was really armored columns moving up on roads and engaging enemy dismounts with RPGs, mortars and recoilless rifles on the other side of the road. Some times they were dug in, some times not. Usually, they were reinforced by technicals."

Leading with a tank platoon, Hilmes began moving toward a key intersection in southeast Najaf, later to become known as Checkpoint Charlie. Almost immediately his company began to take small arms fire, initially from one side of the road, but as they moved forward it increased in intensity and came from both sides. What struck him most was that the enemy was so close.

They were immediately on the side of the road, only about five meters away. Some guys were a little further out, maybe 100 meters. The loaders that day were going nuts with the 240 machine guns. They began engaging these guys immediately on the side of the road. Some times they were pulling out M-4s and M-16s to finish off those engagements. The intensity of the sandstorm made it much more difficult to acquire targets with much more than maybe two to three seconds' advance notice.

First Lieutenant Ryan Kuo, lead tank platoon leader, remembers passing through Checkpoint Charlie and seeing dozens of Fedayeen firing at him from the midst of women and children. "They would use the women to get within five or ten meters of us, shoot, and run away." Throughout his movement trucks would race up and disgorge Fedayeen, who would then run into whatever building was closest and start firing at the column.

> One truck just came screaming right up in front of us and then parked less than ten meters away, and everyone in back started shooting at us. No sooner had we destroyed that truck than another one came up on my left side. It came up to the intersection and stopped right behind a civilian car with a guy in it waving his hands like, "I'm just a civilian. Don't shoot me." The tank behind me saw a bunch of guys in the back with RPGs and AK-47s and engaged right over the top of the civilian. He destroyed it along with most of the personnel that was in it.

Major Michael Donovan, the battalion's operations officer, started moving through Checkpoint Charlie with the engineers. He noted a burning body in a pickup truck and wondered how that had happened, because the vehicle was so close. He could not believe any of the preceding combat forces would let a bad guy get that close without engaging. "Then I looked to my right and saw a minivan come hurtling toward us and slam on the brakes. The door slid open and two guys jumped out with AKs. The only thing I could bring to bear was my M-4 rifle, so I started shooting at them. As we got farther and farther away, I couldn't seem to get them. Then I watched all of the engineers turn their weapon systems on this vehicle and shoot it to pieces."

As the trail company, commanded by Captain Larry Burris, came through Checkpoint Charlie, he ordered a halt to suppress heavy RPG fire coming from his right. Suicide drivers took advantage of his pause to make their attacks.

> Two cars with guys with AK-47s came from the north, right at our vehicles. One of the tanks destroyed the first vehicle with its .50-caliber and it careened off the road. The second vehicle was a taxi, which my fire support officer killed with his coax. Right behind the

two cars, there was a bus, which had apparently been taken over by a couple soldiers. On seeing the two cars get shot, the guy driving the bus made an abrupt left turn, maintained his speed, and was heading straight at my Bradley. I tried to get my driver to move out of the way, but there was no room because we were right up on the back deck of a tank. At this point, my 25mm gun malfunctioned, so all I could do was sit and watch the bus come toward us. He didn't veer off at all. Once he picked up the course, he came right at us. The bus slammed into the left side of my track at full speed. I was able to watch the driver's head plant itself into the rack on the side of the Bradley. At that point, we all quickly breathed a sigh of relief because the bus didn't blow up. We all thought the bus would have explosives on it.

Much like 3-7 CAV on its way to Najaf, Schwartz's battalion had to endure a gauntlet of fire as it moved to link up with the CAV at Objective Floyd. However, by late in the day, it had accomplished the linkup, and Ferrell's cavalry troopers moved off to Objective Rams for a much-needed rest. The 1-64 AR would remain in its new positions stretching from Checkpoint Charlie to Objective Floyd for the next three days, under almost constant attack. Charlie Company's commander, Captain Jason Conroy, describes the action at Checkpoint Charlie, which paralleled what was happening throughout the 1-64 AR's sector:

We saw the bus that was reported to have crashed into a Bradley. One guy on the bus was dead, but another was getting off the bus as we pulled up there. He was shot and killed. I also saw a small truck filled with infantry that had run into a bus stop. Four of them were dead, but two were still alive. One fought us and was killed and the other was captured. There was also a bunker system near the bus stop that had enemy personnel hiding in it. As we showed up on the perimeter, I saw a bus full of civilians with about six armed Fedayeen mixed with them. I dismounted some of my infantry and they killed most of the Fedayeen on the bus with well-aimed shots before the final two surrendered.

As we were setting up our perimeter, I had guys on the ground giving medical treatment to the civilians and prisoners. As we were doing that, eight suicide trucks came in from different directions, driving at full speed straight at our vehicles. They were being shot up and killed as they came in.

Right beside the checkpoint there was a school where a significant number of dismounts were shooting at us with small arms and RPGs. We engaged and killed them, but there was one corner of the

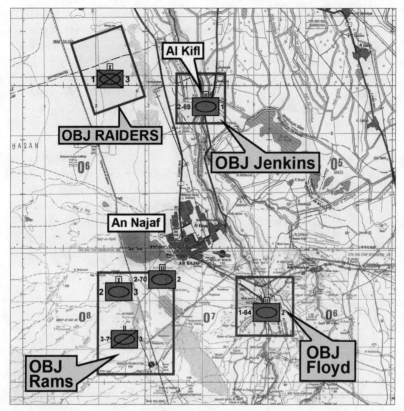

MAP 13. Positions after 3-7 CAV moved to Rams

building where they kept going back to. We stacked four guys' bodies right on top of each other. Every time they went up there, we'd shoot one guy right on top of the other.

We sat there and slowly gained control of the perimeter. Throughout the night, we received mortar, RPG, and small arms fire. Every half hour or so, we'd get two or three dismounts that would come and try to attack our position. They would try to low crawl up to our position. I really don't think they understood we had the night vision capabilities.

For the next two days, we had control of the checkpoint. It was a constant firefight. We'd go an hour where nothing would happen, and then all of a sudden we'd get hit with a mortar barrage and eight to ten guys would race out shooting with AK-47s and RPGs. On the second day we captured the two-star general in charge of the ground forces in Najaf, as he tried to infiltrate through our positions. He was captured with a lieutenant colonel, a major, and several other soldiers. They had two children with them that they were using to carry their weapons, which they had wrapped in rugs.

Iraqi civilians would come during the day and pick up some of the dead. They would not pick up the Fedayeen, because they were from Baghdad. They would only pick up the locals whom the Fedayeen made fight by threatening to kill their families.

This was the first time we encountered the terrorist tactics that we would see a lot of later on. They used women and children as human shields. Several times they used a woman to drive into our positions while they hid in the back seat. As they came up to us, they'd pop up and shoot AK-47s. They also used ambulances and other Red Crescent vehicles to drive up and pretend they were with the hospital. They'd unload some persons and the ambulance would drive off. Inevitably, whoever they left behind would let fly with a salvo of RPGs as the ambulance receded into the distance.

Daily, we had to deal with a large flow of civilians trying to leave An Najaf. They said they were fleeing the Fedayeen who were killing families in the city to encourage the men to fight us harder. As they were fleeing, the Fedayeen targeted them with AK-47 and mortar fire. I assume they were trying to keep them in the city as a protective shield.

On the third day of unrelenting attacks, 1-64 AR was relieved in place by the 1st Brigade of the 101st Airborne Division, which took over the isolation and final assault on Najaf. Schwartz then took his men north, to join the rest of the 2nd Brigade at Objective Spartans and to prepare for the final drive to Baghdad.

14

The Dark Hours

B Y 28 MARCH, the 3rd ID had penetrated halfway to Baghdad and was poised to finish the job. However, that clarity of vision was not evident in the Vth Corps and higher headquarters, all the way back to the Washington. Far removed from the day-to-day battles being fought by the 3rd ID, an entirely different perception of the war was developing. That picture was a lot more troubling then what was visible to the 3rd ID's soldiers. In Washington, military and political leaders, as well as the average citizen, were hearing only about apparent disasters.

The Marines were seemingly stopped after a vicious fight in Nasiriyah left close to two dozen Marines killed. News channels were showing burning Marine armored vehicles every fifteen minutes. When the news was not covering the Marine's troubles, it was reporting on an Army maintenance unit (the 507th Maintenance Battalion), which apparently had gotten lost and was now all dead or taken prisoner— including Private Jessica Lynch.

Moreover, the first reports were filtering out about the near-catastrophic deep attack launched by the 11th Attack Helicopter Regiment (AHR). This unit launched an ill-advised attack with thirty Apache helicopters to seek out and destroy as much of the Medina Division as possible. The Apaches walked into a firestorm. By the time the attack was called off, two helicopters had crashed (with two pilots captured), and the rest of the helicopters were so severely shot up that they were removed from service. For the remainder of the war the 11th AHR was capable of conducting only the most limited missions.

Unfortunately, this was not the only bad military news that was making its way up the chain of command and to the American public. The fanatical attacks of the Fedayeen had come as a total surprise to the U.S. military, and more than a few senior commanders were unnerved. Many were making a big issue of the Vth Corps commander's comment to journalists, "The enemy we are fighting is a bit different from the enemy wargamed against, because of these paramilitary forces. We knew they were here, but we did not know how they would fight." This simple statement of truth was misinterpreted at CENTCOM (Central Command) and Washington as an admission that the Vth Corps was facing something it could not handle.

When unfounded fears of this "unexpected enemy" were coupled with the temporary logistics halt (coinciding with the worst sandstorm in fifty years), it was easy to get the impression that the Iraqis had fought the most powerful military in the world to a standstill. As we saw earlier in this book, the Iraqi supreme command was certain that things were looking pretty good for the home team, and it was at this point Saddam asked his Russian and French "friends" to postpone any plans to call for an immediate ceasefire.

On their televisions, Americans were hearing from "Baghdad Bob" on a regular basis about how their forces were bogged down and on the verge of destruction. Normally, most Americans would have smiled and ignored such reports, as they did later in the war, but at this point in the war Baghdad Bob was not alone. A constant parade of U.S. military analysts, some of them our most respected retired officers (including General Barry McCaffrey, who had commanded the 24th Division during Operation Desert Storm), appeared on TV to castigate the Pentagon's war plan. Over and over again Americans heard that the invasion force was too small and Donald Rumsfeld did not commit enough soldiers to the fight. Most of the talking heads agreed that at the very least the Army and Marines would have to halt in place until the 1st Armored and 4th Infantry Divisions arrived in country.

A distinct air of pessimism, if not yet despair, was becoming pervasive everywhere except among the combat leaders in the Marine Expeditionary Force and the 3rd ID. If you talked to any of the 3rd ID battalion or brigade commanders at this time, you were struck by their uniform optimism. By happy coincidence it was at this time I met Colonel Dave Perkins and members of his staff on the outskirts of Najaf. I was an embedded journalist for *Time Magazine* and was traveling with the 1st Brigade of the 101st Airborne Division, which was coming to Najaf to relieve Perkins's troops.

I got a chance to ask Perkins if the Fedayeen attacks were causing him as much trouble as was being reported back in the United States. He replied, "I didn't expect this many of them, but all that means is that I have to use up more ammo. And I have plenty of that, especially if it means I do not have to face these guys in Baghdad." His operations officer, Major Kevin Dunlop, chimed in, "It is not a fair fight. Trucks with machine guns against tanks and Bradleys can have only one outcome. We were slaughtering them." As far as 3rd ID commanders were concerned, the bizarre tactics used by the Fedayeen were heaven-sent. Rather than having to be dug out of a fortified city in bloody house-to-house fighting, the Fedayeen were opting to charge directly into the massed firepower of armored battalions.

It may not have been the enemy that the Vth Corps commander, Lieutenant General William Wallace, or the 3rd was expecting to fight, but neither was it an enemy that filled their hearts with fear.

After our quick meeting, Perkins left with Colonel Ben Hodges, the 101st Airborne, 1st Brigade commander, to make a tour of the Najaf battlefield. Temporarily left behind at Perkins's assault command post, I fired up my satellite system and checked my e-mail from *Time Magazine*. There I found a note informing me that the cover for the next edition was going to be in big red letters, "WHY ARE WE LOSING," and asking me to find stories that supported the cover.

When Perkins returned I went over and mentioned the title of the cover and asked if he had any comment. I remember him reflecting for a moment and then replying. "Today my brigade leaves Najaf and heads north. Tomorrow we rest, rearm, and refuel. The next day I attack to annihilate the Medina Division. The day after that I will be in Baghdad." He also mentioned that Grimsley's 1st Brigade would be on the Baghdad International Airport at the same time. I did some rapid calculations and realized that *Time Magazine* was going to announce America's defeat in Iraq on the same day that the 3rd ID's soldiers were knocking on the door of Baghdad.

I wrote back to *Time Magazine* that the entire premise of their cover was wrong and they were on the verge of looking awfully stupid. I later learned that this started a huge editorial fight in the New York office. It seemed that I was the only embed they knew of who was saying that things were going well. I explained that virtually every other embed was at a lower level then I was. They were sitting with infantry platoons, where they were ill-fed, dirty, and exhausted. They did not have the larger perspective to understand the true picture. Embeds at levels above where I was, on the other hand, were at such a high level they were hearing senior generals beginning to take counsel of their fears.

In the end, I had to rely on the fact that my reports and information on the war so far had been uniformly correct and they should just trust that I was right. In a major concession, *Time*'s editors changed the cover from "WHY ARE WE LOSING" to "WHAT WILL IT TAKE TO WIN." When a few days later the issue in question hit the newsstands on the same day that the 1st Brigade seized Baghdad International Airport, there was a bit of relief on my part at having made the right call. At the same time there was much joy and mirth at *Time*'s offices because *Newsweek* had gone with "QUAGMIRE" on its cover.

Before Colonel Perkins left me, he got a report that an Iraqi colonel had just walked up to the line and surrendered. "Just like that?" Perkins asked. Captain Cary Adams replied, "He said he was a POW in the last Gulf War, so he has some practice in surrendering when things go bad."

As the sandstorm from hell began to blow itself out, General Blount was becoming impatient with the pause. He had two full brigades massed between Najaf and Karbala and was worried that the longer they sat in the same place the greater the chances they would be hit by artillery. He was particularly concerned that the Iraqis would launch a chemical or biological attack on his static positions. Blount began pressing hard for permission to launch his forces through the Karbala Gap and on to Bagdad immediately. With reports coming in that the gap was wide open, Blount was not even inclined to wait for Allyn's 3rd brigade to close up with the rest of the division. Unsure of the current battle condition of the Medina Division, the Vth Corps refused to consider an early resumption of the offensive.

Looking for ways to keep the momentum and the enemy off balance, Blount recommended a feint towards the Euphrates River at Hindiyah. This attack would serve to further confuse the Iraqis by diverting their attention from the Karbala Gap. Once again they would have reason to think the 3rd ID planned to attack across the

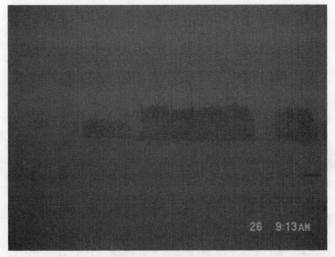

26   9:13 AM

The "sandstorm from hell" turned the air red and convinced
some officers that someone must have "popped a nuke." When
rain came, mud actually fell from the sky.

Euphrates and up Highway 1. Moreover, it was hoped an attack so
close to the Medina Division would draw fire from Republican Guard
artillery, which was currently hiding in scattered palm groves. As they
fired to support the Iraqi forces at Hindiyah they would be detected
by counterfire radar, engaged, and destroyed—removing one more
obstacle on the road to Baghdad.

General Wallace approved this plan and even broadened it into
what has become known in the Army as the "Five Attacks." In addition to Blount's attack at Hindiyah, the 101st would make a feint from
Al Kifl to Hillah, and attack into Najaf, while conducting a strong
armored recon to the west. Simultaneously, the 82nd Airborne would
begin clearing Samawah. The "Five Attacks" were scheduled to start
on 30 March. General Wallace hoped that having to deal with five
events simultaneously would overload the Iraqi supreme command
and cause its collapse. However, he was giving the Iraqi command
credit for being able to perform at an order of magnitude above its
true ability. Asked about their perceptions of the "Five Attacks" after
the war, numerous Iraqi generals claimed ignorance. They had never
even noticed the five attacks. For them the only reality was the tanks
at the tip of the spear. Everything behind them, with a few exceptions,

Troops rest in Objective Raiders, waiting for the order to begin the final assault on Baghdad.

was a mystery to Iraqi leaders. The "Five Attacks" could not overload a command system that was not even developed enough to realize it was under attack.

Blount assigned the feint on Hindiyah (now designated Objective Murray) to Perkins's 2nd Brigade. Perkins in turn assigned the mission to Lieutenant Colonel Phillip deCamp's 4-64 AR battalion, with Lieutenant Colonel Eric Schwartz's 1-64 AR held in reserve. Initially, deCamp was told to make the feint look as much like the main attack as possible. To do this he was told to seize the bridge at Hindiyah and throw at least two full combat companies across it. Just before the attack commenced though, Blount called. With fresh memories of having troops almost trapped on the wrong side of the river when the Iraqis blew the bridge at Al Kifl, Blount warned Perkins that under no circumstances was he to send any forces across the river. DeCamp was supposed to go into Hindiyah and just sit. If things went as planned he would become a "shit magnet."

Lieutenant Colonel deCamp relates: "Very early in the morning, just before the attack, we got a message that the division commander did not want us to drop the bridge or cross it. They just wanted us to come in and hold the bridge, hoping that would be enough to draw Iraqi forces from throughout the area to us." Captain Chris Carter's A Company led the battalion attack. He describes the event:

As we pulled to the outskirts of the city, we were hit by a fairly high volume of RPG and small arms fire. One track was hit in the driver's side with an RPG, which penetrated the armor. However, the driver maintained his composure and continued moving on. He actually made it all the way down to the objective before he stopped and checked himself out—damaged but still combat effective.

Once we got to the bridgehead, we essentially re-task organized the company, leaving one infantry platoon back about 400 meters to the west. We had two Bradleys and two tanks to the south of the bridge and two tanks and two Bradleys to the north of the bridge.

When we arrived at the bridge site, we began taking numerous RPG volleys from the vicinity of a mosque on our side of the bridge.

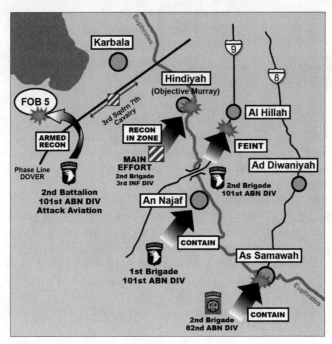

MAP 14. The Five Attacks plan

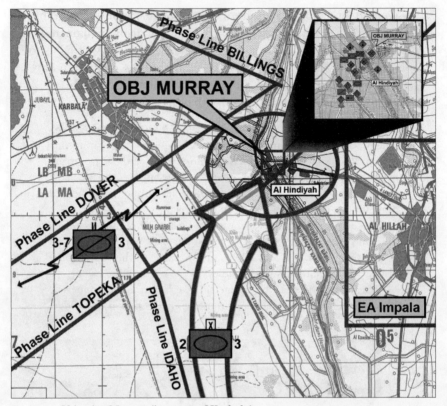

MAP 15. Objective Murray (just east of Karbala)

We absorbed the fire, but did not engage the mosque. When we got our infantry squads on the ground, the majority of the personnel shooting from the mosque turned their attention towards them and we were able to ignore it.

We continued to receive sniper fire from the building just to the east of the mosque. They were shooting from a rooftop and kept it up until we were able to place the company sniper team on top of another building. They killed the enemy snipers that were harassing us.

After we were at the bridge about a half hour, Sergeant First Class Wright identified a woman on the bridge. She waved a couple times, but after that she fell down. We thought she had died. A short time after that, she stood up or sat up again and waved at us. Sergeant First Class Wright and the medics followed me in my Bradley up to the woman. After evaluating the woman and finding out she was good to move, we called a medic 113 forward and evacuated her. Our first sergeant evacuated her back to the field hospital, where she was treated.

Captain Carter rescuing this woman, while under fire, was captured by an AP photographer and beamed around the world. It was later discovered that the Iraqi soldiers or Fedayeen were going to use her as a human shield, but she had walked away. As she crossed the bridge, an Iraqi shot her in the back; the hospital confirmed a .762 wound (the Iraqi caliber). The Iraqis had plenty more human shields with whom to replace her. As deCamp remembers: "I moved my tank right up to the front of the bridge. We could see up the street, vehicles with machine guns were getting ready to rush the bridge. We destroyed two or three of them as they came up the street. Then they started putting women and children in front of the trucks as they were coming up the street. That caused a lot of problems, because we couldn't shoot. We thought this was not the type of battle we wanted to get into, where they were using human shields."

On the outskirts of the town, deCamp had left Captain Phillip Wolford and his company to secure his rear. As deCamp was working out how to deal with an enemy using women and children as shields, what

Captain Carter moves under fire to rescue an Iraqi woman shot by the Fedayeen as she tried to cross the Euphrates to safety.

had been some light skirmishing in Wolford's area grew into a rather intense fight.

> We started taking heavy machine gun and mortar fire, along with RPG fire from a wood line. Also, the mortar fire we had been subjected to earlier was now coming closer. Some Iraqis were in a firing line about fifty meters off the road, but the majority were set back further. I got flanked down a trench line. We began returning fire and the fight escalated for a while. Eventually our firepower overwhelmed them, and during a lull we took twenty-four prisoners and counted twenty-five Iraqi KIA. After that fight, our counterintelligence team went out and checked bodies for usable information. That is when we realized we missed two machine gun positions in the wood line. Staff Sergeant Grissom dismounted his vehicle, threw a grenade, and rushed the bunkers with his 9mm pistol. He pinned them down with his pistol and put a grenade right on top of them. That was the end of the fight. He ended up killing one of them with a grenade and another with his 9 mil. Two more, both captains, surrendered.

With the bridge blocked the Iraqis found a new method to get at deCamp's soldiers. As reported by Sergeant First Class Wright: "Quite a few guys started to come at us in boats, while a number of civilians were using boats to get out of the area. It was hard to tell which boats were coming at us from those trying to flee. From what I could see, it was mainly soldiers coming toward us. There were boats all up and down the sides of the river. You'd look down at the edge and see hundreds of boats on both sides, but there were only about six or seven boats that were coming toward us."

DeCamp talked over his situation with Perkins. He had people attacking with boats and others approaching the bridge by land. In both cases, the Iraqis were using women and children as human shields. Between them they discussed whether it was time to end the fight at Hindiyah, as neither commander wanted to risk significant civilian casualties for what was just a feint. DeCamp finally told Perkins, "Hey, it's probably about the right time to withdraw out of the city." Perkins agreed.

The attack had met some resistance, but it had failed to draw the kind of reaction Blount had hoped for. However, it did turn up some critical intelligence. Some of deCamp's prisoners were from the Nebuchadnezzar Republican Guard Division. At the time, CENTCOM was still showing the Nebuchadnezzar Division as being well to the north in Tirkrit. Somehow, the Iraqis had managed to move an entire division two hundred miles without being detected. A few days after this first contact, Perkins's 2nd Brigade would tear the once-proud Nebuchadnezzar Division to pieces.

Early in the morning, after leaving Hindiyah, deCamp's soldiers rejoined the rest of the 2nd Brigade. By now Allyn's 3rd Brigade had come up from the south, and for the first time since the war started, the entire 3rd ID was massed in one spot. Blount continued pushing for a resumption of the advance, and it appeared that those above him were coming around to his point of view.

The dark days were over!

15

Karbala

(1 APRIL)

THROUGHOUT THE LIGHTNING advance across Iraq, senior commanders had one constant worry—what would happen when they went through the Karbala Gap. The gap was only a few kilometers wide and situated between the western edge of the holy city of Karbala and a large lake. General Blount planned to push the entire 3rd ID through the keyhole along two roads of dubious quality. For a period of forty-eight hours, thousands of vehicles would be jammed into a very small place. During that time they would make a perfect target for Iraqi artillery. Furthermore, if the Iraqis were going to make a stand anywhere, Karbala was the place for it. Digging in along the north side of the gap presented the Iraqis with their best chance of delaying and bottling up the 3rd ID for an indefinite period. Even though there was little likelihood that the Iraqis could have stopped the division from forcing its way through the gap, they could certainly delay progress and inflict losses.

This potential delay was a matter of some trepidation for General Blount. Every hour he was delayed not only meant more casualties for the division, but also gave the Republican Guard forces defending Baghdad more time to improve their positions and prepare a hot greeting for the 3rd ID when it closed on the Iraqi capital. However, all of these fears paled when compared to every 3rd ID commander

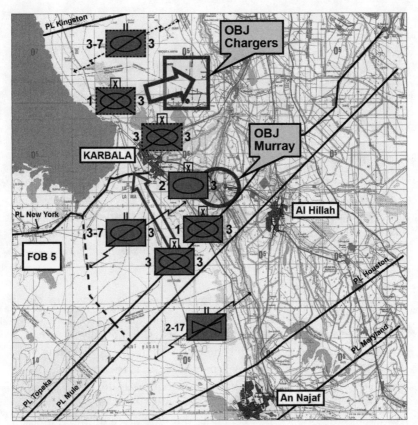

MAP 16. Pushing past Karbala

and soldier's biggest fear—chemicals. If Saddam was going to use any
of his stockpiled chemical weapons, which everyone in the division
was certain he possessed, it would be in the Karbala Gap. He would
never again have such a lucrative target.

Blount knew that, outside of placing his soldiers in chemical protective gear and getting through the gap as rapidly as possible, there
was little he could do about an Iraqi chemical strike except deal with
the consequences. Of more pressing concern was what to do about
Karbala itself and the Iraqi troops positioned in and around it. The
fanatical attacks out of the bypassed cities of Najaf and Samawah had
put the division on alert for more of the same out of Karbala. With so
many vehicles crammed into such a small space, even the slightest dis-

1st Brigade moves through the Karbala Gap. All guns face Karbala, where the 2-69 AR Battalion is fighting hard to secure the city.

ruption would delay the advance for hours and could lead to a major catastrophe.

To prevent this Blount planned to use Colonel Allyn's 3rd BCT to isolate Karbala, destroy any enemy forces in the surrounding area, and, finally, to annihilate any armed force that tried to move out of the city. Allyn and his men, having just rejoined the rest of the division, were uniquely suited to their new mission. For most of the past two weeks the brigade had been guarding the three hundred miles of the division's lines of communication. Allyn's men had become expert at isolating large cities, containing hostile forces, and when required destroying them.

Now, Allyn was tasked to do the same thankless but critical task again. This time, however, there was zero room for error. If any Fedayeen had escaped from Samawah to attack the convoys heading north, it would at worse have produced a minor delay and distraction. If, however, they escaped from Karbala, it could easily lead to a disaster. To accomplish this mission Allyn had his Brigade Reconnaissance Troop, along with Lieutenant Colonel Jeffrey Sanderson's 2-69 AR Battalion and Lieutenant Colonel Wesley Gillman's 1-30 IN Battalion.

Allyn was sure he would meet a significant force in and around Karbala. As he later said, "If I was on the Iraqi side, I would have seen the Karbala Gap as the only and best place to make a significant impact on our forces."

Certain that the Iraqis would make a strong stand at Karbala, the division preceded 3rd Brigade's assault with a massive artillery prep of the entire area. In one overwhelming fire mission, 3rd ID artillery and MLRS batteries opened fire on every Iraqi artillery position that radar and other means had acquired over the previous forty-eight hours. In an instant a large portion of the Iraqi artillery in the area was blanketed by deadly DPICM rounds. DPICM—short for Duel Purpose Improved Conventional Munitions—rounds each release forty-eight bomblets over their target, which float down to earth and on impact jump four feet in the air and explode. No exposed soldier within the target radius of a DPICM round will survive the experience. This massive artillery prep began just as Sanderson's 2-69 AR began moving towards its assault position. As he remembers it, "There was zero percent lume [total darkness], and all you could see was MLRS rockets firing. We were shooting base bleed DPICM, which has a rocket that burns so all you could see were the rounds out in front of you. Then you could here them land." From the ground, the MLRS rounds carrying their deadly cargo looked like a mass of brilliant shooting stars racing across the desert sky. On the receiving end though, that momentary beauty became truly terrible.

As Allyn's battalions began their assault, another massive artillery prep began. This one was orchestrated by Lieutenant Colonel Doug Harding, whose 1-10 FA (field artillery) Battalion was firing in direct support of Allyn's brigade. According to Harding, "We fired a plan that called for a massive artillery prep from all three of my batteries, firing on each intersection in advance of the lead armored company that would come through there. We triggered them based on where they were on the road. At a given point, we'd fire." Harding fired a mix of close to 500 DPICM and high-explosive rounds according to a plan that made use of all the lessons the division had learned since the beginning of the war. His fires were designed to overwhelm the Iraqi Fedayeen, who habitually launched their ambushes from rooftops and intersection overpasses, where they could fire down onto weaker top armor of American vehicles. Harding's prep fire was designed to sweep those high places clear of Iraqi defenders.

One of Harding's senior NCO's later said that knowing they were all the support the 3rd Brigade had was a strong motivating factor for the gunners. "It seemed at times as if they were racing to see how fast they could fire a mission, once a call for fires had come in." For their part, Allyn's troops had the utmost confidence in the professional abilities of the gunners; the lead tanks were often assaulting so close to the last round to explode that the dust and dirt had not even begun to settle. Harding was never sure how many Iraqi defenders were killed by his bombardment, but he was comforted by the fact that Allyn's soldiers reached their objectives without being engaged by the enemy at any of the locations the 1-10 FA fired its prep fires into. As Harding said, "We either killed them, or strongly encouraged them to get out of the way." Lieutenant Colonel Sanderson later said of his artillery support, "We attacked under some of the best artillery you'll ever see. 10th Artillery was everywhere that night. They fired dozens and dozens of missions up and down this road."

As Allyn's troops made their way forward it became obvious that the Karbala Gap itself was either lightly defended or completely devoid of Iraqi troops. The major obstacle to Gillman's 1-30 IN's movement turned out not to be the Iraqis, but an American engineer unit that was apparently moving through the gap early in order to position itself to support the upcoming assault across the Euphrates River. For reasons still unexplained, the Iraqi commander at Karbala had discounted the possibility that the 3rd ID would come through the gap and had instead placed virtually all of his defenses to the southern and eastern sides of the city. Even though the maneuver space seemed much greater east of the city, this was deceptive, as some of Perkins's 2 BCT units found out the next day when they tried to use that route in order to avoid the brewing traffic jam in the gap. Between the Euphrates and the eastern edge of Karbala the land is divided by almost numberless ditches, dikes, irrigation canals, and all the accumulated impediments expected from thousands of years of agricultural use.

Even so, ignoring the gap itself seems a curious oversight by the Republican Guard II Corps commander, Lieutenant General Hamdani, who clearly understood that the Karbala Gap was the one place where he could stop or at least delay the American advance. In his memoirs, he states that he requested an entire division be placed at the northern edge of the gap and in Karbala. His request was refused; instead he was told to keep all of his Regular and Republican Guard forces on the east side of the Euphrates River and well away from Karbala. After the war the Iraqi chief of staff stated that it was Saddam's order to keep these units on the east side of the Euphrates. He was apparently worried that any units on the west side would be cut off and not available to defend Baghdad in the event the Coalition destroyed the bridges. It can also be surmised that the 3rd ID's feints towards Al Kifl and Hindiyah had met one of their purposes, that of deceiving the Iraqis as to the 3rd ID's true intention. The Iraqi supreme command seemed convinced that one of those bridge sites represented the 3rd ID's main effort and that American tanks could be expected to launch a full-fledged assault across the Euphrates soon. They were right about the assault, but wrong about the location.

Still, Hamdani did what he could. He ordered the 14th Mechanized Brigade across to the west side of the Euphrates and gave it an on-order mission to move rapidly to close the Karbala Gap at the first indication the Americans were coming through it in force. When the Republican Guard chief of staff visited him on the day after this movement, in order to review the positioning of his forces, Hamdani lied to him about where the 14th Brigade was located, fearing the chief of staff would order the unit back across the Euphrates, where it would be far removed from what Hamdani sensed was going to be the critical point on the battlefield. In the event, the 14th Brigade failed to react until it was too late. It would first come face to face with the 3rd ID when Lieutenant Colonel Rock Marcone's 3-69 AR Battalion burst out of the gap heading for Objective Peach (see next chapter).

Even without the Regular Army or Republican Guard units there were still substantial numbers of Fedayeen and al-Quds militia in and around Karbala. Unfortunately, because of the unique way Saddam had established his command structure, these forces were not at Hamdani's command. Despite being located at the critical point of Hamdani's defensive scheme, he had no way to control their plans or actions. Like every other Fedayeen and militia unit the 3rd ID had fought, their orders came from Ba'ath political operatives and not from professional soldiers. The Karbala Fedayeen commander, seeing mile after mile of what appeared to be open space south and east of the city, pointed all of his forces in those directions. While that made them hors de combat for the 3rd ID's thrust through the gap, they could still reposition and become a substantial threat to the logistics that would follow the combat formations through the gap. Making sure they did not do so fell to Sanderson and his armored task force.

Sanderson began his attack at midnight with his companies in column. His plan was simple: march or fight his way to each major intersection on the east side of the city. Initially, he was focused on two major intersections leading to Hillia, which he named Grant and Lee. During the night he also decided that to fully isolate the city he needed to move one of his companies north to cut Highway 9, which led to Baghdad, and that was done at dawn. After his companies were positioned, Karbala was effectively cut off. None of the defenders could escape and no one could come to their aid. However, Sanderson did not find the going as easy on the east side of Karbala as Gillman's men were to find it on the west side.

Almost from the moment it began moving towards its objectives, Sanderson's column came under sustained and heavy fire. Throughout the entire march the column was firing at well-hidden enemy positions on both sides of the road. At one point Sanderson said his units stopped reporting actions to him because "there were so many contacts we had about every machine gun in the column engaging somebody to the right or left." As the 2-69 AR advanced, the terrain became more restrictive and the vegetation heavier. After two weeks of fighting in the open desert, this increased vegetation was a bit disorienting. "At times," Sanderson said, "You could be forgiven for thinking you were in a tropical jungle." As movement got tougher and the battalion closed on its objective, Iraqi resistance increased and became more sophisticated than anything the unit had seen previously.

First Lieutenant McKinley Wood, a platoon leader in A Company, noted fighting positions along the road sited so they could fire upwards toward vehicles on the road instead of firing directly at them. "They'd fire at the flanks and up through the armor to try to pierce it where it was weakest." According to Wood, "We also saw a lot of RPG ambushes in the area. They had coordinated attacks from high and low ground, so when you received an attack from the high ground, you won't expect one from the low ground firing positions." Wood's platoon, like each of the other platoons in the column, fought their way through each of these RPG ambushes; despite several RPG hits, no vehicles were lost.

The Iraqi attacks continued for hours after the 2-69 AR seized its objectives, becoming more fanatical as dawn approached. Throughout the night Sanderson's tired troops fought off technical vehicles, which mounted heavy machine guns, and many dismounted attacks. Lieutenant Wood later commented on the numerous vehicles that would launch suicide attacks by racing directly at their positions: "They were destroyed at safe ranges up to about one hundred meters. They were so close sometimes that we never got a ballistic solution. We'd just battle sight our main gun, lower it, and destroy the vehicle."

At one point during the battle Sanderson's tank shot an Iraqi approaching by foot, "Instead of falling down like I expected, he blew up. He was wearing a suicide vest and in another few yards he would have flung himself on my tank."

By dawn, the Iraqi attacks ceased.

Against the possibility that the enemy might be repositioning to the west, in order to interfere with the division's attack through the gap, Sanderson was ordered to attack directly into the city. Captain Carter Price, C Company 2-69 AR commander, described the action in a postwar interview:

> The second phase of this was the fight in Karbala. That piece consisted of us moving in toward the University of Karbala, where we set up a strong point. One of the significant parts of this operation was that we decided to run combat patrols into the heart of Karbala. The mosque area [one of Shi'a Islam's holiest sites] was a no-combat area, so we always ran our combat patrols at least five hundred meters out from the mosque.
>
> The route is seven kilometers from the University of Karbala in to the town itself. At first, it's a slum type of residential area, which changes quickly to a wealthy residential, and then into a commercial area filled with three- and four-story buildings. Two of my patrols went past Karbala's gates and into the commercial area, where we started to see significant amounts of suicide bombers. Other Iraqis were throwing Molotov cocktails from the rooftops and firing RPGs. Within a five-kilometer area, we had thirty to forty RPGs fired. We also engaged several dismounts who tried leaving the area.
>
> As we went deeper into Karbala, we got into a commercial and had to deal with the taller buildings. As all tankers know, you've only got so much elevation. At night time, your .50-caliber's all but useless. It scares people, but that's about it. However, it is the weapon that can fire the highest elevation other than the loader's 240. The elevation problem forced us to call for artillery with VT fuses. [VT is short for variable time—fuses that can be set to explode above the buildings and sweep them clean of the enemy.]
>
> As A Company got into the tight confines of the city proper we started bounding by platoon. The first platoon would draw the enemy's AT ambush out. As they did that the platoon behind them would use your 240s and coaxes to clean their brother's hips as he went forward. The Iraqis would generally try to engage you to the back right

or the back left of the tank. So the tank behind the lead tanks on the left would watch low left and the one on the right would watch low right. If we got into really restrictive terrain we could no longer use that method and had to lay our guns over top of each other.

It's a lot like stacking to clear a room for the infantry, except you're doing it with tanks. You're running close enough that it's pretty hot for your driver because of the exhaust from the engines of the tank in front of him, but it's how close you have to be to cover your buddy.

Generally, the artillery did a great job of cleaning off the rooftops. During our second night in the city I took no contact from any roof. The Iraqis were either destroyed on those rooftops or decided that was not a good time or place to come out and fight. Also, by the second night the fight had gone out of the enemy. It seemed that they were gone, which was fine by me.

The next day Sanderson's forces were relieved of their duties at Karbala by soldiers from the 101st Airborne Division who arrived to take over their mission. Sanderson and the 2-69 AR were given a few hours to rest, refuel, and rearm; then they would join the rest of the division for the assault on Baghdad. Later, Sanderson reflected that the unit had learned some good lessons at Karbala, which "would serve us exceptionally well in Baghdad. Go in under the guns. Fire the artillery. Fire the HEVT [high explosive variable time shells]. Fire at intersections. Fire it low. Fire it high. If the son of a bitch is on a rooftop with an RPG, you'll blow him away. Those were our thoughts as we left Karbala for Baghdad."

16

Objective Peach

(2 APRIL)

BY EARLY MORNING ON 1 APRIL, the 1st Brigade was through the Karbala Gap and consolidating on its far side. For Colonel Grimsley and his battalion commanders the feeling of relief was palpable. Every one of them fully expected to be slimed with chemical weapons as they moved through the gap. Now that they were clear and spreading out in the open desert, they began to feel safe again. The threat was not gone, but it was greatly diminished. The tedious passage through the gap, coupled with the incredible tension of waiting to get hit at any moment by chemical weapons, left everyone in the brigade exhausted and looking forward to a planned twelve-hour rest before beginning the lunge for the critical Euphrates bridges that would open the door to Baghdad.

General Blount had other ideas. As Blount saw it, the lack of resistance in the Karbala bottleneck and Iraq's failure to use chemicals at the division's most vulnerable moment meant the advance had rocked the Iraqis back on their heels, and Blount was not inclined to give them time to recover. He called Grimsley on the radio and asked, "When can you be ready to go forward again?"

Grimsley replied, "I can move at noon."

"Make it ten," Blount said, "We have the momentum. Use it to go on to Peach."

Major General Blount, Commander of the 3rd ID, meets with key commanders just before ordering them to move out and crush the Republican Guard Medina Division.

Ten proved to be impossible, but Grimsley managed to get his lead battalion refueled and roaring towards Objective Peach before noon.

Objective Peach (the al-Qa'id bridge) was a dual-span bridge over the Euphrates River and the final obstacle before Baghdad. It was the last chance the Iraqis would have to slow the American onslaught. General Hamdani had long recognized the importance of the bridge and was determined that it would not be an "Iraqi Remagen." Almost two weeks earlier he had put a company on the bridge under the command of one his best junior officers and ordered him to blow the bridge if he even suspected the Americans were approaching. A week later he sent his chief of staff to the bridge to make sure the defenses were ready and demolitions in place. The chief of staff took it upon himself to countermand Hamdani's order, telling the bridge commander that Saddam had ordered that no bridges be destroyed and that if the captain blew this bridge Hamdani would be executed for it. Though one span of the bridge was damaged in an unexplained explosion, the officer charged with the duty of blowing up the bridge failed to execute Hamdani's orders as 3rd ID tanks approached. Hamdani later said, "Both men acted out of personal loyalty to me, but it was a big mistake. It cost us the war."

Knowing the bridge was still standing, but not knowing how long it would remain that way, Rock Marcone's combat-tested 3-69 AR set a furious pace as it led the 1st Brigade's drive to Peach. Along the way Marcone's troops met sporadic resistance, which only two weeks earlier would have caused the attacking columns to deploy and take precious time developing the situation. But something had happened to Marcone's soldiers, as well as the rest of the 3rd ID soldiers, during the past two weeks—they had become veterans.

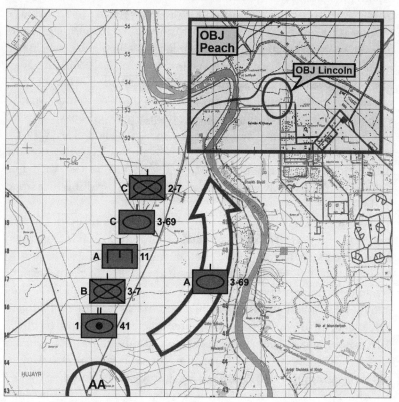

MAP 17. 3-69 AR advance to Objective Peach

Now, encountering the enemy on the line of march was routine, and only the most determined resistance called for a halt. For Marcone's veterans, enemy contacts merited only a quick radio report as armored vehicles destroyed everything they encountered and continued to advance. Radio traffic became a standard litany of targets spotted, engaged, and destroyed. Only at one point did the Iraqis make a serious stand, when two hundred soldiers (identified as Fedayeen at the time, but later proven to be elements of the Republican Guard's Medina Division) fired from behind fortified positions into the flanks of the onrushing armored column. Marcone's Alpha Company veered out of the advancing column and annihilated the position, while the rest of the battalion ignored the threat and barreled north. Fifteen minutes later, Alpha Company had finished its work and was racing to catch up. Iraqi attempts to face the 3rd ID on the battlefield had become instant death sentences for those who tried. What Marcone's troops were reporting as light and sporadic contact was actually the entire 14th Brigade of the Medina Division being ground out of existence. One Iraqi commander later lamented, "The speed at which you maneuver armor is hard to understand. Your ability to isolate Iraqi forces so that they cannot react is unbelievable. And most importantly you do not give the Iraqi army any chance to think or to understand." When asked if there was anything the Iraqi army could have done to slow the American drive he said, "The American soldiers are very disciplined. They fight like robots and engage and kill everything on the battlefield. The Americans did not even seem to react to our defensive plans. They simply fought their way through anything that stood in their path."

Worried about reports that the Americans were through the Karbala Gap and that his front was collapsing, General Hamdani rushed from his eastern sector (where the Marines were about to assault Al Kut) back to the Medina Division's headquarters north of Karbala. While receiving an open-air briefing from the Medina Division commander, Hamdani proudly watched the 1st Regiment of the 14th Brigade form up to launch a counterattack. A regiment in attack formation was a lucrative and rarely found target, and U.S. sensors almost immediately picked it up. Before the regiment could move out of its assembly area, American jets pounced. As Hamdani looked on, the First Regiment was annihilated in an instant of blast and flame. Thirty-nine Iraqis died and hundreds more were wounded.

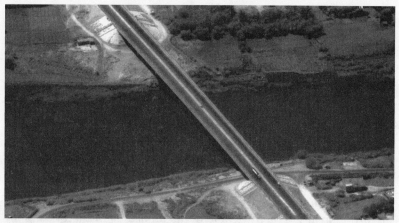

The Iraqi Remagen—A view of Objective Peach from the air. After the 1st Brigade took the bridge intact, the 2nd Brigade poured across to decimate the Medina Division.

Hamdani left with the haunting image of a field littered with severed limbs and burning hulks, where a moment before there had been a proud regiment.

A bit after 1:00 P.M. Hamdani was called back to Baghdad for what would turn out to be the most incredible meeting of the war. All he could do for the Medina's commander was to tell him to hold on as best he could and that he would send what reinforcements were available. It was a comment of despair, because by that time, Marcone's leading tanks had already covered half the distance from Karbala to Objective Peach, and the Medina's 14th Brigade was a wreck.

Grimsley and Marcone had learned a number of lessons from their seizure of the Al Kifl Bridge, especially how the Iraqis set demolitions on a bridge. If the bridge at Peach was like that at Al Kifl, then the explosives would be wired to one detonation system, with a single Iraqi officer manning it. Using the Al Kifl paradigm, that officer was likely to be watching from a building near the bridge's approach. Grimsley wanted that man dead.

When Marcone's troops were only a few miles from the bridge, Grimsley ordered the execution of a sustained multi-battery artillery barrage, followed by a series of pinpoint JDAMS attacks on each of the buildings in the bridge's immediate vicinity. As the soldiers of the 3-69

AR made their final approach, the far side erupted into balls of dust and flame.

Despite the intensity of this preemptive bombardment Marcone could not be sure that the Iraqis would not destroy the bridge as soon as his men started crossing. Remembering that the Al Kifl Bridge had been blown with his tanks on it and fearful of a repetition of that near catastrophe, Marcone decided to take the bridge with a river assault.

Captain Todd Kelly's infantry company (C/2-7 IN), which included one tank platoon, moved up to the edge of the Euphrates and established positions to guard the flanks and provide covering fire for the engineers who would assault the bridge. According to Kelly, "I was just moving my tanks into position, when what Colonel Marcone calls 'idiots' drove up in several trucks and began unloading in plain view of my guns . . . we dispatched them." Kelly's tanks and Bradleys were soon firing into the buildings across the river to kill or pin down any Iraqis willing to contest the crossing.

At the same time, Captain Dan Hibner and his engineers were three hundred yards behind Kelly's line preparing for the most audacious action of the war: a daylight river assault in small zodiac boats!

Racing against time, Hibner's soldiers prepped the unit's zodiacs for an immediate assault. By the time they manhandled the first equipment-laden boat several hundred yards to the river, his men were exhausted, but their morale was high. Gallows humor took over when a sergeant commented on what a beautiful day it was to go on a float down river . . . under enemy fire, which started everyone laughing. Hibner originally planned a four-boat assault, but it would be a considerable time before his men could muscle the next boat forward. Iraqi artillery was already beginning to fall. Fearing the Iraqis might blow the bridge at any moment, Hibner put his tired men into the boat and ordered them across. Since the boat's engine had not arrived, they had to paddle. First Lieutenant Ramon Brigantti, who commanded the first boat, remembers, "We started paddling as fast as we could, but the infantry guys with us did not know how to do it. We were out in the open, being shot at in a paddle boat, which had a big leak, and we had to stop to show the infantry how to paddle. We were also slowly drifting directly towards the building we were receiving fire from. Of course everyone was very pissed off."

Marcone had every weapon he could bring to bear plastering the buildings on the far side of the river to give his men in the boats some

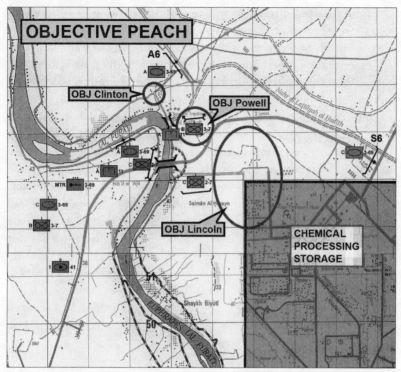

MAP 18. Seizing Objective Peach

protection. After the war he said, "Putting those guys in boats was the hardest thing I ever did. It really bothered me because I expected we might lose a lot of them. I just didn't want to have any of my soldiers' bodies in the Euphrates." He did not know that every soldier at the river's edge volunteered to go over in the first boat, and the squad selected considered themselves lucky.

By the time the first boat was halfway across, Hibner had his second boat in the water. This boat had a motor, but it quit only a few yards from shore. Once again the occupants had to paddle across. After what seemed to Hibner an interminably long time, both boats made it across and began expanding their toehold at the base of the bridge. Job one—cutting wires—fell to the engineers, while the infantry began clearing Iraqis out of nearby buildings. As Hibner got in the third boat (with a working engine) and started across himself, his men were already hard at work.

Hibner started directing the wire cutting activities; he ordered his men to shunt off exposed wires so that stray radio waves did not set off the explosives. Some of the wires were dangling in the water, and one young sergeant jumped into the water to handle the task. With eighty pounds of combat gear on he was immediately sent ten feet to the bottom, whence the unit's embedded reporter fished him out. Hibner let the infantry clear a few nearby buildings, where they found only dead and wounded Iraqi soldiers. However, when they discovered a manned and intact bunker complex, Hibner told them to pull back and set up a defensive position. He did not have enough men to take on the bunkers and wanted his men ready to repel a counterattack. Once the position was secure and Hibner was sure his engineers had cut every wire leading to the bridge, he called Marcone, who immediately sent his tanks across. Hibner, who was awarded the Silver Star for leading this action, later noted, "It was a good feeling to hear the rumbling of the tanks on the bridge. It was much to our joy, as it meant the demise of the Iraqis who were still shooting at us."

Captain Jared Robbins led C/3-69 across the bridge and secured the far side with armor. As soon as that was done, Captain Dave

1st Brigade Engineers cross the Euphrates under fire to seize the far end of the bridge at Objective Peach. The boat engine quit, forcing the engineers to paddle while being shot at.

Engineer company commander Captain Hibner prepares to cross the Euphrates while under direct Iraqi fire.

Benton, commanding B/3-7 IN, led his company through Robbins's troops, and his troops began making their way through the smoke and debris towards a canal bridge on the far side of the objective area. His mission was to get to a position where he could cover the bridge with fire and not allow any Iraqis to cross it. Navigating proved tricky on the wet ground, and it took Benton some time to find a narrow dirt road his Bradleys could use. The road was too restricted for tanks, so Benton left his tank platoon in an overwatch position on a hill to the rear.

Two hundred yards past the bridge, Benton's Bradley ran into a dug-in Iraqi BMP, which he had failed to see in the smoke. He immediately backed up fifty meters and fired 25mm rounds into the Iraqi vehicle until the turret blew off. While he was shooting, a missile from a second BMP struck Benton's Bradley. Not fazed in the least, he quickly dispatched that BMP with 25mm rounds also. By this time Benton was receiving heavy small arms fire and multiple RPGs from entrenched Iraqis. Benton's tanks could not see the ongoing fight or maneuver to his assistance. Worse, the rest of the unit's Bradleys remained strung out on the road behind him and unable to add their fire to the growing fight. With no other choice, Benton ordered his infantry out of the Bradleys to start clearing the enemy entrenchments. Benton continued the attack down the road, as the infantry began their assault. He engaged four BMPs lined up in succession on the road, before his 25mm malfunctioned. Still he continued to move forward, without a main gun, until he found room to maneuver. When he pulled off the road to repair his gun, the rest of the platoon swung past him towards the canal bridge, destroying two more BMPs as they advanced.

When Benton reentered the fight, his other Bradleys already dominated the objective, and the fight had gone out of the remaining Iraqis. None of the Iraqis in the foxholes made any move to indicate surrender, but Benton could sense that they were a beaten force. After the fight, Benton said he could not understand their fighting methods: "They really didn't establish good engagement areas and as far as I could see the infantry stayed in their holes. As my infantry would go through, they would throw grenades in and kill five or ten of them and then spray the hole to make sure there were no survivors to surprise them as they moved to the next hole. They should have surrendered." Benton's company had run into the reconnaissance company from the Medina's 10th Brigade. It was a harbinger that the rest of the brigade could not be far behind.

By 5:00 P.M. Marcone had the 3-69 AR across the bridge and in defensive positions. They met sporadic resistance as they moved into previously assigned fighting positions, but before dark Marcone had five companies of mixed armor and infantry tied into a single defense, waiting for an expected major Iraqi counterattack. For the next several hours the Iraqis made sporadic platoon- and company-sized attacks on Marcone's bridgehead, but they seemed incapable of mounting a major threat. Typical of the actions that evening is one described by First Lieutenant Jim Temple, a platoon leader in C/3-69 AR:

> I had the fight that was north of the canal. I had two tanks oriented north on the road, and my B Section was oriented toward the west, on the left side of the canal. I was also augmented by two Bradleys and dismounts from an infantry platoon. At approximately 2230 I pulled off my shift and let my wing tank take over. About ten minutes later, my wing tank came on the net and said, "What do you want me to do about these thirty people down here?" I thought

he was joking. I didn't think he was telling the truth. I thought he was just messing with me. I said, "30 people? What are you talking about?" I put my gear back on and pulled alongside of him, and sure enough, there were about thirty people about one thousand meters from my position. They were carrying AK-47s. Some looked like they were wearing military uniforms, but we couldn't tell. The majority of them had traditional Iraqi dress, the robes, we could tell they were wearing the headdresses. They were yelling at us.

One key feature really kind of gave them away. All of them had their boots bloused, yet they were still wearing the traditional garb. That kind of gave it away. We still weren't sure. Our first thought was, It's just a bunch of pissed off farmers. They're pissed off because we're blocking the road. These people were out there dancing all over the road with their fists in the air. We fired a warning blast first, which sent them scurrying to the side of the road. But, they did not move any farther then that. We figured most civilians would have taken off running after a warning blast, but they didn't. They stayed on the side of the road.

About thirty minutes later, about three deuce-and-a-halves pulled up and skidded to a halt. They started passing out AK-47s and RPGs to the people on the ground who were all running toward the trucks. Now, I knew it was a military target and fired a main gun volley into it. I shot one round HE and my wingman fired HE as well. That lit the truck sky-high. It was probably carrying a lot of ordinance, because the explosion was a lot bigger than when a single HE round blows up. The explosion went two hundred meters in the air.

Twenty minutes later, everything had calmed down, but there were still people on the side of the road. We thought, "Obviously they know we're tanks. We'll fire HE rounds and they'll back off." Well, they didn't. We started seeing them crawling up on the side of the road. They were pulling people off the road. They were also picking up weapons that they'd found on the side of the road, so we engaged them with coax.

Despite that they continued to push along the sides of the road, though they stopped coming right up the road. They knew it was too easy of a target. I figured the enemy was going to push up the right side of the road, as that was where we had the least amount of visibility. My B Section could see a little bit, but not much because there were a lot of depressions in the area. I figured any time they came up that road, we were going to volley on them with as much as we could. I had all my turrets pointing down that right side of the road.

They came in chains of fifteen to approximately thirty, and every twenty minutes they'd make another push. They made the mistake of assembling where I could have the artillery fire illumination rounds. It was like having a streetlight and I could see them plain as day, massing. At one point, I saw approximately one hundred dismounts at that location, and called indirect fire using Maverick 6 [the task force's mortars]. We had some really good effects down there and they quit massing at that location.

We continued to fight until two in the morning, and at one point they managed to creep within three hundred meters of our positions before being destroyed. After that the attacks stopped, and I assumed they had had enough for the night.

Lieutenant Temple was wrong. The mixed Iraqi Special Forces and Republican Guard attackers were not quitting. They were getting out of the way of the 10th Brigade's counterattack.

While Marcone's men fought their way to and across Objective Peach, General Hamdani was called back to meet with Qusay, along with the minister of defense and other senior military commanders. It was to be one of the more bizarre meetings in the history of a regime that made a penchant of having such meetings. As Hamdani relates:

The minister of defense had a message from Saddam. The message was an order for immediate execution. The minister of defense said that Saddam would not be able to meet during the next two days, but that he had just met with Saddam, and the plan was explained to him. The minister went on to explain that what had happened over the last two weeks was a "strategic" trick by the Americans. He told us American forces were going to come from the direction of Jordan, through Al Ramadi, and into northern Baghdad. Emergency procedures were to go into effect at 0500 the next morning. The Al-Nida was supposed to shift to the northwest of Baghdad under the Republican Guard I Corps. Minefields were to be immediately established to the west and northwest of Baghdad. The talk of establishing minefields made me think that they thought we were fighting Iran again or something.

At this point, Hamdani strenuously objected, telling them that they were wrong and that he was facing the main American attack and that the attack out of Jordan was the trick. The minister of defense replied that he was only the messenger and that there was no further use for discussions since Saddam had spoken. Qusay at least allowed Hamdani to explain his view of the situation:

I said that a minor attack was moving up the Tigris along the line from An Nasiriyah to Al Kut [the Marines' 1st Regional Combat Team]. This attack was actually somewhat of a surprise to me, given the tight roads and poor armor terrain in the area. Another minor attack was pushing up the middle ground from As Samawah to Ad Diwaniyah. However, the main attack was on the west side of the Euphrates River through Karbala and into the southwest side of Baghdad. The U.S. 4th Infantry Division would soon join in the main thrust. I said that the Americans would own Karbala by that night, and they would move quickly to take the bridge [Objective Peach].

After Hamdani finished his presentation, Qusay turned back to the minister of defense and Republican Guard chief of staff to ask what their opinions were. The former could only suggest that he did not know whether Hamdani was right or wrong, but they should still execute the plans that President Hussein had ordered. According to Hamdani: "He said that we should execute the plan as Saddam directed. The Republican Guard chief of staff at first did not answer either way. He repeated over and over, 'we must fight.' The regular army's chief of staff said that he did not agree with my theory and that Saddam was right. He said, 'We must all be 100 percent with Saddam.' The Republican Guard chief of staff then said that I had never executed the plan and that I moved forces without permission. He said that I was to blame for all these casualties."

Qusay remained unsure of what to do, but finally ordered that the Al-Nida Republican Guard Division and the 16th Regular Army Division move to support the Republican Guard's I Corps, which was tasked to defend Iraq from the supposed American thrust coming from northern Jordan. According to Hamdani, "He also directed a withdrawal from Karbala and that all units move to the east side of the Euphrates." Hamdani, realizing the argument was lost, tried to salvage something and asked for permission to destroy the strategic Al-Qa'id Bridge over the Euphrates (Objective Peach). He received Qusay's permission and then went to talk privately to the chief of staff.

After speaking with the chief of staff for only a moment, Hamdani received a call informing him that the Al-Qa'id bridge had fallen. As he recalls, the officer reporting indicated that columns of enemy armor were moving from Jaraf al-Sakhr towards the bridge. "I gave the report to those present, but they did not believe it." Hamdani records the scene as he prepared to leave the meeting:

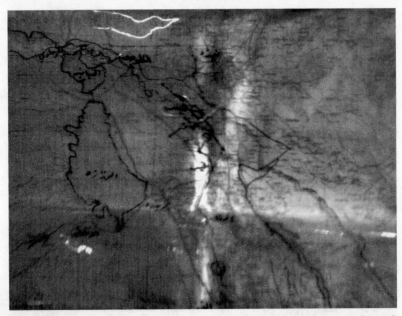

A captured Iraqi map showing they were prepared to defend against the 3rd ID feint east of the Euphrates, but had no idea the Americans were moving in force through the Karbala Gap.

The meeting attendees continued to apply themselves to the question, one that resembled the Gordian Knot, about the nature of the minefields which must be set up around Baghdad. The minister of defense and the army chief of staff were on one side, and the chief of staff of the Republican Guard was on the other side wanting to challenge my comment. They now saw me as their adversary. I could not stay for one more second. To the President's son I said, "Sir, the disastrous fate of Baghdad will happen within the next 48 hours. I hope to be wrong in the opinion that we have chosen to follow the wrong decision. Please allow me to return to my headquarters." He dropped his head down for a moment, and then he raised it so he was looking at me with a sad expression, or it was a strange expression I couldn't read, and he said, "As you wish. Go ahead." I said my goodbyes to him and left sadly. I looked at my watch, which told me it was 1540, and I did not know that I had just seen Qusay for the last time before the American forces killed him with his son and his brother on the 22nd of July, 2003 in Mosul.

Hamdani later commented on the dismal scene saying, "It was the kind of arguments that I imagine took place in Hitler's bunker in Berlin. Were all these men on drugs?" In a mood of utter disbelief, he left the meeting to go back to the real fight, while the generals, Saddam, and his sons dealt with their "imaginary universe."

Hamdani returned to the front to discover that the bridge was still standing and the Americans were across the Euphrates in strength. He ordered limited counterattacks with available troops and newly arriving Special Forces regiments—the Iraqi troops Lieutenant Temple and the rest of Marcone's men fought off all night. At the same time he sent for the Medina Divisions' 10th Armored Brigade and other forces from the recently arrived Nebuchadnezzar Division, intending to build a new defensive line to the north of the American bridgehead. Before he could put those orders into effect, the Republican Guard chief of staff arrived. Informed that U.S. tanks had captured the bridge, he refused to believe it. He was convinced that the bridge was destroyed and foolishly insisted that any American tanks north of the Euphrates must have been carried over by helicopters. When he was eventually convinced that the bridge still stood, he refused to entertain any thoughts of building a new defensive line and emphatically demanded a major counterattack to retake the bridge. Hamdani had no choice but to oblige him.

By 3:00 A.M., Hamdani had assembled a substantial force around the 10th Armored Brigade. He now ordered the attack on the bridge.

> The attack moved forward slowly because we did not have night vision. . . . The Medina Division's commander and I followed the 10th Armored Brigade with our communications groups. . . . At 0200 American jets attacked our force as we moved down the road. We were hit by many missiles. Most of the Medina Division's staff were killed. My corps communication staff was also killed. When we reached the area near the bridge where the Special Forces battalion had set up a headquarters, we immediately came under heavy fire. Based on the volume of fire, I estimated at least sixty armored vehicles.

At this point Hamdani knew all was lost, but pushed by his superiors in Baghdad he ordered one final assault. He personally briefed the commander of the armored battalion that would make the final push. "The tank battalion commander was astounded when I told him his mission and how dangerous it was. He saluted me and said, 'I am a martyr and I promise I will not return without accomplishing my mission.' Within a half hour he fell as a martyr."

By daybreak Hamdani had managed to maneuver several hundred Special Forces soldiers within a few hundred yards of the bridge. They had several trucks filled with explosives that were to join what was left of 10th Brigade in a final rush and then explode the trucks on the bridge. Just as Hamdani was about to give the order for a last suicidal charge, the final disaster struck. "At that moment, a huge number of American aircraft and combat helicopters launched a series of intense attacks. When they were done I did not have a single tank or other transport left to me. They were so accurate. I could not believe how easily they hit targets. All around me were columns of smoke from burning vehicles. At this point, I lost hope and ordered a withdrawal."

For Marcone's men the Iraqi counterattack was a shock. After hours of fighting off small, hastily gathered bands, they had assumed that this was the best the Iraqis could do. They also assumed that with all of the electronic sensors deployed in the theater they would receive some early warning of a major armored counterattack. They were wrong on both counts.

However, Marcone had not left much to chance. After crossing the bridge he had coordinated a linear artillery target area and a close air support kill-box along what he considered the most likely avenue of approach for an Iraqi counterattack. He guessed right. When the counterattack came, the 10th Brigade drove right through both the preplanned artillery coordinates and the kill-box. They met a storm of steel. Bravely, the battered survivors continued to come on, directly into Lieutenant Temple's tired tankers:

> At three o'clock in the morning, we noticed another big push. This time, they were definitely using modern tactics. They were using three-to-five-second rushes and low crawls. We thought this must be something a little bigger than the militia or Fedayeen coming at us. More trucks started coming at us. We had several trucks with crew-served weapons in the back. Then came the big-money targets.
>
> At the time, there was no illumination. We thought these were BMPs, but were not sure. When we fired them up, we fired sabot at first, and that had negative effect. It looked like it just went right through them. So we broke out the HE, and we fired at approximately three tanks. I didn't know it at the time, but later we discovered we killed two with one shot. They were in a line and the round

went through both and blew their turrets right off. They went a good three hundred meters in the air. In fact, from my position almost a kilometer down the road, we had shrapnel coming down on us.

We continued to fight. Steel 6 [Marcone] continued to direct air support for us. We stopped up the column right here. You could tell there was mass confusion. People were falling out of vehicles. They were running back and forth. They weren't exactly sure how much we had done. We just kept raining fire on them. We stopped up column.

The fighting continued until about five o'clock in the morning. It finally stopped. As we drove up the road, there were body parts all over the road. They were on the side of the road. There were bodies everywhere, a sea of body parts. We did a lot of damage to them. A lot of hurt.

The fight for Objective Peach was over. Marcone's 3-69 Armor had first ground the 14th Brigade out of existence in getting to Peach, then annihilated the 10th Armored Brigade when it tried to take it from them. By morning Marcone's supporting artillery was out of ammo and his own vehicles had used up their 25mm HE as well as most of their machine gun ammo. Marcone later said, "If they threw another brigade at us we would have gone zero on ammo, and it would have been hand-to-hand for the bridge." The Iraqis had attacked bravely and at times ferociously, but they were not near a match for what they ran into. In an interview long after the war Marcone remembered: "The way they attacked unnerved me. They kept coming, rolling over their own dead. They should have learned. Fighting for us was easy. Killing at close range though is very hard and unforgettable. I am still dealing with having to kill so many people. Destroying the 10th Brigade still bothers me." Troubled or not, Marcone still had a battalion to command, and the war was not over. With the 2nd Brigade passing through his positions to finish off the last of the Medina Division, he counted on a long rest for his exhausted men. It was not to be.

As his exhausted soldiers loaded up on ammo, Colonel Grimsley ordered that the attack be continued to the Baghdad International Airport (BIAP). Marcone later said, "After a grueling 48-hour fight I had to give an order to attack BIAP in forty-five minutes. No other unit could have done it, but we knew we could do it. I was so proud of my men. It was a euphoric feeling."

17

The Other Side of the Hill

WITH THE BRIDGE AT OBJECTIVE PEACH secured and the engineers busily constructing additional spans over the Euphrates, the 3rd ID's march to Baghdad was entering its endgame. The division was now face to face with the much-vaunted Republican Guard, and the climatic battle was at hand. This is a good time, then, to halt our war narrative to examine the state of the Republican Guard forces as well as the defenses around Baghdad.

In the *Iraqi Perspective Report* my coauthors and I recounted the story of Saddam's regime, its military planning and execution, in great detail. Those who want a more complete picture of the Iraqi side of the war should read the full report. However, this history would be incomplete if it failed to mention what the Iraqi commanders had to contend with and to provide an account of what it was like to be the target of the merciless war machine America was employing.

The Regime's Expectations

Based on dozens of interviews with senior Iraqi generals and government officials it is now clear that Saddam did not expect he would ever have to face a Coalition ground attack with the end of his regime as its final objective. In fact, the evidence clearly demonstrates that when he ranked potential threats to his regime, a Coalition

invasion was a poor third. Both the threat of another Shi'a revolt and
a renewed war with Iran weighed much more heavily on Saddam's
mind than America ever did. He was convinced that what he called his
"international friends"—France and Russia—would make sure that
the Coalition never attacked. In the event he was wrong on that score,
but he remained certain, almost to the very end, that diplomatic pressure from his friends would force the Americans to stop their attack
on Iraq long before it got to Baghdad and threatened the regime.[1]
Based on past experience, he also doubted America's stomach for a
hard fight. After seeing that we failed to topple his regime in 1991's
Desert Storm and our quick retreat from Somalia following the loss
of what to him seemed an insignificant eighteen dead, he was convinced that the United States would never dare a costly city fight to
take "Fortress Baghdad." Saddam was certain that, even if his friends
failed him, the U.S. would be content to seize southern Iraq and allow
his regime to survive. He and his most trusted advisor, best known as
Chemical Ali, even joked about letting the Americans deal with the
troublesome Shi'a for awhile and they would certainly withdraw at the
earliest opportunity.

Moreover, Saddam along with many of his senior commanders
were convinced of the inherent fighting superiority of the average
Iraqi over the Americans. All they needed, by their estimation, was a
battlefield that would negate the American technological superiority.
They considered the cities perfect for that purpose and adjusted their
strategy and tactics accordingly. Saddam was so taken with the events
depicted in the movie *Blackhawk Down* that he gave copies to all of
his commanders and ordered them to study it. He was certain that
what took place in Somalia could be replicated on a massive scale in
every city in southern Iraq, and it would not be long before mounting
causalities caused the notoriously squeamish Americans to give up
the fight.

---

1. In an interesting side note to the war, Saddam was so buoyed by optimistic reports
coming out of his southern cities that he was convinced he was winning the war. In early
April he told the Russians and French to stop pressing for a halt to the Coalition attack
so that he had time to further humiliate the United States. He was making this demand
at the same moment the 3rd ID was rushing through the Karbala Gap.

The Regime's War Plans

Ever since Desert Storm the Iraqi military had been planning for—and, to the best of its limited abilities, rehearsing—a specific plan for the defense of Iraq. There were numerous problems with the basic defense, not the least of which was the Iraqi military's inability to carry out the plan. Still, this plan represented the best thinking of Iraq's professional military officers, and while it probably would not have stopped the Coalition offensive, it would certainly have made it more costly and time consuming.

All this planning and preparation proved a massive waste of time, because just months before the war Saddam threw out the entire plan and presented a new one. On 18 December 2002, the chief of staff of the Republican Guard gathered his commanders together and announced a new concept for the nation's defense. It was both original and bold in conception—and totally impractical. This new plan threw out the previous plan, which had been based on a defense-in-depth and a gradual phased withdrawal as American pressure increased. In the new plan, the defense of Baghdad became the focus of all military efforts—hardly surprising in a country whose leader considered his survival the paramount interest of the state. In a postwar interview, the commander of the II Republican Guard Corps reported how the news of the new plan was reported and received:

> On 18 December 2002, the Republican Guard Chief of Staff called all the commanders [Republican Guard Corps, division, and air defense commanders] to meet at the Republican Guard Command Center. When I asked why, I was told that they had a new plan for the defense of Baghdad. I thought to myself that we were supposed to be defending all of Iraq, not just Baghdad. When we got there, we found that Qusay Hussein was also present.
>
> The Republican Guard Chief of Staff briefed in front of a large wall map that covered just the central portion of Iraq. The map showed Baghdad in the center with four rings. Every ring had a color. The center ring was red. Approximately ten kilometers out from the red ring was a blue ring. Then approximately seven kilometers out from that one was a black ring. Finally, the last circle was marked in yellow, which was designated for reconnaissance forces only. The Republican Guard Chief of Staff explained the plan in a very crude and ugly way.
>
> Things like "the Republican Guard Hammurabi Division defends in the north of the city, the Republican Guard Medina Division in the

south, the Republican Guard Al Nida Division in the east, and special forces and the Special Republican Guard in the west." When the Americans arrived at the first ring and, on order from Saddam, the forces would conduct a simultaneous withdrawal. The units would then repeat this "procedure" until reaching the red circle. Once in the red circle, the remaining units would fight to the death. With this incredible simplicity and stupidity, the assembled Republican Guard officers were told that this was the plan for the defense of our country. Qusay said that the plan was already approved by Saddam and "it was you who would now make it work." I disagreed and told Qusay that a proud army with an 82-year history cannot fight like this. We were not using our experience. I was told by Qusay that there would be no changes because Saddam had signed the plan already.

At a whim, Saddam had imposed on his commanders a radical new plan for the defense of Iraq that was contrary to their best advice. Moreover, it was a plan that failed to take into account simple things like geography. For Saddam, obstacles such as rivers, swamps, and canals simply did not exist. Worse, the new plan did not take into account how the Iraqi army was to retreat uniformly from one ring to the next while simultaneously being pounded from the air and the ground. It is doubtful that superbly trained American forces could pull off such a feat. For the poorly trained Iraqis it went several steps beyond hoping for a miracle.

For the plan to have even the slightest hope of success would have required a high degree of coordination between units and, if time permitted, rehearsals or at least map exercise to ensure commanders understood the concept and the problems that could arise. This unfortunately was impossible within Saddam's Stalinist regime. Commanders were not even allowed to bring copies of the new plan with them to study, and they were forbidden to make notes. Given the paranoid nature of the regime, there was also no chance that they would try to coordinate plans among themselves. As far as Saddam and his security services were concerned, the only possible reason that two generals could possibly have to talk together was to plan a coup or otherwise conspire against the regime. In a country where even the most senior officials often disappeared without a word, nobody wanted to take the risk of a conversation being misunderstood. Generals rarely socialized together or even spoke with each other. All of them still remembered the fate of one of their number who had the temerity to offer Saddam advice the dictator did not like. He was cut up into little pieces and his dismembered body delivered to his wife the next day. This was the kind of lesson that the generals could easily to take to heart, and they simply stopped associating.

It is hard to overstate the pervasive fear that imbued every level of the Iraqi armed Forces. There were at least five security agencies keeping an eye on the military and each other. Each of them had multiple spies and informers in every military organization, all of them looking for something negative to report so they could make a name for themselves and move up the promotion ladder. Senior commanders worked hard to make sure they knew who all the spies were and found ways to make sure they invited them to all of their meetings and conferences. It was considered very dangerous for a military commander to have a meeting and even inadvertently exclude one of the spies, since the spy's next message to the commander's bosses would be all about the "secret" meeting.

In the Republican Guard, division and corps commanders could not make decisions without the approval of the staff command. Division commanders could only move small elements within their command. Major movements such as brigade-sized elements and higher had to be requested through the corps commander to the staff command. This process did not change during the war and in fact became more centralized.

Such a lack of trust had a direct effect not only on the commander's ability to lead his unit but also the unit's ability to take advantage of its knowledge of the ground to prepare an optimal defense. In many cases, staff officers in Baghdad who had never visited the area still managed to forward precise deployment locations for even the smallest units directly to division commanders. The Baghdad commander continued: "Only the Republican Guard staff command directed maneuvers and it did not allow subordinate commanders to make suggestions. If a commander made a decision without the Republican Guard chief of staff's approval, he would be punished. The only commanders who had any protection were those from Tikrit [Saddam's hometown]. They were allowed to make their own decisions because the government trusted them more." In such an atmosphere it was impossible to build the trust that is essential to the cohesiveness of a military force. Without such cohesion there was a high likelihood that much of the Iraqi army would melt away when put under stress—as did happen.

In the end commanders were presented with a plan in which they had no confidence, which they were not permitted to discuss among themselves or rehearse, and coordination between various units was forbidden. There is little reason to doubt that to Saddam the mere issuing of a decree was sufficient to make the plan work. For him the Iraqi Army required neither coordination nor further planning to make his conception effective.

The Worst Parts of the Old Plan

The new concept for the defense of Iraqi primarily affected the Republican Guard and Regular Army units near Baghdad. There was just no time between the delivery of the new concept and the start of the Operation Iraqi Freedom, three months later, for the bulk of the Regular Army to make the adjustments required to enact the plan. In the event, it put the Iraqi Army in the worst possible situation. The old plan had been discarded, but the on-the-ground reality was that nothing had yet replaced it. The plan called for a ringed defense of Baghdad and a few other key cities, but when the war started the Army found itself still positioned to enact former priorities.

Furthermore, the fact that the new plan did nothing to supersede Saddam's previous priorities crippled it from the start. Even as he planned for the defense of Baghdad, Saddam still considered a Shi'a revolt his most dangerous threat. This is the reason that so many intact bridges fell into Coalition hands. During the Shi'a revolt of 1991 Saddam had tremendous difficulty imposing control on southern Iraq because so many of the bridges had been destroyed. Not many in the United States realize what a near thing Saddam's overthrow was in 1991, but Saddam never forgot how close he came to his final end. With that image still burning in his mind, he forbade the destruction of any of the bridges over the Tigris or Euphrates Rivers. If the Shi'a revolted again he was certain to need them to crush their uprising.

Just as damaging or maybe even more so was that the new plan did nothing to address the Fedayeen and Al-Quds militia forces that were created after 1991. The original intent had been that they would be available to crush another uprising before it could get beyond the smoldering stage. In case of a Coalition invasion, Saddam put a lot of faith in the ability of these forces to bleed the American Army dry in a series of ferocious urban battles. However, in direct violation of the principle of unity of command, these units were not under military control. They were private armies of hopefully fanatical quality, but they were never integrated into any overall coherent defense effort.

Military Effectiveness

Besides the pernicious effects of the regime's focus on every military threat except a Coalition invasion, there were other things that sapped the ability of the Iraqi military to fend off an invasion. Near the top of any list were the debilitating effects of sanctions. For more than a dozen years, United Nations sanctions had attacked the very fiber of the Iraqi military by making it difficult to purchase new equipment, procure spare parts, or fund adequate training. One Republican Guard officer described the insidious effect of sanctions on the military in the following terms:

> The government made rapid efforts to limit the negative direct and indirect effects of the savage sanctions on the weapons and activities of the military forces. Unfortunately, they were the wrong kind of efforts. The army continued to fight the schemes of the Military Industrial Commission, which played an important role in promising secret weapons it would never deliver while most types of things we needed were neglected. These people received large amounts of financial support, but the army could not get simple things. As time passed, President Saddam Hussein set aside many resources for the commission departments that were difficult to afford.

By the time the Coalition invaded, the Iraqi regular army was in a sad state of disrepair and possessed only a fraction of the combat power their table of organization implied. However, this was not true of the Republican Guard. Most of the Guard's combat formations were at full strength, and by cannibalizing the regular army's equipment the Guard also was able to keep most of its combat equipment in a satisfactory state of repair.

The military effectiveness of the Iraqi Army was also severely eroded by Saddam's growing need to hear only good news. After 1991, commanders became very wary of giving Saddam bad news, and no one contested his view that his eviction from Kuwait in 1991 was a glorious victory. As far as Saddam was aware, his military was as ready for war as it had ever been despite the effects of sanctions. Honest reporting of military readiness and capabilities became the exception, not the rule. Many commanders simply became afraid to put their positions, possibly their livelihoods or even lives, at risk by challenging the given truth. One senior minister noted, "Directly disagreeing with Saddam Hussein's ideas was unforgivable. It would be suicide." Another official said that there existed an almost reflexive tendency to pass on good news and never to contradict what they had previously told Saddam. According to one former high-ranking Ba'ath official: "Saddam had an idea about Iraq's conventional and potential unconventional capabilities, but never an accurate one because of the extensive lying occurring in that area. Many reports were falsified. The ministers attempted to convey a positive perspective with reports, which were forwarded to Saddam's secretary, who in turn passed them up to Saddam."

In one instance, Saddam commissioned a series of reviews and studies of lessons learned after the 1991 Gulf War with the Coalition. One might assume this would have represented a singular opportunity for the military to bring some reality into Saddam's conception of the world. Just the fact that he was calling for a lessons-learned discussion could be interpreted that perhaps Saddam recognized something had gone wrong. However, these reviews and studies started from the assumption that Saddam's decision to invade Kuwait was militarily sound. Therefore, the "lessons learned" efforts did not take into account the complete scope of Gulf War experiences. The opportunity was too much for the military commanders to handle. Presented with a one-of-a-kind opportunity to tell the truth, they passed. During one recorded review of a post–Desert Storm study, the commander of the Republican Guard strode to the podium with confidence and listed the "great" accomplishments of his forces during the "Mother of All Battles," among them:

- Creating impenetrable and perfectly camouflaged command bunkers.
- Analyzing the battlefield and deploying in such a way as to make the American nuclear-tipped Pershing missiles useless. [No mention was made of the facts that the United States did not deploy Pershing missiles during the war, or that, by dispersing their forces to avoid nuclear attack, the Iraqis became easy prey for the massed Coalition armor.]
- Determining the specific method and timing of U.S. operations so that "once the attack began, we were clearly expecting it." [Nothing was in the presentation about how the Iraqis were helped by President Bush giving them an ultimatum and countdown.]

According to the then-Republican Guard Commander:

> As a result of all these successful preparations, our losses were not as devastating as the arsenal that was used against the Iraqi Army during the period should suggest. So this clearly shows that the Republican Guard and the other Iraqi armed forces were able to dig in and deploy wisely, and thus minimize the damage of the aerial power.

In Saddam's conception of victory, the ability to escape total annihilation equated to military success.

The Iraqi military's dwindling capability to win on the modern battlefield was further weakened by the almost always irrelevant guidance it received directly from Saddam. According to one Iraqi general, "All military planning was directed by Saddam and a selected few. It was much like Hitler and his generals after 1944." After 1991, Saddam's confidence in his military commanders steadily eroded, while his confidence in his own abilities as a military genius strengthened. Like a number of other amateurs in history who dabbled in military affairs, Saddam began to issue a seemingly endless stream of banal instructions. He could not resist giving detailed training guidance at the same time he became fascinated with the ethereal military capabilities promised by the Military Industrial Commission. Dozens of surviving memoranda mirrored the 2002 Iraqi top-secret document "Training Guidance to the Republican Guard" (described below). They all hint at the guidance that military officers received from Saddam on a regular basis. One chapter from the Training Guidance document, "Notes and directions given by Saddam Hussein to his elite soldiers to cover the tactics of war," charged them to train in the following ways:

- train in a way that allows you to defeat your enemy
- train all units' members in swimming
- train your soldiers to climb palm trees so that they may use these places for navigation and sniper shooting; and
- train on smart weapons

Similar instructions were repeated in almost every training manual issued to the armed forces. In time, Saddam's wisdom became a substitute for real training.

In Saddam's view, such simple guidance was necessary to keep his commanders focused on what he considered the important issues in combat. For him, the key to all things military was violence of execution. In discussing the proper employment of the Republican Guard, he reminded his generals that "it should be kept away from skirmishes. I mean, if it is sent in, I want it to be decisive. The Republican Guard will consider anyone on the battlefield an enemy. I don't want to complicate things for them."

Another major factor in the Iraqi military's decreasing effectiveness grew out of Saddam's growing paranoia. He trusted only one person—himself. However, no single man could do everything. Where he was forced to enlist the help of others to handle operational details, Saddam pursued a unique set of hiring criteria. As one senior Iraqi leader noted, Saddam selected the "uneducated, untalented, and those who posed no threat to his leadership for key roles." Ability or talent was never high on Saddam's list of attributes for a new hire. As one of Saddam's closest confidants, Chemical Ali, noted, "Saddam was always wary of intelligent people. While Saddam liked having men around him with strong personalities, he did not like for those men to show off."

Describing Saddam's approach to choosing those charged with making decisions that directly affected the military, one Republican Guard Corps commander commented after the war: "Saddam Hussein was personally a brave and bloody man. But, by his decisions he threw out the clever men, or the clever men learned not to involve themselves in any decision-making. They were then replaced by hypocrites who cared not for the people or army, but only cared about pleasing Saddam."

Always wary of a potential coup, Saddam remained reluctant to entrust military authority to anyone too far removed from his family or tribe. To Western observers, the Republican Guard represented the bulwark of the regime, but for Saddam the Guard was the military force best positioned to overthrow him. Consequently, in 2001 he placed his youngest son, Qusay, at its head, despite his limited military experience (which consisted of a short stint at the Iranian front in 1984, where he saw little, if any, real combat). According to the minister of defense: "My working for Qusay Hussein was a mistake; Qusay knew nothing—he understood only simple military things like a civilian. We prepared information and advice for him and he'd accept it or not."

Despite his lack of expertise, Qusay exuded confidence and attempted to play a dominant role in the final planning of Iraqi deployments against a Coalition invasion. As the "honorable supervisor" and son of Saddam, Qusay had the final say in significant military decisions unless Saddam himself chose to intervene. His purview included such fundamental matters as what key terrain to defend and when and how to shift the remaining Iraqi forces during the war. Several senior officers privately questioned many of his decisions, but few were willing to do so in an open forum. After the war, senior military officers constantly remarked on Qusay's lack of military knowledge and his unwillingness to take their "good" advice.

However, this is too simplistic a formulation to explain everything that went wrong. The evidence shows that many who were in a position to advise Qusay were, in fact, unqualified to do so, while those who were qualified were often silent even when given an opportunity to speak.

One of those at the heart of the regime who proved incapable of providingsound military advice to Qusay was Major General Barzan 'Abd al-Ghafur, the commander of the Special Republican Guard. Before the war, Coalition planners generally assumed that the quality—and loyalty—of Iraqi military officers improved as one moved from the militias to the regular army, to the Republican Guard, and then on to the Special Republican Guard. It stood to reason that the commander of the Special Republican Guard would therefore be a highly competent, loyal, and important personality in Iraq's military system. After all, the regime was entrusting him with the duty of conducting the final defense of the homes and offices of the regime's elite.

Coalition planners considered the Special Republican Guard the elite of the elite; by logical extension, their commander would surely be the best Saddam could find. This piece of conventional wisdom was wrong. After the war, the peers and colleagues of the Special Republican Guard commander were all openly derisive of Barzan's performance as an officer and commander. Saddam had selected Barzan, as one general noted, because he had several traits that Saddam held dear: "He was Saddam's cousin, but he had two other important qualities which made him the best man for the job. First, he was not intelligent enough to represent a threat to the regime and second, he was not brave enough to participate in anyone else's plots."

This general, the man who was to command the last ditch stand of Saddam's Guards, spent most of the war hiding, reportedly drunk in his mother's basement. The selection of such a man for an important military position appears counterintuitive, but given the imperatives of Iraqi politics, it was the only possible rational decision Saddam could make.

The case of the minister of defense, General Sultan Hashim Ahmad al-Ta'i, is strikingly different. Here, by all accounts, was a competent military commander who, upon reaching the pinnacle of power, apparently decided silence was the better part of valor. A number of senior Iraqi leaders identified General Sultan as one of the best and brightest among Iraq's military leaders. His peers described him as a "mountain of morals" and compared him to Jafaral Askari, minister of defense in the 1930s and considered the "father of the Iraqi army." Judging from the scope of his military record alone, he appears to have been an impressive soldier. During his forty-year career, Sultan commanded two brigades, three divisions, and at least two corps of regular army troops. In so doing, he fought in every war after 1968 and developed a reputation as a creative, dynamic military leader. However, Sultan's elevation to minister of defense changed him as well as his colleagues' opinions of him. The specific reasons for the change are no doubt complex, but his actions during the meetings and planning conferences prior to the Coalition invasion suggest an explanation. In one telling event during the final planning, he remained silent when more junior officers voiced concerns over Saddam's new plan for the defense of Iraq. As one corps commander who was present later noted, "Some of the senior military leaders present only competed to please Saddam. The minister of defense was an honorable man but he gave up his strategic vision in order to keep Saddam's favor. This was very unfortunate for Iraq."

The Ba'ath Armies

The final factor negatively affecting military readiness was the rise of the Al-Quds and the Fedayeen, which was outlined in Chapter 4 above. Anyone who signed up for one of these armies was automatically exempted from military service in the regular army. Since the training and attendance commitments of the Al-Quds was minimal and the Fedayeen provided its members with valuable privileges and status, it is no wonder that Iraq's best and brightest youths headed for their recruiters. This left the regular army with society's tailings for recruitment.

Besides having to make due with the worst elements of Iraqi society, the army was further weakened by being the primary supplier of arms and equipment for the new political armies. Because of sanctions it was impossible to procure new equipment for the forming armies, so everything they required had to come directly from regular army stores. Moreover, because of their political clout, these armies were often able to select the best equipment for themselves and leave the army with worn out materiel.

The professional army, after years of neglect, tried to make do with poor recruits and inferior equipment, but it is really no wonder that the bulk of it dissolved on impact with the 3rd ID.

18

Saints and South

(3–5 April)

WITH ALLYN'S 3RD BRIGADE securing the Karbala Gap and one of Grimsley's battalions sitting on Objective Peach, the time had come to launch Perkins's 2nd Brigade north towards Baghdad. Leaving Lieutenant Colonel Stephen Twitty's battalion to secure the area around Peach (as Grimsley's 1st Brigade headed for Baghdad International Airport), Perkins was going to take his other two assigned battalions, plus Lieutenant Colonel Charlton's 1-15 IN north to the outskirts of Baghdad. Once there, he planned to turn the brigade east to the intersection of Highways 1 and 8 (Objective Saint).

According to Perkins:

> My intent was to go into Saints and then come down from the north to hit the Medina Division from the rear. I wanted 1-15 IN to secure Saints and set up blocking positions facing north to stop any counterattack from the Special Republican Guard. It would be awkward to be hit in the rear as I was attacking into the Medina's rear. Once the blocking positions were in place, 1-64 AR would attack along Highway 8 into the Medina's 2nd Brigade, while 4-64 AR would head down Route 1 into the Medina's 10th Brigade.

But first, Perkins had to get his brigade through the Karbala Gap and across the Euphrates at Peach. Originally, division headquarters

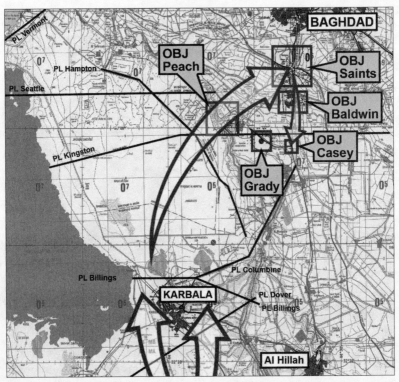

MAP 19. Attack to Objective Saints

had told Perkins to bring his entire brigade through the Karbala Gap,
but when his lead elements arrived he found what his executive officer later described as a "cluster-fuck." The entire 3rd ID was trying
to get through the gap at the same time and nothing seemed to be
moving. General Austin asked Perkins if he could skirt the east side of
Karbala and avoid the gap all together. Perkins said he would try, and
he turned his brigade around to try a route they had not planned for
or reconned. They would have to do what one officer called "recon by
Braille" as they moved through the night's blackness.

Perkins had planned to have his brigade through the gap in a couple of hours and at Peach by the afternoon of April 2. But as Lieutenant Colonel Charlton's lead battalion advanced east of Karbala, they
found themselves sinking deep into marshes, blocked by canals, and
unable to navigate through thick palm groves. What everyone hoped

would be a quick road march turned into what the soldiers called the "march through hell."

Alerted to Charlton's problems, Lieutenant Colonel Schwartz turned his battalion onto a road closer to Karbala itself and was immediately engaged by the enemy. Schwartz, in addition to having to fight off Iraqi attacks, found that his new route did not help him avoid many of the terrain problems Charlton was facing. Perkins now had two battalions mired in swamps, and one of them was under fire. Reasoning that a cluster-fuck was better than trying to have his next two battalions fight their way through a swamp in the dark, he directed Lieutenant Colonels deCamp and Twitty to revert to the original plan and head through the gap.

That done, Perkins had to inform General Austin of the change of plans. According to Perkins, Austin listened sympathetically and then asked how long it would take him to get through. "When I told him seven hours or all night," Perkins said, "He told me to do the best I could, but he sounded disappointed." Eventually the brigade emerged out of the morass and headed for Peach. It was now about 3:00 A.M. on April 3rd and Austin was pushing to get the brigade attacking out of Peach by 6:00 A.M. Perkins had a quick huddle with his battalion commanders and learned that only half the brigade was through the gap; the rest would be dribbling in over the next few hours. Perkins wanted the entire brigade to attack north together, but if he waited until the whole force was mustered and then crossed the bridge at Peach he would not be able to attack until 9:00 A.M. or later. To maintain momentum, Perkins decided to go across Peach with whatever elements of the brigade were already present and then mass combat power on the far side as it arrived.

It was another nondoctrinal solution, and Perkins later remembered that none of his commanders were very happy with it. "They all knew the Medina Division and other Republican guard units were on the other side of that bridge and they wanted all of their combat power with them when they crossed." Perkins told them that the entire division was lining up to use the bridge and it "was use or lose it." Not wanting to be left behind in the decisive attack, each of his commanders nodded and began sending their companies across as soon as they refueled.

As Perkins finished his meeting, Lieutenant Colonel Eric Wesley approached and asked, "Well boss are you enjoying this moment?"

He was referring to Perkins being the commander of an armored brigade about to fight its way across the Euphrates Valley and into Baghdad. While it would be hard to find a colonel in the United States Army who would advocate war as anything but a last resort, it would be equally hard to find a combat arms officer who would not have made a deal with the devil to change places with Perkins. Wesley reported that Perkins thought a moment about the question and smiled.

The brigade finished crossing the bridge at Peach before dawn and by 6:00 A.M. it was massed and ready to head for Saints, with Charlton's 1-15 IN leading. Marcone's hard-fighting, but exhausted, 3-69 AR was still holding the far side of Objective Peach out to about a mile, and its guns dominated for another mile past that. The 2nd Brigade had been able to mass on the far side of the bridge under Marcone's protective umbrella, but as soon as Charlton's lead unit stepped beyond it they were in a fight.

As 1-15 IN attacked along what the brigade had named Route Cubs, they ran into what Perkins called "very significant resistance." All along the route they encountered a series of small fortified garrisons. These garrisons had, in some cases, been in position for years and had spent significant portions of that time digging in. According to Perkins it was a "continual gauntlet of fire."

More troubling to Perkins were reports from the 3rd ID Intelligence Section that Iraqi helicopters were flying Republican Guard reinforcements into Saints and that it was likely that upwards of 4,000 trained soldiers would be waiting for him when they arrived. Perkins had some doubts about the Iraqis being able to fly that many helicopters right under the nose of the U.S. Air Force, but he could not afford to completely discount the reports. If they were true, he would be fighting a reinforced combat brigade on Saints with two unscathed Medina brigades in his rear. Perkins did take some comfort in the fact that if there really was anything waiting for him on Saints the Air Force was in the process of beating the hell out of it.

As his extended column barreled down Route Cubs, Perkins put aside thoughts of what might be waiting for him at Saints. By this time in the war he was supremely confident that his men were more than a match for whatever they met. Besides, at that moment he and his soldiers were consumed by the present. The column was meeting fierce resistance, but the Iraqis were not making much of an impression on Perkins's tanks or Bradleys. For the armor, just barreling through

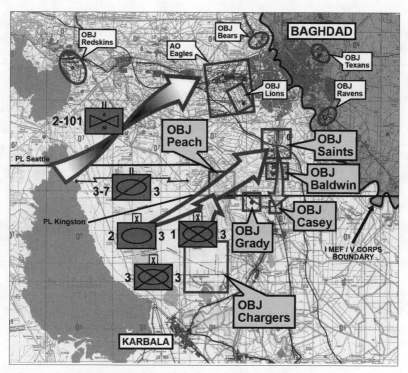

MAP 20. Moving from Peach to Saints

to Saints would have been easy, except that this time they could not leave the thin-skinned logistics vehicles behind to fend for themselves. When they arrived at Saints, Perkins's armor would require fuel and ammo resupply immediately. So the armored units moved slowly and took the time to engage every target until it was destroyed, or they passed it off to the combat unit following behind.

About 1:00 P.M. Charlton's tanks roared onto Saints with all guns blazing. On the objective they found a lot of dismounted infantry, tanks, air-defense guns, and artillery. What they did not find was a coherent defense capable of standing up to the concentrated fire of a U.S. combat battalion. In short order, Charlton's men annihilated the enemy force at Saints and turned north as ordered, to establish blocking positions.

Much later, Perkins talked about one of his tank commanders, Sergeant First Class Pyle:

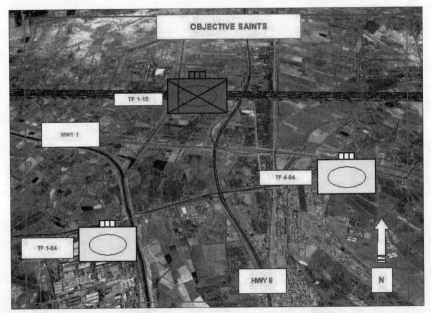

An aerial view of Objective Saints just south of Baghdad. Thunder runs were launched from here.

Pyle ran out of coax ammo, and .50-caliber ammo, as did his loader. All he had left to engage Iraqi infantry with was SABOT.[1] Our gunners learned that the SABOT is embedded with large metal pellets, and as the main round goes down range, the petals shoot out like a shot gun blast, reaching out 1,000 meters at mach 5. The effect on exposed infantry is devastating.

By the time Pyle got to Saints his tank was on fire, he was out of ammo, and he has been shot in the arm and shoulder.

I saw him walking up to me with his arm in a makeshift sling. He stopped, looked at me a moment, and said, "Sir, I need another tank." Think about it. He just fought his way through hell and has two bullets in him. But, all he was concerned about was getting another tank so he could get back into the fight.[2]

---

1. SABOT is an incredibly fast tank round designed to penetrate the thickest armor. Until this moment it had generally been considered useless against infantry.

2. Perkins had brought a surgical unit with him to Saints, so they were there to treat SFC Pyle. Perkins said, "The surgeons seemed fine with it. They had no idea that they were not supposed to be tucked up right behind the lead combat brigade as it was fighting. Corps HQ, however, wanted my head for putting their surgeons in danger."

Before the rest of the brigade arrived, Charlton's battalion was in five blocking positions heavily engaged with dug-in armor that had remained hidden in palm groves on the northeast side of Saints. It took a heavy artillery bombardment and an air strike before this force was finally destroyed. The 1-15 IN also handily dispatched a counterattack from the south that was led by three T-72 tanks.

With Charlton's troops still engaging some Iraqi stalwarts, Perkins turned his attention south. The brigade was now in the rear of the Medina Division, and he did not want to give the Iraqis time to recover. It was part of Perkins's military philosophy to create as much chaos as possible. "We operate very well in chaos, the Iraqis, well, not so well," he would say with a smile, "The delta is huge." As his other two armor battalions rolled into Peach, Perkins turned them south. Schwartz's 1-64 Armor attacked down Highway 1, while deCamp's 4-64 AR attacked down Highway 8.

Almost a week before, when I had met Perkins on the battlefield, I had asked if he thought his brigade could take on the Medina. He replied, "They are beat up, looking the wrong way, and they don't know I'm coming. My battalions will rip the heart out of them." Now Perkins had two heavy battalions attacking into the rear of the Medina Division, and he was doing just as he promised. In an order that should be a model of conciseness Lieutenant Colonel Schwartz launched his battalion south by saying, "Find tanks and kill them."

The 4-64 AR almost immediately ran into a dug-in motorized rifle company defending highway 1. It took just a few minutes for the lead company to destroy the ten Iraqi BMPs, and the battalion was soon on the move again. The advance continued for the next fifteen miles, before lack of fuel became a factor. Perkins's primary objective for the day had been to secure Saints for future operations. Turning two battalions to the south was basically a raid to make sure that the Iraqis were incapable of mounting a dangerous counterattack during the night. DeCamp was told to turn his battalion around and return to Saints to rearm and refuel. There would be time enough tomorrow to finish off the Medina.

Schwartz's 1-64 AR received the recall order at the same time as DeCamp. However, he was forced to delay his return for a few long minutes when his Charlie Company, commanded by Captain Jason Conroy, found itself in what amounted to a knife fight with tanks. While moving through the town of Mahmudiyah, Conroy discovered his

tanks were sharing the narrow streets with seven Iraqi T-72s. As his first
tank turned into the town's main street, two T-72s loomed up directly
ahead. Conroy's lead tank squeezed off a main-gun round and the one
of the T-72s exploded in a massive fireball. The other Iraqi tank fired
at the advancing M-1, but his shot went high and left. By that time the
M-1 had reloaded and fired. The HEAT round impacted, but it was not
clear how much damage it did. Unexcitedly, the commander of the
second tank online ordered, "One round. SABOT! Move out and fire."
The depleted uranium penetrator on the SABOT sliced though the
T-72's front armor and it exploded in a flash of flame and smoke.

Just as the second of Conroy's tanks fired, the driver spotted another
tank in the adjacent alley. The tank was so close and the alley so narrow
that the M-1 could neither maneuver nor turn its turret to engage. The
tank commander shouted a warning to the first tank, which swiveled
its gun towards the alley. The gunner looked through his scope at lowest magnification and saw nothing but a metal mass filling the entire
frame. It was so close he was not sure it was a tank and asked if everyone was certain. The tank commander screamed fire and the gunner
pulled the trigger. Another Iraqi tank exploded, raining flaming debris
down on the two American tanks.

Conroy's tanks continued to move gingerly though the town, hunt-
ing tanks at ranges they had never considered before. While the M-1
was close to impervious to anything the Iraqis could throw at it, the
125mm gun on a T-72 fired at point-blank range could easily ruin an
M-1 crew's entire day. This was definitely a see-first/shoot-first fight.
Four more times the company engaged Iraqi tanks at point-blank
ranges, before exiting the far side of town and rejoining the rest of the
battalion. It had been a harrowing experience for the company, particularly the lead platoon, but it was a tremendous rehearsal for what
they would encounter in Baghdad in just forty-eight hours.[3]

When the order came to return to Saints, Conroy took his company around the town, rather than through it.

The next morning Perkins sent his two battalions down the same
route, but this time much farther. All along both routes the 2nd Brigade soldiers engaged and destroyed vehicle after vehicle. At one
point, three T-72s fired from under cover at the 4-64's lead company.
The company commander matter-of-factly reported:

---

3. A full account of this fight can be found in Jason Conroy's book *Heavy Metal: A Tank
Company's Battle to Baghdad* (written with Ron Martz).

2nd Brigade tanks in a town south of Objective Saints destroyed seven Iraqi tanks at ranges so close the tankers called it a "knife fight in an alleyway."

As we were moving south along the highway, we came under fire from three T-72s west of Highway 1 in a grove of trees. Red platoon was on the southbound lane; White was in the northbound lane. A T-72 fired from the tree line at C11 coming up short. Red platoon responded by firing 3 main gun rounds from C12, C11, and C14, destroying the entire Iraqi T-72 platoon.

Without pausing, the 4-64 AR continued to roll past the burning Iraqi tanks. Soldiers became more afraid of being hurt by flying debris than they were of Iraqi fire. In this battle the 2nd Brigade held all the advantages, and the Iraqis knew it. As the battle became, in the words of the soldiers who were there, "a grand turkey shoot," more and more Iraqis deserted their positions. Long before the run to the south was called back, the 2nd Brigade was destroying mostly abandoned tanks, BMPs, and artillery guns. After wreaking carnage for almost thirty miles, the two attacking battalions were recalled. In their wake, they had left a shattered Medina Division.

Before them sat the city of Baghdad—the final prize.

19

The Cavalry Heads West

(3–7 APRIL)

A FTER BEING RELIEVED at Objective Floyd, Lieutenant Colonel Terry Ferrell's 3-7 CAV made its way to Objective Rams, where it was able to get a much-needed rest after almost a week of nonstop movement and fighting. Samawah, Ambush Alley, and the battle for Najaf were behind them, and the squadron was a long way from the green troopers who had crossed the border. They had met and destroyed everything the enemy could throw at them and were sure they were more than a match for whatever else came their way.

Their world, however, was about to change.

Since crossing the border the 3-7 CAV had been fighting Al-Quds and Fedayeen in a very up-close and personal kind of war. But now they received orders to head north and screen to the west of the division (Objective Montgomery), as 1st Brigade headed for Baghdad International Airport and 2nd Brigade continued its fight at Objective Saints. The paramilitaries were gone. From this point forward the 3-7 CAV would be facing the tanks of the Republican Guard. Still, the 3-7 CAV troopers remained unfazed. After all, many of them had spent their entire military careers training to fight a tank battle in the open desert. Besides, there was a widespread assumption that after two weeks

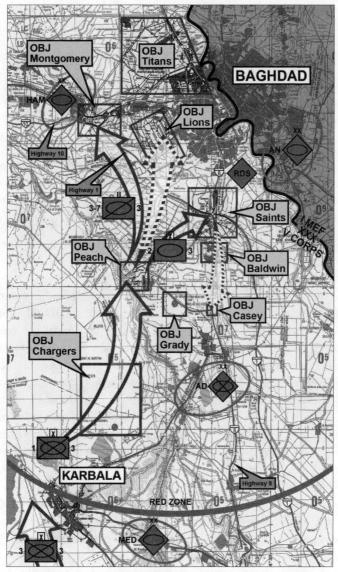

MAP 21. 3rd ID attack on Objective Saints, Objective Montgomery, and the Baghdad International Airport

of pounding by the Air Force, attack helicopters, and long range artillery, most of the fight was drained out of the Iraqis. As Sergeant First Class Matthew Chase relates, most of these notions vanished as the unit approached its screening positions (Objective Montgomery):

> We were expecting to come up and destroy abandoned vehicles. I thought that by now the Iraqis had been hit with so much artillery and the CAS that self-preservation would kick in and they would leave. When we started taking direct fire from T-72s, we got focused real quick. That changed our game plan. We stopped worrying about RPGs and whether our coax was going to jam up. Now, we went to the main gun. Gunnery training comes back into effect and you make sure you have good lazes, your lead is put into your ballistic solution, and you kill the targets.

When the CAV approached Montgomery it found itself engaged in the fiercest armor on armor battle of the war, against an enemy that was far from defeated.

Lieutenant Colonel Terry Ferrell was already moving his squadron across the bridge at Objective Peach when he got a call that General Blount wanted a face-to-face meeting on the far side of the bridge. As Ferrell relates: "Our meeting lasted approximately thirty minutes, just long enough for Blount to explain that the enemy picture to the west was unclear, but he anticipated we would encounter one of the Republican Guards divisions attempting to counterattack from the west. Actually, the enemy situation was so vague, he thought we might see composite units from multiple Iraqi divisions attempting to block the division's progress. The meeting was more of a pep talk to let me know of his confidence in the squadron."

With Clay Lyle's Apache Troop once again leading the way, the other two troops and the squadron's artillery headed northwest from Objective Peach. Because of intelligence reports of a significant threat in the region to aircraft (reflecting the battering the 11th Attack Helicopter Regiment had endured the week before), the squadron's air troop was left at Rams. As a result, the squadron lost its eyes in the sky, which would have given them early warning about what was in front of them.

Crossing the Euphrates was uneventful as the 1st Brigade had, by this time, cleared several miles to the north of the bridge. The squadron moved unmolested to its release point and headed to Objective Montgomery. As they moved from Rams to the release point, soldiers were amazed at the reception from the locals. Thousands of Iraqi civilians were now lining the route waving, smiling, and cheering. Some of the younger women were even bold enough to blow kisses at the troopers. It was a far cry from the reception the squadron had received along the roads of "ambush alley." Despite this reception, the troopers kept their guard up, as word was already filtering around about the heavy resistance that the 2nd Brigade was encountering on its way to Objective Saints, only twenty miles to the north.

Almost as soon as the squadron left the 1st Brigade's cleared zone, they engaged dug-in Iraqis. At first it was just more of the same. According to Ferrell:

> The contacts were similar to that we previously encountered: technical vehicles, prepared dismounted positions, and RPG teams lined the highway. Apache Troop rolled down the highway utilizing all four lanes and simultaneously engaged Iraqi positions on both sides of the highway as it moved. There was also a lot of what appeared to be civilian traffic on the highway and secondary routes. However, it was pretty easy to tell which civilian cars were being used by the enemy, mostly because they stopped and emptied out so the passengers could fire RPGs at us. After which, they would attempt to move to and occupy prepared fighting positions. They were rarely successful.

For the next ten miles, Apache Troop and the squadron's command vehicles were in almost constant contact. Rather than just continue in column through another gauntlet of fire, Crazyhorse Troop maneuvered off the highway, allowing the squadron to attack with two troops abreast, spread out over fifteen miles width. Captain McCoy, Crazyhorse's commander, was forced to maneuver through farmland cut with numerous canals, but for almost ten miles he advanced without contact, though two M-1s were lost when they slid into canals.

Crazyhorse's luck could not hold up. As they came over a low ridge line they ran into a well-organized force using heavy artillery and air defense guns in the direct fire mode. As Ferrell later reflected, "We were only fifteen miles beyond where we had been cheered by waving women and children, and now we were once again fully engaged in another hellish battle."

Captain McCoy, who was traveling with his troop in line abreast, was able to mass every main gun and machine gun he possessed on the enemy bastion. In a matter of moments the Iraqi fire ceased as each of their positions was obliterated under a hail of fire.

As both Crazyhorse and Apache Troops moved just west of the airport, resistance tapered off to almost nothing. Apache Troop moved up to Objective Montgomery and in a final rush seized it. At first, resistance was light, only a few technical vehicles with dismount squads. Familiar with this type of threat from long days of engaging thousands of fanatical Fedayeen, the troop quickly destroyed the enemy and occupied defensive positions. Within minutes of moving into their positions, two technical vehicles attacked the squadron's tactical command post. The command post troopers, including Lieutenant Colonel Ferrell, fired every weapon on hand. Personal sidearms joined with the Bradley's main gun before the two vehicles blew up. Because of their determination Ferrell started to think he had another Objective Floyd on his hand: "We knew it would be a very long night."

Before nightfall Crazyhorse and Apache were in their defensive positions and had found time to clear back through the zone to eliminate any pockets of Iraqis that were bypassed as they rushed the objective. Bonecrusher Troop, which was trailing approximately six miles behind Apache Troop, was sent to the east side of the objective to tie in and screen the 1st Brigade as they attacked Baghdad Airport. Within fifteen minutes of occupying their position, Bonecrusher's commander reported that he sent a platoon to help a 1st Brigade scout team that came under attack as they probed the outer ring of the airport.

Sergeant First Class Hector Camacho (whom we last saw risking his life to save the crew of a stricken M-1 north of Objective Floyd) took his tank platoon to the rescue. He destroyed the technical vehicle that had attacked the scout team and continued on. The scouts were still under heavy fire when he arrived at their position. Camacho placed his armored vehicles in a protective circle around the scouts and dismounted. While under fire, Camacho gave a wounded scout first aid and saved his life. For the second time in the war, Camacho had left the relative safety of his armored vehicle to go to the rescue of a stricken comrade while under heavy fire. Ferrell later made sure he was awarded the silver star for bravery.

As night fell, Ferrell's fear that he was going to face another battle like Objective Floyd was borne out. Iraqis, still not taking the 3rd IDs ability to see at night into account, began a series of attacks against Apache Troop as soon as darkness fell. Still dressed in civilian clothes, they continued their attacks, which included several attempts to ram vehicles loaded with explosives into the CAVs tanks, for the next fifteen hours. With fanatical determination the Iraqis rushed Apache's positions with trucks, buses, cars, and anything else that would move up the road. Repeatedly the main guns of the tanks and Bradleys barked as they unleashed a torrent of fire into suicide vehicles one after another.

At about 1:00 A.M. the suicide trucks stopped coming, but Apache's fight was far from over. At approximately 3:00 A.M. on 4 April, Captain Lyle observed an enemy armored column attempting to bypass his troop and get to the airport, to attack the flank of the 1st Brigade. Captain Lyle saw three T-72 tanks and two other armored vehicles moving in front of his position. To Lyle the enemy attacked as if they were unaware of his being there or thought they were invisible in the dark. Even as the lead tank erupted in a ball of flame, the others continued along as if they were on peacetime parade. The rest of the small Iraqi column was quickly dispatched. Throughout the rest of the night, other armored formations sporadically moved along the same route, seemingly oblivious to the danger, despite the burning vehicles of those that preceeded them. In the morning, Ferrell said, "It looked like an armored graveyard in front of Apache."

Only one enemy prisoner survived Apache's armor battle, a lieutenant who was blown from the hatch of his tank. According to Ferrell:

> For the first time since entering Iraq, we confirmed we were fighting Saddam's Republican Guard. The prisoner said he was assigned to the 15th Mechanized Brigade of the Hammurabi Division, which until two days prior had been located in Tikrit. After our medics and doctors stabilized him, we moved him to the division medical company for further treatment. Before he left us, however, we learned the designation of his unit, and the fact that they had serious maintenance problems with their equipment. He also told us that many soldiers deserted on the day the order came to fight. Based on his company's determination, though, I knew this would not be the last of the armored fights.

For Ferrell, the best thing about that night was that the rest of the Squadron's zone stayed quiet. As he relates: "Crazyhorse Troop had only a few more encounters with dismounts during its entire stay and no armored vehicles entered their zone. Captain McCoy's troopers had plenty of time to clear the zone and found numerous ammo caches and unmanned artillery pieces, which they subsequently destroyed."

For Apache Troop, the excitement was not quite over. Later in the day they would fight one more major tank battle, but at the moment they had another preoccupation. As Ferrell describes:

> The section of Highway 1 that Apache Troop defended became known as the highway of death; literally hundreds of Iraqis were lying dead directly in front of Apache's positions. It was very difficult for the troopers to sit looking at the death and destruction, knowing they were responsible for it. I initially considered forming burial details to clear the Iraqi bodies, but my leaders advised me against this. There were still a lot of Iraqis waiting outside the perimeter to kill us if we let our guard down.
>
> I was able to get a psychological operations team into the local village to broadcast appeals for the locals to police up their dead along the highway and we were all amazed at the rapid response of the local population. Within an hour the highway was cleared of all but a few bodies. Interestingly, we learned that the bodies left behind were foreign fighters. The locals would only take Iraqis. They wanted nothing to do with Syrians or other foreigners.

Ferrell's relatively peaceful day ended when the Vth Corps air operations officer called the squadron's tactical air controller to tell him a pair of F-15s, returning from a corps mission, spotted at least a tank battalion dug in two miles to our northeast. Skipping the 3rd ID Division staff, the corps tactical command post said they were directing aircraft to destroy the targets and then wanted the 3-7 CAV to move forward and confirm the destruction. Ferrell's first act was to notify division headquarters, which led to a thirty-minute discussion on how and why he was receiving orders directly from Corps. Eventually General Austin approved the movement and, since the enemy location was close to Apache's northernmost blocking position, the mission fell to them.

Based on the Corps report and the promise of multiple aircraft sorties in support of his attack, Ferrell thought it safe to take only a portion of Apache Troop, along with his command vehicle, north. The rest would remain at Montgomery, continuing their screening mission for 1st Brigade. In all, Ferrell was moving to engage a fortified armored battalion with seven tanks and five Bradleys. As they approached the reported Iraqi positions, Coalition air elements struck. Ferrell reports:

Right on time, the first two Tornados made their initial bomb run and dropped four 1000-pound bombs. Immediately after that, a second pair of Tornados executed the same drill. After these two passes, we waited for the secondary explosions that indicated the targets had been hit. However, there was no black smoke coming from the target area. We continued watching as two A-10s made bomb runs and then made a pass with their 30-millimeter cannons, but still we saw no secondary explosions from the target area. Since I was expecting twenty or more T-72 tanks, the lack of secondary explosions made it plain something was wrong.

Before giving Apache Troop the order to move forward, I directed the squadron's artillery battery to fire a concentration into the target area. After that I saw some secondary explosions, but nothing of the magnitude expected. When the last artillery round fired, I ordered Apache forward. Within minutes enemy tanks began firing from the south side of the highway, not the north as reported by the aircraft.

Ferrell's troops had walked right into the prepared kill-zone of an armored battalion. Sitting out in the open, they were being fired on by T-72s, BMPs, and heavy artillery at ranges between eight hundred and a thousand meters. It was an ugly position to be in, which was redeemed only by the training, courage, and incredible discipline of the CAV troopers.

Sergeant First Class Paul Wheatley, who was in the lead tank, tells the rest of the story:

We were in a 7-tank, 2-Brad staggered combat column. I was the lead tank. My wingman was behind me. My A section, my platoon leader, and his wingman were on the right side of the road. As we came up the road I was expecting to see twenty or more T-72s on the north side of the road. As we got closer to where the Air Force had struck I halted; everyone began scanning their sectors looking for the targets the Air Force reported. We were stopped for about thirty seconds when a T-72 hidden behind an overpass eight hundred meters ahead fired on us. That's when all hell broke loose.

We were under fire from the south and we had everyone of our guns oriented to the north. As we turned the turret to face the enemy I backed up probably one hundred meters and got off to the side of the road.

Everybody behind me backed up the same amount while still acquiring and engaging targets. Without being told, everybody started spreading out to get some depth to our position, so that when they fired they wouldn't interfere with other tanks trying to engage. As we backed up and spread out, everyone continued to engage. We were all talking back and forth on the radio, telling each other what we saw, what we were engaging, and what was shooting at us.

It was thrilling!

There was some small-arms fire, a few RPGs coming from a strong point on the north, but it was the Iraqi armor that worried me most. Our tanks focused on those while the 25mm on the Bradley tore up the Iraqi infantry positions.

We were destroying tanks with HE rounds, and a couple of my tanks fired MPAT rounds. It was just blowing the turrets right off them. We discovered some BMPs firing from the north side of the road, but our .50-caliber guns were destroying them. I mean totally destroying them, cooking off the ammo that was inside them so that they blew up in huge fireballs.

As the Iraqi tanks and BMPs started burning, it helped us use our thermal sights. It became a lot easier to acquire targets that weren't already burning. So we didn't double-tap any of the targets that we shot at.[1]

This wasn't our first fight. We'd been fighting ever since we crossed the border. But the intensity of a tank firing at you instead of an RPG pushes it up a notch. Other than that everybody reacted and did their drills the way we're supposed to and the way we trained. It was different, because you could hear it and then you could see it. And then we destroyed it. It was just that simple and that fast.

In the rear of the column Sergeant First Class Mathew Chase spotted another threat. Through his thermal sights he was able to see hot spots at about a thousand meters distance, but they were so small he was unable to get the reticle of his sights to lay on them. It turned out that he was looking at the top machine guns of a company of hidden BMPs. Hiding behind thick earthen berms, the BMPs assumed they were safe from direct fire. As Chase relates: "We started cross talking on the troop net, and I was talking with the Red 2 element and he started marking the targets I was describing with his tracers. Once we got a good idea where the targets were we started lazing the berm with our laser range finders. We ignored the small target signatures and aimed beneath them right through the berm. We got a good target effect from that. From what I saw, it was real smooth and methodical.

---

1. "Double tap" being the military parlance for putting a second round into a target.

We kept talking with Red 2, so that they wouldn't double tap a target we already hit."

In less than fifteen minutes Apache Troop had annihilated its ambushers and begun to withdraw back to Objective Montgomery. To ensure the destruction of the Iraqi positions Ferrell asked for and received permission to fire an MLRS concentration on the position. Later it was learned that the Apache's seven tanks and five Bradleys had destroyed more than four times their number of Iraqi armored vehicles, more than thirty of them being T-72s.

As they returned to Montgomery the troopers were euphoric. Sergeant Chase continues the story:

> On the way back there was a lot of chatter on the radio, a lot of feeling good about what we did. We were successful and no troopers were hurt. I could hear a lot of the leadership ribbing each other by saying things like, "Thanks for coming out and supporting me." But there were a lot of very honest feelings. I was talking to Red 2 on the way back, and gave him a real honest thanks. There was lot of honest thanks and praising others going on. The espirit was just unbelievable going back down that highway to Montgomery. It was through the roof. It was a good feeling, winning against such a large force and bringing every soldier back home.

Three hours after hearing the first reports from the Air Force, Apache Troop was back to its previous blocking positions. The next day Ferrell was told that the Colonel Allyn's 3rd Brigade would pass though his positions on its way to Objective Titans. The 3-7 CAV had fought its last battle of the war. Its next order was to move to occupy Objective Saints so that Colonel Perkins's 2nd Brigade could focus on their thunder run into Baghdad.

20

Before the Crash:
Under the Sniper's Scope

B Y MIDDAY ON 4 APRIL, the bulk of the 3rd ID's combat
power was through the Karbala Gap and on the outskirts of
Baghdad. Its soldiers had mostly obliterated the Medina Division and crippled two other Republican Guard divisions that had
entered its sector. Still ahead, though, was the city of Baghdad itself
defended by fanatical Fedayeen and the Special Republican Guard.
Large elements of the Nebuchadnezzar Division, which had hastily
redeployed south from Mosul, were also reported to be preparing
defenses in and around the city. Moreover, the 3rd ID staff was getting reports that the powerful Al-Nida Division was redeploying to
the west—directly in the path of the 3rd ID. This came on top of
reports that a number of other units were also on the move, all of
them heading towards the 3rd ID and away from the Marines. A
number of early histories of the war interpreted these Iraqi moves as
representing the regime's belated recognition of the mortal threat
the 3rd ID now posed. It is now clear, however, that most of these
units were not trying to interpose themselves between the 3rd ID
and Baghdad, but were actually trying to follow Saddam's orders to
move west of Baghdad to prepare to defeat a phantom threat coming
from Jordan.

Still, had this final desperate maneuver of the regime succeeded, it would have placed the better part of three Republican Guard heavy divisions directly in front of the 3rd ID just as it made its rush to Baghdad. On the plus side, however, any units that were in the process of moving west would present their exposed flank to the onrushing 3rd ID armor. Furthermore, they would be caught totally by surprise. After all, Saddam had just informed them that the American attack from the south was a ruse. As always there was no reason for doubt once Saddam had pronounced the truth. Nevertheless, even if caught by surprise these units still possessed formidable combat power—on paper. To understand the remainder of the battle and the Republican Guard's poor showing, it is important to understand what they had endured over the preceding two weeks and the effect it had had on them.

Psychological Destruction

From the beginning the Iraqis had convinced themselves that any American attack would, as in 1991, begin with a prolonged air offensive. Saddam apparently believed the Coalition would limit its entire assault to air attacks; most of his senior military officers, still mentally stuck in the Gulf War paradigm, believed that any land assault would come only after weeks of sustained air operations. It was a shock to many of them when the Coalition offensive began with a simultaneous air and ground attack, coupled with a comprehensive psychological operations campaign aimed at undermining the rank-and-file's willingness to fight.

It is now obvious that Coalition planners did not fully appreciate the psychological effects that precision firepower would have on Iraqi combat units. Lieutenant General Majid Husayn Ali Ibrahim Al-Dulaymi, commander of the Republican Guard's I Corps, told interviewers after the war, "Our units were unable to execute anything due to worries induced by psychological warfare. They were fearful of modern war, pinpoint war in all climates and in all weather." The general added that psychological operations were "the bullet that hits the heart before hitting the body. . . . When it hits, it makes a fearful man; he walks without a brain. Even the lowest soldier knew we couldn't stop the Americans." Though the staff at CENTCOM were worried that the post-strike battle damage assessments were not demonstrating sufficient damage of Iraqi materiel to provide commanders

a high level of confidence about the attrition suffered by the Republican Guard, they failed to take into account the psychological damage
caused by the air strikes.

Besides the normal tools of a psychological campaign such as leaf-
lets and radio broadcasts, General Husayn emphasized the impact
that precision weapons had on the morale of Iraqi soldiers. He himself received a severe shock during a visit to the Adnan Republican
Guard Division shortly after one of its battalions had unwisely moved
into an open field, and air power had almost instantly obliterated it.
In his words, "The level of precision of those attacks put real fear into
the soldiers of the rest of the division. The Americans were able to
induce fear throughout the Iraqi Army by using precision air power."

The story of the Al-Nida Division, which was the most powerful
and best-equipped division in the Iraqi military, underlines the devastating psychological effects of Coalition airpower. Considering that the
Al-Nida Division never really engaged Coalition ground forces during
the course of the war, what happened to it suggests that psychological
operations, integrated with precision fires, created a general dread of
seemingly inevitable destruction—a combination which quite literally
broke the will of the many Iraqi units subjected to it.

Even the Coalition's leaflet drops (which the Iraqi generals called
trash) had a devastating psychological effect not foreseen by CENT-
COM planners. For the average Iraqi soldier, the regime's inability to
stop U.S. aircraft from "flying 8,000 miles to drop its trash" on them
proved Iraq's military impotence. What made it worse was the fact
that the Coalition seemed to know exactly where to drop the so-called
"trash."

According the General Husayn's account, "It made every soldier in
the Republican Guard feel as if they were in 'a sniper's sight.'" Even
when Coalition firepower hit decoy positions, the psychological effect
was devastating. Many Republican Guard units had prepared a number of decoy positions to trick the Coalition as to their actual positions. In more than a few cases the decoys were effective and became
the focal point of concentrated Coalition firepower. The first reaction of Iraqi commanders was a touch of glee that they had been able
to fool the Americans. However, that emotion soon turned to dismay
when, soon after the attacks, their forces began to melt away. What the
average Iraqi soldier saw was not the Americans being fooled, but the
systematic, hole-by-hole destruction of positions often directly to their

South of Objective Saints Iraqis who have had enough of the fight discard their uniforms and go home or . . .

. . . surrender.

front. They made the obvious deduction: "The Americans are blowing up every hole and I am in a hole." It was time for them to leave.

The Al-Nida commander offered the following opinion on the psychological effects of Coalition air attacks on his troops:

> The air attacks were the most effective message. The soldiers who did see the leaflets and then saw the air attacks knew the leaflets were true. They believed the message after that, if they were still alive. Overall they had a terrible effect on us. I started the war with 13,000 soldiers. By the time we had orders to pull back to Baghdad, I had less than 2,000; by the time we were in position in Baghdad, I had less than 1,000. Every day the desertions increased. We had no engagements with American forces. When my division pulled back across the Diyala bridge, of the more than 500 armored vehicles assigned to me before the war, I was able to get fifty or so across the bridge. Most were destroyed or abandoned on the east side of the Diyala River.

In effect, precise airpower and the fear it engendered reduced an entire Republican Guard division to combat ineffectiveness. In this case, the Iraqi unit was not so much destroyed as dissolved. It is doubtful, however, that the psychological effects of the air strikes would have been so pronounced if Coalition airpower had not also been destroying significant amounts of Iraqi combat power. The reality of the situation was that airpower was doing a magnificent job of chewing up anything that attracted attention. In one air attack, Coalition aircraft had spotted the 41st Brigade's 153rd Artillery Battalion. The battalion had dispersed itself in three distinct locations: it had hidden its artillery pieces in an orchard, the soldiers in a second position, and the ammunition in a third location. The division commander said he had been shocked when "the air attack hit all three locations at the same time, and annihilated the artillery battalion."

Continuous air strikes essentially wore away the adjoining 42nd Brigade. The division commander relates: "In the 42nd Brigade sector, the troops were in their prepared positions and were hit very effectively for five days. The continuous nature of the attacks did not allow us to track the number of losses. When there was a pause in the attacks, many of the soldiers 'escaped' [a euphemism for deserted]."

Every unit of the Republican Guard endured the same pressure. Some collapsed like the Al-Nida Division, but others held on grimly and patiently waited for their chance to meet the American in an upclose fight. Some Iraqi commanders even at this late date thought

The aftermath of an Air Force JDAMS strike on an Iraqi command center.

there was still a lot of fight left in the Iraqi army and that it would soon show its teeth. After the war General Hamdani summed up his current view of the situation. "During this time there were heavy air attacks on the Medina Division, but we were surprised at how few fell on the Al-Nida Division. The attacks were effective against fixed sites such as communications and logistic facilities, but much less so on the forces themselves. We had multiple positions for each vehicle, and the troops remained dispersed. The Nebuchadnezzar Division took some damage from air attacks during its move into position during this time, but it was not seriously hurt. The real effect was on the morale of the troops. But at this point morale had not broken. My soldiers were still prepared to fight." The 3rd ID was about to test their mettle.

21

Baghdad International Airport

(4–5 April)

O N THE MORNING OF 3 APRIL, General Blount had reason to be satisfied with the situation. Grimsley's 1st Brigade was holding the bridge at Objective Peach and had decimated the Republican Guard's counterattack. Perkins's 2nd Brigade was already moving across the bridge, heading for Objective Saints, in order to complete the destruction of the Republican Guard, while the 3-7 CAV was enroute from Ram to screen the division's left flank. Blount's troops were knocking on the very doors of Baghdad.

In front of him was Baghdad International Airport (BIAP), and Blount was determined to seize it. The Vth Corps had spent long hours discussing the best way to seize this key objective; they had always leaned towards taking it by a massive air assault by the 101st Airborne Division. Because the terrain approaching the airport and all around it looked more like a jungle than a desert, it was assumed BIAP would be a deathtrap for heavy armor. Blount, though, knew two things that the corps staff did not. First, he had seen his troops completely dominate the fight in closed, jungle-like terrain at Karbala and elsewhere. More importantly, Blount, who was always up front with the lead combat elements, had a sense of the battlefield. He knew that the Iraqis were rocked back on their heels, and Blount was not inclined to give them a chance to recover.

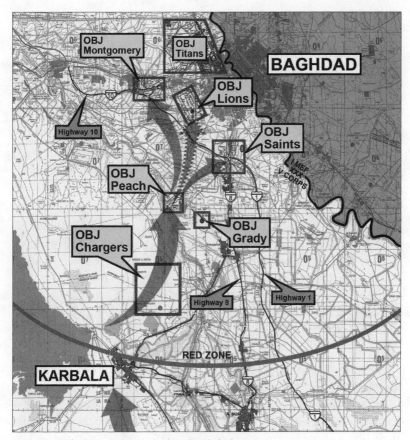

MAP 22. Vth Corps plan to isolate Baghdad

Blount called Lieutenant General William Wallace, Vth Corps commander, and asked for permission to attack the airport immediately. Wallace hesitated, but Blount insisted, "Sir, we trained for this. . . . We prepared for this. . . . We're ready for this. . . . We need to go now." There was a long silence on the radio before Wallace replied, "Have a good fight. Victory Six, OUT."

Blount traveled to Colonel Grimsley's command post, now at Objective Peach, to break the news in person. Grimsley had anticipated the order to head for BIAP. Even before Blount arrived at his command post, he had told his commanders to prepare for the mission. However, he assumed the attack would be ordered for the next morning. He was counting on a full day to rest his exhausted soldiers, particularly Marcone's 3-69 AR, which had just finished a thirty-hour nonstop fight.

When Blount asked him, though, how long before he could start attacking north again, Grimsley assured him the brigade could move out by late afternoon. Lieutenant Colonel Marcone remembers receiving the order:

> I am thinking we are going to get a break, so I call the brigade headquarters and they tell me to take the airfield. I said, not us again. I thought we were going to take it the next morning at 0600, and we had planned to get a good night's sleep and refuel and rearm. At 1200 Brigade called again and said get moving in two hours. We had a problem with the timeline because we had fought all night and hadn't refueled yet. All of my tanks were less than half full and we were critically short 25mm HE for the Bradleys. I sent my executive officer, Major Johnson, to the rear to find fuel and ammo and we figure we will rearm and refuel on the fly because we have to move out no later than 1430.
>
> This was the mother of all worst nightmares. We were about to conduct a movement to contact, at night, without any reconnaissance, and zero intel on where the enemy is. Moreover, we have to attack in column due to the terrain.

Despite his unhappiness, Marcone's 3-69 AR moved out before 3:00 P.M. At first the battalion made good progress, as they were moving in the wake of the 2nd Brigade and 3-7 CAV. Any Iraqis left unmolested by those two units as they drove past were not inclined to try their luck against Marcone's men. But as darkness fell and the terrain became more restricted, Iraqi defenders became bolder. As Marcone remembers:

> It was just the craziest night movement. We were traveling in column with canals everywhere. My scout team was ambushed and the lead truck was hit by an RPG. There was two wounded, one of them serious, who required evacuation. [This incident was referred to in the previous chapter when SFC Hector Camacho came to the scouts' rescue.] We actually get there in pretty good order, though some of the ambushes in the early evening were pains in the ass.
>
> We were in this jungle-like terrain filled with palm trees and they would hit us out of the darkness. Most of the time we would just roll over the top of these guys while the Bradleys put out a massive rain of 25mm. I didn't want to put infantry out in the groves, as I didn't want them to get decisively engaged. My objective was the airport, and I did not want to get bogged down fighting in this morass. Still, their

fanaticism was amazing, but it was also pissing my soldiers off. By this time, we were very tired of killing and we wanted them to stop being stupid. A Bradley would come up and kill everything and everyone in a position and they would just reseed the position with more knuckle-heads for the next Bradley to kill.

The 1-41 Field Artillery, commanded by Lieutenant Colonel James Lackey, was following directly behind Marcone's battalion and was ambushed as it was executing a fire mission in support of Marcone's advance. Even as they continued to fire the mission, a small band of artillery soldiers, led by one of the battery commanders, fought off the attack. However, in this engagement the unit took seven of the nine casualties it suffered during the war, including the death of the head-quarters battery commander, Captain Tristan Aiken.

Despite having to defend themselves in a series of close engage-ments with Iraqi dismounts, the artillery men never faltered. They fired every mission requested, usually within a minute or two of receiv-ing the call for fire. By the time the airport was secured, the 1-41 FA had fired more than a dozen emergency fire missions while on the move and dozens of other normal missions. In just two days they fired more than two thousand rounds, which were critical in breaking the Iraqi Special Republican Guard's will to fight.

Eventually Marcone's men fought their way to the airfield perime-ter, which was enclosed by a ten-foot-high concrete fence. After spend-ing a few minutes fruitlessly searching for an opening, the lead tanks blasted a hole through the wall, which ignited the dry underbrush lin-ing the wall. The illumination from the fire was enough to discern a gate just north of where the battalion was piling up. Captain Todd Kel-ly's Charlie Company led the way into the airport compound: "As my lead platoon came up, it was a mix of two tanks, two Bradleys, followed by another mix of two tanks, two Bradleys, followed by my infantry platoon. We moved directly up to the airfield and established a fir-ing line along the southern end of the airfield. We were set in posi-tion, it was pitch black; however with thermals and other night vision devices working, it was an outstanding view of the airfield. We had not received any fire since coming though the gate, and our arrival must have been a surprise.[1] Once we got into place, we were told to wait until other 3-69 elements came in."

---

1. Keep in mind that artillery, MLRS rockets, and close air support continued to pound the surrounding area. Any sounds Marcone's men were making as they approached the airfield were thus masked.

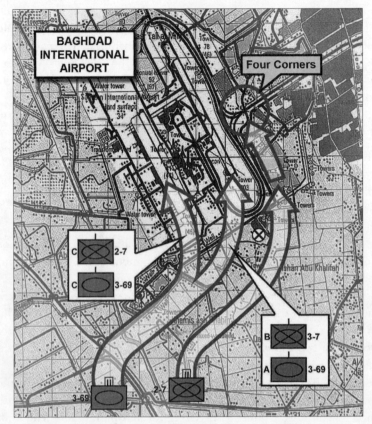

MAP 23. 1st Brigade assault on Baghdad International Airport

The silence was unnerving. Marcone's men expected to meet at least a brigade of the Special Republican Guard on the airfield; instead they were faced with dead silence. With his entire battalion on line, Marcone prepared to sweep across the airport and see what he could rouse. As he remembers: "It was around 2300 and it was very eerie. Baghdad was blacked out [the power had gone out in Baghdad hours before], all the lights were out on the airfield, and there is no natural illum. Everything just stopped. No shooting, no nothing. I used artillery and close air to shape the battlefield by targeting every position I thought the enemy might defend from. After a great artillery prep my companies swept towards the center of the airfield. Except for two abandoned tanks there was no sign of any Iraqi defenders." Marcone did not have long to wait. "At 0430 an unbelievable thing happened. All of the Iraqis woke up. They had been sleeping deep in their holes and bunkers waiting for an air assault. So, they wake up, scratch their ass, make their tea, and holy shit the American army is two hundred meters away. They started coming out of the ground like ants and the whole world just goes nuts for two and half hours."

For the next several hours Marcone's soldiers fought off a determined enemy. Unfortunately for the Iraqi defenders, they once again found themselves outgunned and outfought. When prisoners were interrogated later, they said they were expecting an airborne attack from the 82nd Airborne Division and never expected to see tanks. They had no clue how to react to tanks. Though hundreds of Iraqis stayed and fought desperately, prisoners also reported that six hundred or more of Saddam's best threw off their uniforms and ran when they saw what they were facing. One of those who tried to run was the Special Republican Guard brigade commander responsible for the defense of the airfield. According to Captain Jared Robbins: "We found the Iraqi brigade commander with a 7.62 round through the center of his head. What was unusual about this was that he was beside his personal civilian vehicle and it looked like he was abandoning his men. He was away from the main Iraqi defensive line when the round hit him and he had his car keys still in his hand. I consider him being killed as he was abandoning his men a bit of poetic justice."

3rd ID Bradleys seize Baghdad International Airport (BIAP).

Despite the overwhelming fire they were facing and their commander abandoning them, a number of the Iraqi soldiers fought
hard and well. The 3rd ID soldiers found that many of the bunkers
were so close and well-sited that the main guns of the tanks could not
engage them. Infantry began to rush out of their Bradleys, joined by
some tankers, to launch dismounted assaults on the Iraqi bunker complexes. Marcone later said, "It was unbelievable; our infantry was chas-
ing guys down and killing them. They had not rested or eaten a real
meal in a couple of days, but here they were assaulting bunker after
bunker as if it was a training exercise." As one of his company commander relates part of the fight:

> The enemy company commander defending the bunker I approached
> was determined to fight. He charged out of his bunker, but was
> instantly killed by coax fires from my White Platoon. The rest of the
> positions were so close we couldn't engage with the main gun, and
> coax wasn't having any effect on them. Sergeant First Class Ponder,
> one of my tank platoon sergeants, dismounted and, with his loader
> covering him, he walked up in a half crouch and tossed a grenade
> into a bunker. After it goes off about thirty clowns come out of this
> bunker to surrender. If we had fired our main gun into that bun-
> ker we would have killed all of the enemy, but we probably would
> have been injured by secondaries, as there was so much ammo stored
> in those bunkers it was dangerous to fire into them. As he was tak-
> ing the surrender of the Iraqis another bunker began firing on Pon-
> der. My gunner spotted them and took most of them out. The rest
> surrendered.

Securing the airport was the last hard fight for Marcone's soldiers.
A few days later they were ordered forward to secure several of Saddam's palaces and to link up with the 2nd Brigade. In their last skir-
mish the battalion engaged and destroyed a company of Iraqis wearing
red berets. They learned from some captured survivors that they were
part of a special service unit that was covering the escape of high government officials leaving the city. Marcone now knew for sure that the
ability of the Saddam regime to resist was rapidly collapsing. He was
happy for his soldiers. After three weeks of almost constant fighting
and killing, they needed a break.

General Blount and Colonel Grimsley had only one more important mission at the airport: they had to tell the world they owned it.
According to Grimsley,

Early on the morning of the 4th, I'm standing next to my Bradley and the Fox News guys say, can we go live? I say, sure, let's go live. And as the information minister [Baghdad Bob] is trumpeting something about a parade the regime was running in downtown Baghdad and telling the world that the Americans aren't anywhere near the airport, we go live to the world. Just the day before he had brought the international press out to the airfield to prove that the Americans were nowhere nearby. He is announcing that again as the Fox guy pans wide and shows that we're obviously at the airport. We told the world we were winning, though the BBC still seemed to doubt it.

If the hard fighting was over for Marcone's 3-69 AR, it was only just beginning for other 3rd ID units. Even as Marcone's men were clearing the airport bunker complexes—a job which took two full days and the help of one of the 101st's airborne battalions to complete—Lieutenant Colonel Scott Rutter's 2-7 IN was skirting his positions and moving to the east side of the airport. Here the battalion planned to occupy a major road intersection, known as four corners. If the Republican Guard tried to retake the airport, they would have to come though four corners. Rutter was positioning his battalion to make sure any counterattack was crushed before it could get started. But as 2-7 IN occupied four corners they were engulfed in the most effective counterattack the Iraqis launched during the war.

As the tactical operations center began to occupy positions near four corners they came under immediate small arms and accurate mortar fire. Worse, as the 2-7 IN was using the cover of darkness to occupy its positions it failed to notice it was sharing the ground with a number of hidden T-72 tanks. It was not until a chemical reconnaissance vehicle was fired on and a Bradley actually was hit by a T-72 main gun round that the battalion became aware of its immediate peril.

The Bradley was saved only because the 125mm round hit a soldier's rucksack strapped to the outside of the vehicle. Still, the impact was powerful enough to toss the vehicle commander out of his hatch. With boots and spare clothing still flying through the air, the Bradley driver threw his vehicle in reverse and dashed behind a small berm. As the Bradley retreated, a four-man infantry team armed with the new Javelin anti-tank missile climbed onto a nearby overpass to engage the T-72.[2] Less than a kilometer from the tactical operations center they

_____

2. The Javelin is a fire-and-forget top attack weapon. Unlike earlier anti-tank missiles, which had to be wire-guided to the target, once the Javelin locks onto a target the

spotted three T-72s hiding behind a wall to the battalion's south. Shooting right over the tactical ops center, the first Javelin slammed directly into the top of one of the T-72s with a deafening roar. The Javelin's impact sent the tank turret flying fifty feet in the air and created a fireball large enough to ignite a nearby second T-72. As secondary explosions wrecked the tank, a second Javelin streaked out to ensure the destruction of the burning second tank. As the third T-72 frantically tried to move out of the area, a third Javelin struck it, but this time the damage was not catastrophic and the tank limped away. It was destroyed later by an M-1 that spotted it moving towards Baghdad's city center.

In another section of four corners, the battalion mortar platoon leader and sergeant were doing a dismounted security patrol of their area when they heard the rumble of tanks behind them. Looking back, they saw two T-72s only a hundred yards away. Horrified, the men split and ran in opposite directions. The tanks followed the platoon leader, Captain Matthew Paul, who ran into a palm grove and ducked behind a berm. Both tanks stopped less than thirty yards from the platoon leader and began firing their machine guns into Paul's protecting berm. With his face pressed into the dirt, and trying to make himself one with the mud, all Captain Paul could do was wait and pray.

As Paul kept as still as possible, his platoon sergeant, Sergeant First Class Robert Broadwater, had made it back to the mortar platoon and began to organize a rescue. Broadwater was just about to move out when an M-1, towing a disabled tank, drove into his position looking for the maintenance collection point. Told that there were T-72s only a couple of hundred yards away, the M-1 swung in behind them while still towing the crippled tank.

Captain Paul could hear frantic screams in Arabic as the T-72 crews became aware of the M-1 pulling into a firing position directly behind them. It was too late for them to react, and both tanks blew up in succession, tossing their turrets high in the air and spraying debris in every direction. As T-72 parts continued to rain down, a mortar platoon vehicle pulled up and rescued their leader.

As the mortar platoon dealt with rampaging T-72s, the battalion

---

shooter can forget about it and either take cover or fire another weapon. Furthermore, the Javelin can be programmed to jump up before it reaches its target and slam down on its thin top armor.

tactical operations center (TOC) came under sustained attack by dis-mounted Iraqi infantry. Rutter had ordered his engineers to knock large holes in some of the many high walls in the area to clear field of fire for his battalion. No sooner had they started punching out these holes than the Iraqis started to pour through them directly into the center of the battalion. For the next forty minutes engineers, medics, and headquarters personnel fought off repeated assaults in a fierce close-combat battle. At one point the battalion aid station, which was filling up with 2-7 IN wounded, came under direct fire; armored vehi-cles had to be placed around it to absorb the enemy fire and protect the wounded.

As the Iraqi attack gained momentum Sergeant First Class Paul Smith mounted an M-113, from which vantage point he was the first to see a large counterattack developing just a hundred yards away. Climbing down off the vehicle, Smith stood in a breach in the wall and directed his engineers to put in a hasty defensive position, while he sent for a Bradley to give them some support. One of his soldiers said, "He told me to go get some 40mm grenade rounds, while he calmly stood in the open picking off attacking Iraqis one by one." As an engineer M-113 moved to the wall breach to support Smith, it was hit by an RPG, wounding the driver and two soldiers inside. Smith entered the burning vehicle three times to extricate the wounded men to safety.

When he got back to the fight, Smith found his engineers were being engaged from every direction. They were completely pinned down and taking fire from the surrounding walls and three guard tow-ers. Sergeant Derek Pelletier later said, "Nobody backed down from the fight. I fired five anti-tank rounds at two of the towers, but they just kept coming."

"It was non-stop shooting," reported Private Michael Seaman, "The Iraqis just kept spraying fire over the walls, hopping up to fire RPGs and dropping mortar rounds on us."

Engineer casualties were mounting and it did not appear that any help was on the way. Worried about the wounded, who were lying exposed in the open, and also about his men in the Iraqi kill zone, Smith made the decision to order them back to more easily defensible ground. In order to cover their movement, Smith got in and drove the still-burning M-113 to the center of the wall breach and mounted the .50-caliber on top. As he engaged the enemy he called for a driver to maneuver the vehicle around as necessary. Private Seaman, who later said, "I would follow that man anywhere," leapt aboard. Seaman could hear the .50-caliber firing as Smith engaged over a hundred Iraqi attackers single-handedly, only pausing to tell Seaman to pass him up some more ammo.

As Seaman passed him up his fifth box of ammo, the firing stopped. As he later said, "I looked at the ammo can and gun and could see rounds were still loaded. I couldn't see him and was wondering what had happened to him when I saw him fall in through the hatch." Seaman exited the M-113 and screamed to the retreating engineers that Smith was hit. Several of them immediately counterattacked back towards Smith and fought their way to his vehicle. By this time, an M-1 had arrived on the scene; using it for protection, the engineers loaded Smith on a litter and ran back to the aid station. Sergeant First Class Smith died a half hour later. His platoon credited his selfless heroism with saving many, if not all, of their lives that day. As Smith stood exposed on top of a burning M-113, his actions broke the back of the enemy counterattack. What was left of the Iraqi force retreated back into the wood line, leaving close to a hundred dead around Smith's position.[3]

For another half hour or so the 2-7 IN continued to fight off enemy attacks into their positions, destroying two more T-72s. However, Sergeant First Class Smith's heroic stand seemed to have broken the counterattack's back, and there were no further major assaults. By dawn, Rutter's soldiers held uncontested control of the four corners intersection.

The 3rd ID was on Baghdad International Airport to stay, and the end of the Saddam regime was near. All that remained was to give it that little extra push that would bring the entire edifice toppling down. Blount had just the solution. He called Colonel Perkins and told him to have his brigade ready to enter the heart of Baghdad.

Blount was ordering the first of two thunder runs into the center of Saddam's power base.

---

3. When his wife, Birgit Smith, his daughter, Jessica Smith, and his son, David Smith, went to the White House to receive the Medal of Honor their father had earned, *Time Magazine* covered it in five words. Neither *Newsweek* nor *U.S. News & World Report* thought it was worth covering at all.

22

Thunder Run I

(5 APRIL)

B Y NOON ON APRIL 4TH, the 3rd ID was in firm control of Baghdad International Airport and was busily wrecking the apparently paralyzed Medina Division. As far as the Vth Corps was concerned, the 3rd ID's campaign was about over. All that remained was for Blount to send a brigade around the city to Objective Titans and slam the door shut from the rear. With Colonel Allyn's brigade already moving forward to do just that Vth Corps was satisfied that they had Saddam and his army right where they wanted them. With the 3rd Division to the south, west, and north, and the Marines to the east, Baghdad was effectively isolated.

Fearful of taking heavy casualties in a bloody street fight in "fortress Baghdad," Vth Corps had dictated that this was as far as the 3rd ID was to go. From this point forward, Baghdad would be isolated and the surrounding Army and Marine divisions would conduct raids into the city to take out key objectives. These pinpoint raids would continue until the regime collapsed.

From the very beginning Blount had not thought much of this plan, but he had remained silent. He had other more pressing issues with the Corps planning staff, such as getting permission to go west of the Euphrates instead of the more urbanized and defensible route east of the Euphrates that Corps had selected. He would pick his battles with them, and his concern was with immediate issues. There would be ' time to address the takedown of Baghdad as he saw how the campaign developed. Well, now he was on the outskirts of the city, and every bit of military sense he possessed told him that the Corps plan was wrong.

For one thing, it would have his men fighting their way into the city and then giving up ground they had fought for, only to have to do it again and again as new targets were identified. Blount could not think of a faster way to demoralize his men than to make them fight and bleed for the same ground twice. Moreover, he doubted if laying siege to a city of five million people was a wise move. He dreaded the global outcry that would arise as the media started beaming out pictures of prolonged suffering being endured by a mostly innocent population. Besides, every day that the siege continued gave Saddam and his international friends just that much more time to force a diplomatic settlement that might leave Saddam in power.

Mostly though, Blount was absolutely sure that a prolonged siege was not a military necessity. His troops had now fought more than half a dozen urban engagements, and the results had been the same every time—Iraqis crushed and minimal losses to the 3rd ID. He was certain that his armored columns could penetrate into Baghdad and take on anything the Iraqis had, and do so with minimal risk. Blount knew that the 3rd ID had the initiative, and he was loath to give it up. With the Iraqis battered and on the ropes, he formulated his knockout combination.

What he came up with was a Thunder Run. Blount wanted to send a heavily armored column from 2nd Brigade in the south of Baghdad towards the center of the city. After penetrating a couple of miles, the column was to turn west and cut across the richest area of Baghdad (where most of the regime's senior functionaries resided) and head for the airport, where Grimsley's 1st Brigade would be waiting. It was a bold plan, but it required a soft sell. To get Corps' permission, Blount sold his plan as nothing more than a small movement to open a shorter line of communication between his widely separated brigades. Blount was not sure if the Corps commander fully comprehended what he was up to, but since he never called to say "no," Blount fell back on an old military maxim—silence is permission.

About 4:00 P.M. Perkins called Blount to tell him his battalions were back at their starting points at Objective Saints. He also told him that he believed that the Medina Division was shattered, and that he planned to rearm and refuel his two battalions and launch them south again in the morning to finish off the remnants. Blount took the report and then announced a change of mission. He wanted Perkins to take an armored column into Baghdad and see what the Iraqi defense was made of.

Perkins was wholeheartedly behind the mission; he selected Lieutenant Colonel Eric Schwartz and his 1-64 AR Battalion for the job.

Perkins called Schwartz to his TOC and gave him the word. Without thinking, Schwartz replied, "Sir, you're fucking crazy."

Perkins hesitated before answering. The other officers in the TOC were silent. "Rick we gotta do this," Perkins said, "and I am coming with you."

Unfortunately for Perkins, the upcoming thunder run was not the only mission on his plate that evening. He would also be sending Lieutenant Colonel Twitty's 3-15 IN to the Euphrates to finish off the Medina Division's 14th Brigade, and Lieutenant Colonel deCamp would attack south again the next morning to finish the job south of Objective Saints. Perkins would later describe the next day's events— all three of his battalions fighting at the same time in widely separated locations—as a starburst attack from his center. By far the biggest and most important of these fights was the one in Baghdad itself.

After his initial comment, Schwartz accepted the mission, and as far as anyone could tell he exuded confidence as he returned to his own headquarters. His biggest worry at the time was trying to figure out how he was going to break the news to his company commanders. One of his commanders, Captain Larry Burris, remembers: "I walked into the battalion TOC and the staff was chattering about a new mission. We were all so tired that it took a minute to sink in, but it suddenly dawned on all of us company commanders that we were going into Baghdad. After Schwartz briefed us, we all just stared at him as if we were looking at a crazy man." Burris's biggest fear upon leaving the TOC was exactly what Schwartz had been feeling only a short time before—how was he going to tell his men. As it turned, out he need not have worried. "My guys were excited about it." This turned out to be the most common reaction of the troops involved. When Captain Ronny Johnson had to tell the soldiers in his company that they were being held in reserve during Thunder Run II, they became visibly upset and angry about missing out.

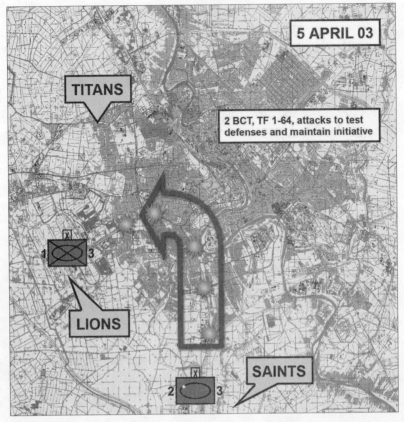

MAP 24. Thunder Run I

With only five hours' warning the company commanders went about preparing their men for the fight ahead. Told they were going to leave all wheeled vehicles behind, they had to reconfigure loads and soldiers to make sure they had enough ammo and soldiers to fight the expected battle. Short on time and with a lot to do, no one in the company chains of command was getting any rest.

For Schwartz, there was little to do after the order had been given and a short rehearsal conducted. But he found it impossible to rest: "I didn't have the luxury to get down with each company commander like I did at the NTC [National Training Center, in California]. At 0100 in the morning I saw the XO and the S3 stirring around and I thought, those guys are not getting a wink of sleep, and then I looked around the TOC and everybody else was up also. Nervous energy was

THUNDER RUN I   209

keeping everyone awake. We knew that we were starting the beginning of the end and this could be the most significant event in our lives. But it was possible that there could also be a significant loss of life. All those things kept running through my mind."

Before dawn the 1-64 Armored Battalion (The Desert Rogues) was lined up and ready to go; Wildbunch (A Company) was leading. The entire squadron heard the static on the radio as Schwartz came in: "Wildbunch this is Rogue 6. Let's move."

"This is Wildbunch 6, moving."[1]

With that simple statement the Rogues started their move into Baghdad. It was going to be what Schwartz later said was the longest day of his life.

Two minutes after the battalion started moving, the A Company commander, Captain Andrew Hilmes, was on the radio again, "This is Wildbunch 6, contact small arms. . . . Contact RPG. . . . Contact squad in trench." The fight was on. A moment later the battalion was being hit by torrents of Iraqi fire, but it was giving as good as it got. Captain David Hibner, commanding the battalion's engineers and directly behind Wildbunch, remembers:[2]

> The enemy was everywhere. They fired from trenches and bunkers on the sides of the road, from windows inside buildings, and from rooftops. Bullets cracked and zipped, and the sounds of battle increased as the task force moved into the enemy's kill zones.
>
> Our tanks were shooting targets inside buildings and laying down an incredible suppressive fire with their .50-calibers, coax, and main gun. The Bradleys fired their 25mm guns with a fearsome effect as the enemy presented themselves. Dawg [the engineers] fired .50-caliber machine guns and M-16s with a sustained precision that suppressed and killed the enemy in large numbers. I had never before seen so many enemy dismounted infantry in one place. They ran and moved from hole to hole with the tops of their heads protruding from the tops of bunkers and trenches. Soldiers like Sergeant Mulcahy and Private Northcutt fired their weapons with such lethal accuracy that I could see the plastic helmets shred.
>
> As we moved we continued to receive heavy small arms and RPG fire, while all along the sides of the road twisted and mangled

---

1. The "6" is the normal radio designation for the commander of any particular unit.

2. David Hibner is the twin brother of Captain Dan Hibner, who led the boat assault at Objective Peach.

bodies of the enemy were piling up, some barely recognizable and some just looking as if they were sleeping. The ones that fought from the trenches and bunkers were all in uniform. They wore olive green shirts and pants, black leather boots, and sand-colored plastic helmets. Mortar tubes and anti-aircraft guns lined the sides of the road [many already destroyed by Wildbunch or Rock] with their operators lying dead beside them.

I was scanning on the right side of my track, engaging dismounts in their holes and trenches and a few that actually ran right at the column. Suddenly, I saw a white technical truck speeding right towards our flank. I keyed my CVC and shouted, "Technical, technical, technical!" while firing my M16. By the time I said technical the third time, the truck had been consumed in a hail of bullets that stopped it in its tracks.

More technicals were appearing all the time and would speed out of alleys on our flanks or come up from behind or in front of us right on Highway 8. As each one appeared it was smothered in a hail of fire. One technical stopped on a side ramp and managed to fire a few shots from its mounted machine gun before a 120mm heat round turned it into a ball of flame and smoke. Once again I was amazed at the pure tenacity with which these soldiers fought. They didn't fight smart or with any obvious tactics. They just threw themselves at us and most died in the process. It was as if they had accepted that they were going to die that day and were determined to take as many of us with them as they could.

Under such a blizzard of Iraqi fire, it was only a matter of time until a round found its mark. When Staff Sergeant Jason Diaz felt a thud on the side of his tank he thought nothing of it. His tank had already been hit by close to a dozen RPGs since entering Iraq and he knew it was impervious to them. But when the fire alerts lit up and smoke started to fill the interior of the tank he knew he had a major problem. An RPG round had struck the auxiliary power unit on the back of his tank, and leaking fuel had ignited when it came in contact with the tank engine.

Schwartz had a decision to make: halt the column under heavy fire and try to save the tank or keep moving and abandon it. No one wanted to leave an M-1 behind in Iraqi hands, so Schwartz ordered a halt.

Sergeant Diaz and his crew exited the tank and began fighting the fire, while a platoon of M-1s surrounded the stricken tank in order to shield the firefighters from direct fire. Diaz and his crew used up their

Engaging targets with .50-caliber machine gun on Thunder Run I.

fire extinguishers and those of the surrounding tanks in putting out the fire, but as they attached a tow bar to another tank, their tank reignited. The battalion XO, Major Rick Nussio, left his tank and started bringing over five-gallon cans of water to drop on the flames. For more than ten minutes Nussio, Diaz, and others fought to save the tank.

In the meantime, the Iraqis were taking full advantage of the opportunity the stalled tank presented them. Captain Conroy remembered the moment: "The enemy kept sending a lot of suicide trucks our way, and we received a lot more fire after we stopped. I increased my suppression fires, trying to give the guys fighting the fire some protection. We expected to receive RPG and AK-47 fire like at Najaf, but this was seriously ridiculous." And from the Battalion operations officer, Major Donovan: "The psychology of losing an armored vehicle is large. The guys on my tank were monitoring the radio and everyone was getting hammered just like we had in Najaf. They were just

hurtling buses, technical trucks, you name it, at us. Vehicles came flying up and dropping guys off one hundred meters from our vehicles.
It was insane to watch these guys jump out and just get mowed down."
As Captain Hilmes relates though, the pause was not without some
benefits:

> It was not all bad. By that time we had expended an enormous amount
> of ammunition, and the stop was a wonderful opportunity for gun-
> ners and loaders to re-link a lot of coax and get ready for the real
> push through the heart of Baghdad on Highway 8. People were emp-
> tying spent brass boxes and I even had several tank commanders who
> traded out .50-caliber for 5.56. It was a great chance to cross level class
> five [ammo]. If we had not done that I don't know if all of our tanks
> and Bradleys would have had anything to fire when we really needed
> them as we pushed into BIAP.

All during the fight around Diaz's crippled tank, the 1-64 soldiers
were astounded to see civilian traffic on the other side of the highway divider continue down the road as if nothing was going on. Captain Hilmes had this to relate: "Civilian cars continued to attempt to
take the ramp onto Highway 8, causing White Platoon to fire warning
shots to turn them around. Eventually, one car didn't take the hints
and I moved a Bradley up to block the ramp. Almost immediately two
cars came up and crashed into the stationary Bradley. The second car
had an Iraqi Republican Guard colonel in it. Two infantryman rushed
out of the Bradley, snatched him out of his car and stuffed him in
the back of a Bradley with several other unhappy prisoners they had
collected."

The colonel later told interrogators that he was on his way to work
and had no idea that there were American tanks anywhere near Baghdad. He was convinced by the official government reports he had been
hearing on the radio that the Americans had been stopped two hundred miles away and were suffering tens of thousands of casualties.

When after a while it became apparent that the tank could not
be saved, Perkins was anxious to get moving. The enemy was massing fire at the damaged tank and it was only a matter of time until
they took out another one or shot one of the soldiers fighting the fire.
He began pressing Schwartz to get the column moving. Schwartz later
said, "There was tremendous reluctance to leave a tank behind. Andy
[Hilmes] was holding his own, Rock was holding his own, Dog was

doing well, and Cobra was fighting the fire. There was no reason to charge out of there in haste and risk adding chaos to the mix. We tried for as long as possible to save the tank and I purposely tuned out the brigade commander's calls to move out immediately; however, a point came where we had to go."

The 1-64 AR was moving again, down one tank and with two-thirds of the trip still to go. Captain Hilmes, whose Wildbunch was still leading, picks up the story:

> The Cobra tank couldn't be recovered, we didn't know why, but we knew we were moving again and we thanked God we were.
>
> As we continued the attack I saw trucks and even buses spilling Iraqi soldiers onto the highway. Most of them immediately started ripping off their uniforms and took off at a full sprint, hoping to avoid the steady stream of coax, main gun, and 25 "mike-mike." But a lot stayed and fought. They died.

As Wildbunch approached the "spaghetti junction" it became impossible to find the highway signs pointing to the airport. The smoke became too thick, and the Iraqi soldiers were too numerous to ignore even for a moment. Red Platoon missed the turn for the airport, but realized it quickly and turned around without costing the column any time.

The volume of Iraqi fire increased with every yard the column advanced. RPGs were flying thick through the air and skidding off the pavement. Dozens of them were also hitting the column's vehicles, mostly without major effect. One RPG round, however, did penetrate a Bradley and broke the leg of Private Sean Sunday. Thinking that the Bradley was on fire, he opened the ramp and fell out onto the tarmac and into the middle of a firefight. As the Bradley commander tried to figure out what had happened, an M-1 and another Bradley pulled up to shield the lame Private Sunday. Staff Sergeant Jeffrey Empson, who commanded the assisting Bradley, was reluctant to expose the infantry in the back of his vehicle to the deadly fire swirling around outside, so he jumped down and went to Sunday's rescue himself. Under fire, Empson ran to Sunday and assisted him back to his own vehicle. Then, still under fire, he hooked a tow bar to the crippled Bradley and towed it to the airport.

The battalion had now taken other casualties in addition to Private Sunday. On one Bradley in Captain Conroy's company two soldiers were seriously wounded as they tried to engage nearby enemy soldiers

Thunder Run I starts under Iraqi artillery fire.

from an open fighting hatch. Conroy's executive officer, First Lieutenant Jeremy England, added to his commander's concerns when he announced he had been shot in the head. Conroy, thinking that if he was able to talk it could not be that bad, told him they would examine it at the airport. England, who later dug the bullet out of his Kevlar helmet, was enraged and possibly personally offended at the insult of being shot. He shouted into the platoon radio, "Those motherfuckers tried to kill me. Shoot them all. Kill them all." His platoon redoubled their fire.

Adding to Conroy's troubles, one of his tanks, with a damaged gun tube, had made a wrong turn in the smoke and dust and was now heading into the center of Baghdad. Putting aside his executive officer's troubles, Conroy was shooting with one hand and trying to talk the lost tank back to where it belonged.

Eventually the lost tank came to a traffic circle, which was filled with Iraqi soldiers and vehicles getting ready to move up to engage the column. With its main gun out of commission and finding it too late to turn around, that tank commander, Staff Sergeant Roger Gruneisen, ordered full speed and charged into the intersection with machine guns blazing. Surprised but reacting quickly, two Iraqi cars raced to the entrance of the intersection and tried to block the tank's escape, a useless effort. The tank rolled over them, killing at least one driver. Another brave Iraqi stepped out to the middle of the road and shouldered an RPG to take a shot into the rear of the rapidly retreating M-1. Sergeant Gruneisen killed him before he could pull the trigger.

While Conroy sorted out his multiple problems, Colonel Perkins was doing his best to coordinate supporting artillery fire and close air support. He was getting constant JSTARS and UAV updates from his executive officer, Lieutenant Colonel Eric Wesley, so he had a good idea of what the Iraqis were doing around him. It was no easy job to coordinate supporting fires while also in a firefight with nearby Iraqi fighters. Wesley later said, "I would tell Perkins several times a day that he needed to stay clear of the fight, as he was too important to lose. He would tell me that he was staying safe and not to worry so much. . But, as he was saying it I could hear his .50-caliber shooting."

At one point, a truck filled with Iraqi soldiers charged the column and was engaged by the battalion executive officer, Major Nussio. The hail of bullets caused it to crash, but a lone fighter brandishing an AK-47 charged Perkins's vehicle. His gunner was in the process of changing out an empty box of ammo and had nothing to shoot at the charging Iraqi. When he was close enough, he did throw the empty ammo box at him. Perkins was dumbfounded, "An entire armored battalion around me and this guy literally waltzed up to my vehicle unscathed." Perkins drew his pistol and killed him.

Perkins was trying to manage the far fight, but the close fight was taking a turn for the worse. Reports came over the radio that Staff Sergeant Stevon Booker had been killed. The news stunned the battalion. Sergeant Booker was one of those bigger-than-life characters, known and loved by everyone in the battalion. If anyone was supposed to be indestructible, it was Booker. Early in the movement his .50-caliber had jammed. The halt to rescue Diaz's tank had afforded him an opportunity to exchange his .50-caliber ammo for more ammo for his personal weapon, an M-4 carbine. After the war Captain Hilmes wrote about the event:

> Approximately 8 kilometers into the move, Booker's tank had already had several near miss RPGs fly by, as well as a few that didn't miss. Sergeant Stevon Booker had been engaging the Iraqi soldiers with his

M-4 carbine, exposing himself to heavy fire in order to engage anyone who threatened his tank, his crew, and his platoon. Everyone in
Team Wildbunch had been doing the same up to this point in the
run, but SSG Booker had been doing it with a lot more intensity than
the rest of us. Of course, Booker was not leaving us very many to shoot
at either.

With Booker hit I had a hard decision to make, it was a tough
spot to try to evacuate a casualty, but if he was still alive it had to
be done. Fortunately (or unfortunately, depends on how you see it),
Blue 4's Bradley took a direct hit from a rocket-propelled grenade
disabling the vehicle and ejecting the driver onto the road. Now we
had to stop, and tanks and Bradleys surrounded Booker's tank so that
the medic vehicle could move up and extract him in relative safely.

Once Booker was in the medics' vehicle they found there was little they could do for him. From the looks of his wound the medics
assumed that an RPG round had glanced off the vehicle and hit him
in the face. The medics covered his gruesome wound with bandages
so as not to shock the rest of the company when they saw Booker at
the airport.

General Blount, who was at BIAP watching the entire fight on a
UAV feed, called Perkins to give him the option of turning around.
Blount could see thousands more Iraqis moving towards the column's
route. On live TV he saw Iraqis putting barriers both in front of and
behind the column. It was clear that they were trying to trap the battalion and cut it into easily destroyed pieces. Not even considering the
option, Perkins informed Blount that he was "coming on the airport."
Blount, still worried, ordered Colonel Grimsley to get one of his battalions ready to move to rescue Perkins and Schwartz if necessary.

With Booker and the other wounded loaded onto vehicles, the column started moving again. The pause had given the Iraqis time to concentrate more men on the road, and their volume of fire was reaching
a crescendo. In a hurry to end this fight now, the 1-64 soldiers raced
down the highway lashing out with every weapon they possessed. If
the Iraqi fire was heavy, the 1-64 AR fires were simply overwhelming.
Every soldier realized that their survival depended upon keeping the
Iraqis buried under a blizzard of fire. Each Iraqi target that presented
itself was immediately smothered in shell and flame. What few targets
were not annihilated were passed off to following vehicles and continuously engaged until destroyed. Schwartz kept up a constant calm
refrain on the radio, "Pass them off and keep moving."

Alerted by Perkins that a concrete barrier was being placed in front of him, Schwartz had just begun considering his options when the lead platoon leader, First Lieutenant Robert Ball, solved the problem for him.

Spotting the concrete barrier, Lieutenant Ball reported it to his company commander. Hilmes was about to order one of his other platoons forward to provide covering fire for breeching operations, when Ball, not hearing any instructions, lowered the plow bolted to the front of his tank and increased speed. His tank smashed into the barrier at full speed and leapt several feet into the air. The barrier did not budge, but it was crushed to half its size when the seventy-ton monster fell on it. Right behind him, the tank that had been Sergeant Booker's also plowed into the barrier at full speed. By the time the fourth tank had barreled through, the barrier had been ground into dust.

The battalion was in the final stretch now, but there was one last moment of panic to endure. Lieutenant Ball radioed Hilmes one final time, as Hilmes relates.

"I have tanks."

You could hear the hearts hit the floor with Ball's words. I was looking at Blufor Tracker screen and I can see friendly units to our front. I asked Ball, "Can you identify?" A moment went by and he said, " Roger, I have an M1A1 to my front."

I exhaled deeply and then said to the company, "Ok, we're done."

The Desert Rogues of the 1-64 AR rolled onto the airport with every vehicle scarred by RPG impacts. Many of them were on fire and more than a few were virtually crippled. All of them were covered in empty brass from the hundreds of thousands of rounds the battalion had fired in the last four hours. Grimsley had everything waiting for them: medics and medevac helicopters were waiting to whisk the wounded away, and an area had been set aside for the battalion to assemble under the protection of the 1st Brigade's guns.

The first priority for everyone was getting the wounded taken care of. Then a crew from another vehicle came over to clean up the blood in Sergeant Booker's tank, saying, "It was not right that the guys who were with him might have to do that." Once the wounded were away, it was time to take stock and reflect. Soldiers milled around their vehicles and just stared at the damage. Often they would just shake each other or hug in confirmation they were all alive. There was some congratulations going on, but not of the high-five variety. They were congratulating each other on making it through.

Schwartz went from vehicle to vehicle, mixing with his men, checking on them, talking to them as a father. His battalion had just pulled off the most spectacular mission of the war, but as he made his way around the battalion he was quiet and subdued. His battalion had done what had been asked of it and come through, but one of his soldiers was dead and several more were seriously wounded. Schwartz, one of the toughest warriors in the 3rd ID, was not in a celebratory mood. He found Captain Hilmes standing over Sergeant Booker's bagged body, crying. Schwartz led Hilmes away and then he himself walked off alone. For the next twenty minutes, Schwartz sat beside his tank, alone and quiet.

Then he went back to work.

At the airfield, Blount had come over to speak with Perkins and ask about options for the next day. Perkins told him the key to ending this war was to place tanks on the grounds of the government's palaces. Blount told him he would look at options and discuss them with his staff; then he went over to talk with and take the measure of his soldiers.

By the time Perkins got back to his TOC, Blount was on the radio telling him he wanted to conduct a similar raid the next day. This time Blount wanted him to head towards the central government buildings, but then turn around and return. After judging the Iraqi reaction Blount would discuss going for the main prize. Blount also told him that for this second thunder run, Perkins was to take all three of his battalions.

While he was at his TOC, Perkins learned that Baghdad Bob was denying reports that any American units had been in Baghdad. Worse, BBC reporters in Baghdad were confirming the Iraqi reports. Perkins wanted the U.S. journalists embedded with his brigade to go on the air and announce that they were in Baghdad, but was astounded when most of them refused, claiming that they did not want to take sides in the dispute. Perkins went on Fox News live and was told that the BBC had not seen him in the city. Perkins only reply was, "I had not seen the BBC in Baghdad either."

Perkins now knew he was in an information war as much as a shooting war. He figured that a lot of the fanatical resistance he was still facing was rooted in the fact that no one had told the Iraqis they were defeated. As far as most of them knew, the Americans were getting their ass kicked by brave Iraqi soldiers hundreds of miles from the city. As Perkins and his staff began putting together their plan for the next day's thunder run, he knew he wanted two things: an option to stay and a Fox News camera team so he could go live from inside Baghdad. The next time his soldiers went into the city, he did not want to leave any room for doubt that they were there.

Afraid that Blount would say no, Perkins did not ask him for permission to stay in the city. He held it as his own private option if conditions were right, once he arrived at Saddam's palaces. His XO, Eric Wesley, considering the option, remembered what Perkins had said many weeks ago back in Kuwait: "One way to bring this war to a rapid end would be to place tanks right on Saddam's palace grounds."

23

Titans

(4–8 APRIL)

WHILE PERKINS WAS BEGINNING preparations for his first thunder run on 4 April, Allyn's 3rd Brigade was relieved of its duties around Karbala by the 2nd Brigade of the 101st Airborne. The 3rd brigade immediately moved up to Objective Peach and went into a desert lager to prepare and plan for its next move. The plan called for Ferrell's and Grimsley's troops to isolate Bagdad from the west and Perkins's brigade to do the same in the south; Allyn would swing west of Bagdad and seal it off from the north. With the Marines moving up on the east, U.S. forces would soon effectively surround the city.

By 0300 the morning of 5 April, Allyn and his staff had completed their plan. The brigade would drive north from Peach approximately forty miles to link up with Ferrell's 3-7 CAV, already holding Objective Montgomery. It would then conduct a passage of lines through 3-7 CAV and travel another forty-five miles to sweep down on Baghdad from the north. In keeping with the football theme for naming objectives near Baghdad, the 3rd Brigade was going to seize Objective Titans. More specifically, it was to seize three critical bridges over the Tigris, which were both the only way Baghdad could receive reinforcement from northern Iraq and also the Republican Guard's only escape route from Grimsley's and Perkins's armor, which was chewing them up in the south. The three bridges were named Objective Monty, Objective Rommel, and Objective Patton. Patton was much farther to the north than the other two, which bordered on the city's edge.

After sending an e-mail with the attack order to each of his battalion commanders, Allyn was on the move by 0400 with Sanderson's 2-69 AR Battalion leading. He met up with Charlton's 1-15 IN and Harding's 1-10 Artillery along the way (both units had been attached to Perkins's 2nd Brigade to help clear Objective Spartans). For the first time since Tallil, the 3rd Brigade was back together again. Allyn later claimed one could feel the energy from the commanders all being together again.

Lieutenant Colonel Sanderson outlines the start of the attack: "The attack started at 4 o'clock in the morning, but it was not until 0530 that the battalion was fully across the line of departure, which was the Euphrates River. We followed that up with a one hundred km uneventful road march to the objective. For the first sixty km we went through a lot of friendly forces and eventually conducted a forward passage of lines with 3rd Squadron, 7th U.S. Cavalry. The minute we conducted that forward passage of lines, the task force came into contact."

Allyn later stated that Captain Lyle of the 3-7 CAV told him that he had had contact to his front all night and once my Brigade was three hundred yards in front of where he was standing it would be engaged hard. "Truer words were never spoken." Almost exactly three hundred yards past the CAV's positions, Allyn's leading elements started taking RPG and small arms fire.

Sanderson continues his recounting of events: "For the next 60 hours my battalion and the Brigade were in constant combat. Almost immediately after completing the forward passage of lines, we began taking RPG fire down the entire column. However, speed was of the essence, and we could not stop to clear out pockets of resistance. We continued to attack towards Titans, engaging Iraqi resistance as we moved."

Following close behind Sanderson's battalion was Doug Harding's artillery. Armor plating adequately protected his Paladin guns against most threats, but many of his thin-skinned support and command vehicles found the experience harrowing. One junior officer describes part of the trip:

When we came off the main road and made a U-turn over the canal, I'll remember that the rest of my life. There were a bunch of vehicles off to the right side of the road, mostly shot up. There were dead people everywhere. We were passing dead people all along the road. We had to turn to the right, and small arms come out of the woods. So here we are, artillery guys, riding in plastic-doored Humvees. It kind of got a little nerve-wracking. You could hear C Battery in the front saying they were taking small arms fire, and we're right behind them. So you know when they're going through a spot, we're going to be going through it right after them. I think everybody was feeling it. Everybody heard the chain of command trying to keep them calm, letting the soldier know that "Hey, these guys are alright, so we're going to be alright too." It was wild.

The dead Iraqis the artillery was passing all along the road were what Sanderson's soldiers were leaving in their wake—the result of dozens of failed ambushes. According to Lieutenant Wood, who was leading the point platoon, "I had to pull my wing tank back because he was destroying so many Republican Guard troops and vehicles that he was running low on ammunition." Eventually Sanderson's column was on the edge of its objective area. Amazingly, though, despite the continuous running gun battle the Americans had fought the entire way, the Iraqis in and around Titans appeared surprised by their arrival. Captain Stu James, commanding Sanderson's lead company, relates:

> We encountered a mechanized infantry platoon reinforced. However, our speed and the fact we were coming from the north so surprised them that they did not have a chance to man their equipment. We literally found them still brewing tea as we came on to the objective. They got to their bunkers and started to fight from there, but the shock effect of the armor column coming on them so quickly caught them off guard.
>
> There were two T-72s on the objective, but they were unmanned as we came up. I believe the crews were hiding in the wood line. The shock effect of seeing an armored column just roll up out of nowhere made running away their preferred option. We did receive some RPG fire, but we saw large numbers of RPGs left on their stands, ready to shoot at us as we came on. The only real resistance came from a bunker complex on the south side, which my infantry had to dismount and clear bunker by bunker. We took several friendly wounded, as they cleared the complex, killing four determined Iraqis and taking two prisoners.

As each of Sanderson's companies roared into Objective Titans, he sent them in differing directions to seize and occupy the three key bridges (Objectives Rommel, Monty, and Patton). Sanderson was now responsible for a vast battle space, but he had very few troops with which to cover it, even after asking for and receiving another infantry company from Allyn. Sanderson was on Objective Titans, but he had only four combat companies to hold more than sixty square miles of territory that the Iraqis desperately wanted back. According to Sanderson, "I recommended straight up to the brigade commander, 'let's drop this bridge' [Objective Rommel]. I said, 'We need to drop [destroy] this bridge immediately.' I was out of combat power, I had over 60 km of battle space and it didn't seem like any friendly forces were closing on me fast enough to be of any help. Of course when you drop a bridge, that's a big deal, so it went all the way up the chain of command. When it came back down, I was told, 'don't drop this bridge, drop the bridge at Monty;' which, in hindsight, turned out to be a better decision."

Fifteen minutes after the decision was made to drop the bridge at Objective Rommel, F-16s dropped their first bomb but missed. The second, only a moment behind the first, collapsed the bridge. Sanderson now stripped combat power away from Objective Montgomery and spread it over the rest of his battlespace. As the Iraqi counterattacks gained momentum, this extra firepower would be sorely needed throughout Sanderson's sector.

Captain Stu James had just settled his ten tanks and fourteen Bradleys into positions around the bridge at Objective Rommel when the Iraqis counterattacked. He picks up the story for us:

> They began their counterattack with one T-72 trying to cross the bridge while six more T-72s lined up behind him. It looked like about a tank company minus was moving to retake our objective. They definitely did not want us on the bridge. Once that lead tank was destroyed by my White 2 tank, the rest stayed in a circle on the far side, just milling around. By now we had a lot of CAS [close air support] racked and stacked over our heads, which came in and took the circling T-72s.
>
> Even as we were engaging the tanks there were a lot of dismounted attacks coming from all sides. In fact, we were on the receiving end of RPG fire for about sixty hours. Initially, we were also receiving a high volume of mortar fire, however, counterbattery from 1-10 Artillery quickly took care of that.

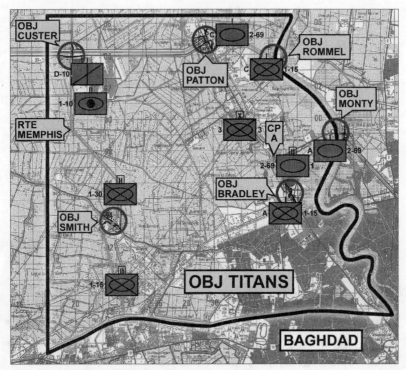

MAP 25. 3rd Brigade's Objective Titans

Destroying the tank on the bridge effectively cut that route off for any further Iraqi mechanized counterattacks, though later in the evening they came up with a crane and tried to remove the debris from the bridge in order to reinitiate a counterattack. My Red 2 tank destroyed the crane, which put an end to Iraqi efforts to breech the bridge obstacles.

Since it was impossible to bring tanks across, they started firing volleys of RPGs from the other side of the bridge high into the air to create airbursts, which were loud but ineffective. They kept trying to reinforce the bridge by going up a staircase on their side and getting on top of it. Effective .50-caliber and .762 fire put a stop to that. But, it was remarkable how long they persisted in trying to get on top of and over the bridge under murderous fire.

I kept at least four tanks on the bridge all night with my B-FST [artillery coordinator]. So between the 120mm guns on the tanks

and the 25 mike mike on the Bradleys, we were able to destroy anything that came on the bridge. We dominated them through overwhelming firepower. We did not allow the enemy to breathe. Every
time they tried to counterattack they were met swiftly, both with overwhelming platform-mounted firepower and dismounted infantry,
which destroyed dismounts in the wood line to the south.

Still, the Iraqis continued to counterattack, mostly from the
south. They definitely wanted that terrain back. They had some
FRG-7s back there, along with at least forty trucks with air defense
systems mounted on them, which were causing the A-10s some problems there. Eventually, I ordered an attack to the south for about five
kilometers, which destroyed the truck-mounted air defense guns and
cleared the area for the CAS guys.

Because of the destroyed Iraqi tank on the bridge we couldn't get
across the river either, so we kept hitting the far side with CAS and
artillery. They kept stacking up a lot of men and equipment to face
us, which was providing the CAS and artillery with lucrative targets.

At one point though there was so much RPG fire coming at us
that I had to call on 1-10 FA to shoot final protective fires. That effectively destroyed them and we did not receive and RPG fire for about
three to four hours.

In this commentary Captain James's mention of having the artillery fire its final protective fires (FPF) is almost off-hand. To combat
arms soldiers, though, calling for the FPF is very serious business. It
usually means an American unit is close to being overrun or at the
very least is facing a lot more than it can handle. Normally, every artillery unit in range stops whatever it was doing and begins firing at the
coordinates of the FPF. Since calling for the FPF strips artillery away
from every other unit needing fire support on the battlefield, no commander would make the call except in dire emergency. Once the FPF
is called, every gun in range starts firing as fast as the gunners can load,
and they keep firing until their ammo is exhausted, the gun tubes
melt, or the commander calling for the FPF reports the enemy attack
is broken. During the first 12 hours that 1-10 FA was firing on Titans,
it shot about 2,300 rounds of all types. Lieutenant Colonel Harding
believes that close to half of them were fired during the thirty-minute
FPF alone. Colonel Allyn later said that "if the 1-10 had not been firing in support at Rommel I am not sure we could have held it."

If anyone up the chain of command had any doubt that the fight
at Titans was serious business, James's call for the FPF erased it.

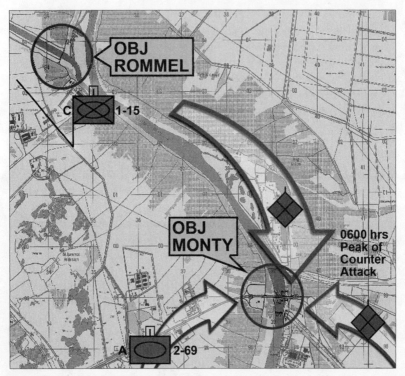

MAP 26. Iraqi counterattack at Titans

After James called off the FPF, a lull in the fighting allowed him to bring up bulldozers and put some berms in front of his armored vehicles to give them better protection against a future mass RPG assault. The lull continued, so James decided to have one of his tank platoons nudge aside the destroyed T-72 on the bridge and cross to see what the enemy was up to. The indefatigable Lieutenant Wood was given the task.

> Captain James ordered us to cross the bridge to see what the Iraqis were doing. He mostly wanted to know if he could expect another counterattack. Myself, my wing tank and my platoon sergeant started moving across the bridge. While we sat in place on the bridge, we observed several uniformed Iraqi soldiers on the far side of the bridge taking off their uniforms. We began engaging an Iraqi military compound and several bunkers on their side of the bridge, destroying all of their positions.

We were on the bridge about five minutes when they detonated their first charge. They must have thought we were beginning our attack across the Tigris River. After they detonated that first charge we began to back off. As we were moving off the bridge I saw several un-uniformed Iraqi soldiers running with RPGs away from the bridge. As soon as they were out of sight a second, even larger, charge exploded on the far side of the bridge.

Not sure how badly the bridge was damaged, Captain James settled in for a long two days of fighting off incessant dismounted attacks. However, elsewhere in Objective Titans another fight was brewing. Colonel Allyn, along with the brigade's trains, was moving to establish brigade headquarters inside what appeared to be a deserted school but what was in fact the Arab Petroleum Institute.

They discovered it was not deserted soon after pulling into the school's courtyard. According to Lieutenant Colonel Sanderson:

I brought my logistics team and my headquarters to collocate with the brigade headquarters at the Institute. I put my headquarters inside the buildings and put my trains in the main compound. However, I left an ammo truck and two fuel trucks sitting outside the compound to rearm and refuel units as they pulled back from the perimeter. I also kept two scout Humvees outside the compound to provide security for the ammo truck and tanker.

As we moved into the building, no one fired on us, so it looked like it would be a good headquarters location. But, at about 1700 that night, I was talking to the brigade commander and he had just finished the division update. We walked around behind the building, and we began receiving massive amounts of enemy fire. The lead Hemmet, which was an ammunition Hemmet and full of 120mm ammunition and 25mm ammunition, was hit almost immediately. A lot of things were now happening simultaneously. I had a truck filled with explosives on fire, there was an Iraqi walking and the enemy was shooting at us from three directions.

The Brigade Assault CP was back in a corner of the compound. Allyn immediately headed there, jumped in his Bradley and headed out the gate to the attack. I jumped on my tank and followed right behind him. Initial reports indicated that besides the burning Hemmet, there was also a scout Humvee hit and burning. At this point we had several injured soldiers outside the compound. Staff Sergeant Jimmy Harrison, my medical platoon sergeant, scaled the fence and leaped down to help the wounded. He was the first man on the scene to help. He found Private Pruett with most of his leg blown off, but he was still laying down suppressive fire on the enemy. Harrison literally covered Pruett with his body, to protect him from being wounded again, as he worked on him.[1]

Harrison was only out there alone for a brief moment before a whole bunch of other great soldiers from both the Brigade Assault CP and my trains leapt the fence and got into the fight. As they were climbing the gate my tank and Allyn's Bradley burst out of the compound. We got on both sides of a road that led to where most of the enemy fire was coming from and advanced.

At that point, one of the fuel trucks caught on fire, and the ammo truck started suffering secondary explosions. The secondary explosions were so dangerous that no one could approach to move the second fueler for a while. Eventually, we did manage to save one fueler as fire engulfed this second one. By now I've lost an ammo truck and a fueler and I have at least one great soldier critically wounded.

I kept moving down the road killing everything that was left down there shooting at my men.

Long after returning to the United States, Allyn reflected on that night. "My battle captain and my radio telephone operator, Private First Class Aiken, joined by cooks, radar operators, and Air Force personnel all jumped that wall to go help the guys stuck outside with the burning vehicles. Nobody ordered them out there and they were not trained combat infantrymen. But, without considering their personal safety they rushed towards the shooting to keep a bad situation from getting worse. They literally dashed away from positions of safety and ran to the point of most danger to rout the enemy. That night I saw what I believe is the epitome of what it means to be an American soldier."

Though two more days of incessant fighting would follow at Objective Titans, the Iraqi backbone was broken. The next day Colonel Perkins would lead his second thunder run into the heart of Baghdad and the day after that Colonel Allyn would lead his brigade into Baghdad from the north and link up with Perkins in the center of the city.

---

1. Private Pruett was evacuated to the aid station, but he later died from his wounds.

24

Thunder Run II: Collapse of the Regime

A FTER THE FIRST THUNDER RUN into Baghdad, one soldier is reported to have said, "There is a terrible rumor going around that the colonel is going to order us back into that hell again. I pray to god it's not true." As he and the other soldiers in the 2nd Brigade soon learned, however, it was true. Fortunately, our reluctant hero's thoughts on the advisability of going back into Baghdad were not widespread. Postwar interviews indicate that reactions ranged widely: enthusiasm dominated in the two battalions that had missed out on the first thunder run, while in Schwartz's 1-64 AR the ruling emotion was "if it has to be done let's do it." As one commander said, "Everyone knew the shortest route back to the USA was through Baghdad." After taking a bit of time to settle their emotions, Schwartz's men found themselves emboldened by the success of the first thunder run. They had absorbed the hardest punches the Iraqis could throw and, though they had not gone unscathed, they knew that Baghdad was theirs for the taking.

Perkins felt the same way. He was never a big fan of the idea of hit-and-run raids into Baghdad meant to convey the message that the Coalition could enter the city with impunity. And besides, that was not the message being transmitted. Instead, Baghdad Bob was broadcasting tales of American defeat and the bloody repulse of the 3rd ID. Worse, most of the international media were picking up the same line. The first thunder run was rapidly being transformed into a major American defeat, and Perkins was wary about feeding this media impression with another raid.

Still, the thunder run concept fit very nicely with the Corps plan to isolate the city and eventually bring down the regime through a series of raids aimed at critical points. As far as General Wallace was concerned, the thunder runs were "proof of concept." General Blount was less certain of the overall impact of the in-and-out missions, but having played a bit loosely with the corps staff to pull off the first one, he was not ready to upset their applecart by asking them to throw out their entire isolation plan.

Perkins, on the other hand, had no such qualms. He also had never much liked the Corps plan, and from the very beginning of mission planning he told his staff to put in an option to stay the night in Baghdad. Afraid that if he told the 3rd ID staff what he was planning someone would tell him no, he saw no reason to trouble them with the details. At one point during the planning process, Generals Blount and Wallace did discuss the possibility of Perkins staying, but Wallace had stated that the corps was not ready yet. Still fearing another Somalia, Wallace was not sure that he could get help to Perkins if he went too far into the city and got trapped. After some thought, Wallace told Blount that the 2nd Brigade was not to go downtown. Blount had his staff pass the word to Perkins, but Perkins never received the instruction. When the second thunder run began on April 7, Perkins knew he had not told anyone he planned to go downtown, but as far as he knew nobody had forbidden him to do so.

In the event, Generals Wallace and Blount discovered the 2nd Brigade was heading for Saddam's palaces when they saw it on the BLUFOR Trackers. Everyone was caught by surprise. Blount had General Austin call Perkins to ask him what he was doing. Perkins replied, "I am going downtown." At Vth Corps headquarters a staff officer called a technician over to fix the screen on his BLUFOR Tracker. It was showing 3rd ID forces in the center of Baghdad and that was impossible. At CENTCOM headquarters, back in Doha, another staff officer started clicking the screen with his forefinger in a futile effort to make the blue squares, signifying the 2nd Brigade, fall back into their proper place.

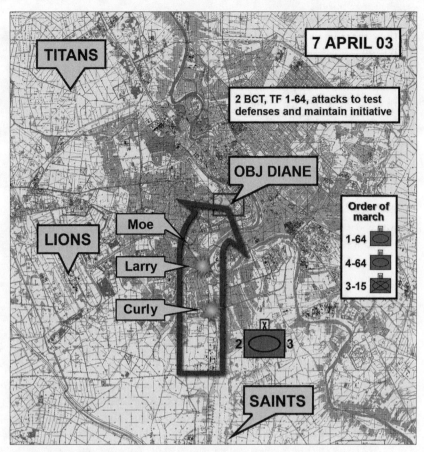

MAP 27. Thunder Run II

Once Perkins had made the final turn, he was committed; there was nothing left for Blount to do but to call Wallace and tell him there had been a change of plan. Blount, however, did not discuss the staying option since it was still not in his own plan and it was far from certain that it was even possible. Rather, Wallace and he saw this as an opportunity for an enhanced propaganda victory. Knowing Perkins had a camera crew from Fox News with him, Wallace thought it would help the overall effort immeasurably for them to get some film of tanks on Saddam's palace grounds before they departed the city again.

Once Perkins was sitting on Saddam's palaces Blount called and said, "You made your point. Now move back out." That is when Perkins first mentioned that he wanted to stay. At first Austin was against the idea, but Perkins told him, "I spoke with my battalion commanders and they think we can stay. If we stay here for the night, the war is over in the morning." The three-way discussion continued for more than half an hour, but eventually Blount and Austin were convinced that the 2nd Brigade could hold where they were without undue risk. All Blount had to do, then, was sell the idea to Wallace. General Wallace, however, had been monitoring the conversation and had heard all of the right questions being asked about fuel, ammo, and evacuating the wounded. He also knew enough to sense when one of his commanders had created a war-winning initiative, and he had enough courage to throw out a carefully crafted plan and seize an opportunity when it came his way. But we have gotten ahead of ourselves in the story; first, the 2nd Brigade has to fight its way into Baghdad.

Soon after Baghdad fell, Colonel Perkins laid out his planning thoughts.

> My mission was to conduct a raid and to be able to offer options to my higher HQs. I wanted to make sure they had more options to pick from than just finishing the raid and coming back to Objective Saints. We developed a plan that turned into a brigade deliberate attack. Rather than a one-battalion raid, like thunder run one, we planned a three-battalion deliberate attack. To go into Baghdad and stay meant that we had to go into the city and win the tactical fight. Next, we had to secure tactically defensive terrain, ground we could hold and fight from all night. Thirdly, we had to secure the lines of communication (LOC) so resupply could come forward to us. When we did that analysis it was clear we would need all three of my battalions.
>
> We had learned some lessons on the 5th on how to win the tactical fight. For instance we learned that road intersections are key terrain. If you control the intersections then you control all lateral movement on the battlefield. By extension, we also knew that on an operational level if you control all the elements of the Saddam regime's power, such as ministries and palaces, you now control the government. By holding key places in the city the regime, while it might still be alive, was made irrelevant.
>
> Even after we took critical points in the city, however, we still had to secure the LOCs. Unless we could bring in the refuel-rearm (R2) package, there was no way we could stay in the city, even if we broke the Iraqi Army's back. The first decision was how we were going to sequence ourselves for the attack. Doctrine would dictate that the

lead battalion attack up Highway 8 to secure the intersections and make sure we had an open line of communication. That accomplished, the rest of the brigade would barrel through the cleared corridor to the objective. The problem with that is the whole brigade would be sitting on its ass at Saints while one battalion slugged it out on the highway. That would both cost us momentum and alert the Iraqis that we were coming in. So, I made the decision to do just the opposite and have the trail battalion seize the intersections and overhead bridges.

That meant the lead battalions would fight their way to the palaces and the trail battalion would clean up behind them and hold the key intersections along the route. The key was to maintain momentum by passing off targets and not stopping for anything, including disabled vehicles. The other problem in making the lead unit secure the intersections was that the trail units would have to conduct a passage of lines while under fire. A passage of lines is hard enough when no one is shooting at you; it is a very dangerous endeavor when in contact.

In basic form the plan called for 1-64 AR to enter the downtown area and peel left as 4-64 AR follows them in and goes to the right. Behind them 3-15 IN would secure and hold open the line of communication back to Saints. After deciding that, we put a lot of time deciding on what the critical decision points were for staying overnight. We took a long look at the time line and saw the main problem was that an M-1 tank consumes about 56 gallons per hour whether it's moving or not. That meant each tank had enough fuel for eight to ten hours. We used eight hours to be safe and divided it in half—allowing for a return trip to Saints if necessary. That made the 4-hour mark a point of decision.

The next problem was that if we were going to stay how were we going to refuel ourselves. We decided that, despite the risk to the vulnerable logistic vehicles, we would bring our R2 package [rearm and refit] into the city. Once I was certain we had examined the problem from every angle, I told the commanders to plan on staying in the city and we will make the final call at hour four or five.

As Perkins's soldiers took the first real rest they had in the war, rumors started to leak out that the staff was planning another attack into Baghdad. After the war, Captain David Hibner, commanding the 1-64 AR's engineers, wrote down his memories of the war. His reflections on 6 April are worth quoting in detail, both because of what they say about the events of the day and for what they show us about the emotions and feelings of the soldiers and officers being asked to go on this very dangerous mission.

I got a call from the task force TOC at about 1700 telling me to come to the TOC for tomorrow's mission brief. I was wondering what tomorrow had in store for us when it came over the radio that we may be going back to Baghdad first thing in the morning and commanders needed to report for a warning order. Everyone around my track heard the message on the speaker and they just stood there quietly, trying to digest going into Baghdad again. They were remembering fighting the enemy the way we did yesterday, from which the relief they felt after making it through alive had barely soaked in. Now we were going to do it again.

I sat down and just thought about it for a few minutes and before long several of my company's senior leaders approached me and expressed concern about the mission. They said that if we didn't have an engineer mission other than to fight as infantry, then we might want to consider whether or not we should be going at all. I told them I didn't necessarily disagree with their feelings and I'd talk to the staff about it when I got to the briefing.

I walked into the TOC and found the staff busily planning the next day's mission. No one minced words this time. We were going to attack Baghdad . . . again. I talked to CPT Ferrell who told me that we were attacking the palaces this time and we might be staying overnight. I said "What do you think the threat is going to be like on this one? Worse than last time?"

"Well, we are attacking his house and his government," Ferrell said. "It's probably going to be worse." He then explained what worse meant in more detail, and I shook my head in disbelief. It was just amazing to me that we were going back into Baghdad. I talked to LT Schwimmer to see what they were thinking for the task organization for the attack. He said that they hadn't really talked about it yet.

I wanted to know if they intended to take engineers on this mission. Dawg Company [the engineer] was the only company that didn't have anyone killed or seriously injured in the last attack; it was generally accepted across the task force that it was a miracle we made it through as we did.[1] CPT Ferrell told me that they might be looking at minimizing all M113s going into this fight and then said, "Dude, I don't think you guys need to be going on this one."

---

1. The engineers traveled in M-113s, which did not have nearly the armored protection of the Bradley. These vehicles were easy penetrated by RPG rounds and even heavy machine-gun bullets.

When all of the company commanders came together at 1700 hours, the task force issued the warning order. Task Force 1-64 would attack along Highway 8 as part of 2 BCT. The order of march was Rogue, Tusker, China.[2] I looked over at Larry Burris and he said, "Someone is trying to get us killed." I agreed, still astonished that after the fight we had just finished, we were being thrown back to the lions. Being first in the order of movement meant that our battalion would take the brunt of the enemy fire. At the conclusion of the warning order MAJ Donovan stated, "What they put out was all they knew, and the details would be published at the brigade order." The meeting broke up and the field grade officers started gathering their materials to go to the brigade TOC.

I saw MAJ Nussio outside and asked him if they intended to take any M113s. He said that they were. I asked him if he thought that the engineers really needed to go. He said, "I think you should have serious reservations about it."

After some reflection I told him, "I think we shouldn't go unless the task force needs engineers for this particular fight. Otherwise, I'm not sure it's worth the high risk. This is supposed to be a harder fight and it's amazing we survived the first one." He looked at me and told me that he agreed that if we weren't needed for a specific mission then we shouldn't go, but that I needed to talk to LTC Schwartz about it. I asked if he thought LTC Schwartz would be receptive and MAJ Nussio said that he thought he would.

I knew that LTC Schwartz would listen to what I had to say. He always had; he was that kind of leader. Input from his commanders was taken under consideration and scrutinized as needed. He never returned negative criticism or questioned intentions. He just gave honest feedback and sound advice. I looked forward to talking to him.

I found him on his tank and said, "Sir, I've got some concerns about Dawg going on this mission. If we aren't needed for a specific engineer task, then I think we should consider staying back on this one. It's not that I don't want to go fight. I just feel that I owe it to my soldiers not to take them on a mission that they may not be required for. I think it was a miracle we made it through the last fight and this one is supposed to be worse. We are the most vulnerable force in these battles."

He responded without hesitation. "Dave, I think you're right. There isn't a specific mission for you guys so I think you should sit this one out."

---

2. Rogue was 1-63 AR; Tusker was 4-64 AR; China was 3-15 IN.

I didn't expect that response. "Sir, I'm not saying I don't want to go," I blurted, "If we need to go we will; that's what we want to do." He said, "No, you're right. You guys shouldn't go on this one."

I didn't know what to say. I suddenly felt terrible, like something was taken away from me. I said, "Sir, I feel like crap over this. Maybe we should go. I really wasn't trying to get out of the mission. I just felt like it was the right thing to ask, for my soldiers."

His mind was made up and he smiled and said, "You've done the right thing. Sometimes it doesn't feel right, but you've done the right thing and you're right about this."

I was about to leave but I couldn't. I felt as if I had let him down. If there was one thing in the world I didn't want to do, it was to let this man down. He was my commander, my leader, and even my mentor. I felt as if I was abandoning the task force and I wished I'd never said anything. I wished I could go back to when I was leaving the TOC and just continue out to my vehicle. I looked at the battalion commander for a few seconds, trying to find words. Finally I said, "Sir, we've been on every fight with this task force and we are a part of this team. When you guys LD tomorrow I'm going to wish I was there. I'll feel left out and empty inside."

"I know you will," was all he said.

I left to go back to my Humvee and return to the company with my stomach turning inside. On the way I walked by MAJ Donovan and felt compelled to tell him about the decision. Maybe, I thought, he'd tell me it was fine and I'd feel better. I should've known better. "What?" exclaimed MAJ Donovan, "How can you guys not go on this mission? There's no engineer specific task, but your mission is to fight like infantry."

I said, "Maybe you're right sir. Maybe we should go."

"We need you guys," he replied. "You kill a lot of shit out there for us and you shoot what the tanks and brads can't. I think you should go back and talk to your guys." With that he left. My heart agreed completely with MAJ Donovan. The thought of the task force going into Baghdad without us was almost unbearable. My mind was telling me I did the right thing for the company, but my heart wasn't. As soon as I drove up I saw LT Phillips, LT Gacheru and First Sargeant Troutman. I told them I needed to talk to them in private, and we walked into the grove under what little daylight remained. I started by saying, "I talked to the battalion commander about not going on this one if there's no engineer specific mission for us, and he agreed."

They all said something on the theme of, "Wow, that's great. Great news. That's good."

I looked at all three of them, one at a time and said, "I need some help with this then. If this is so great, then why do I feel like shit about it? Why do I feel like we're letting them down? Why do I feel empty inside?" No one responded, so I asked LT Phillips what he thought.

"Sir, I think you did the right thing," he replied. "If we're not needed then we shouldn't go."

I looked at 1SG Troutman, "First Sergeant?"

He said, "Sir, I feel the same way about this that you do, but it's the right thing. You made the right call."

"Ok, Gacheru?"

Gacheru started beating around the bush. "Well, I don't know, sir. I guess it's good. I don't know. I guess it's the right thing. I feel like you do though, I feel empty, like we're letting them down."

I closed the discussion by saying, "Ok, for right now the plan is stay here, but we are going to get ready anyway. I want both platoons to prepare like they are going."

I went over to my chair to brood over the situation.

Walid walked up and said, "I heard that you are not going to the fight in Baghdad tomorrow."

I lifted my eyebrows and shook my head a little bit. "Nope, we are sitting this one out."

He said, "That's ok. You have fought enough." Even Walid could tell that I was being eaten alive by the situation.

Then I made up my mind. I was going to walk up to the battalion commander and say, "Sir, I was not right. I was wrong. Dawg is going on this mission sir!" I was rehearsing it in my head. I was going to do it at the OPORD briefing.

Then, as if fate were stepping in, we got a call from LT Schwimmer in the TOC saying that a minefield had just been found on our route to the TOC. Suddenly, we had a mission—a specific engineer mission! He said the minefield was reported to be five hundred meters deep with no bypass and we were going to remove it.

The minefield was discovered almost accidentally, when the brigade logistical officer insisted on going outside the brigade perimeter to find a base to place the R2 package for the next day's attack. Despite being warned by Captain Burris that everything north of him was infested with enemy soldiers the officer went anyway. He soon made contact with more than a dozen vehicles and ran for his life. Burris sent one of his tank platoons north to "save his ass" and remembers being infuriated at having to put his soldiers at risk because "some staff officer had a whim to go exploring."

However, the officer did bring back news of a substantial minefield directly in the path of the 2nd Brigade's planned assault. The minefield itself was massive—five hundred meters deep—but it was all surface laid. The brigade engineers were busily reviewing options on how to handle this unexpected problem, but their favored options did not suit Captain Hibner—the man who would have to execute their decision. After discussing the matter with the engineer battalion staff, Hibner went to talk it over with the 1-64 AR leadership.

> I came out of the track. MAJ Nussio, MAJ Donovan, and LTC Schwartz were all sitting around the map.
>
> "What are they telling you, Dave?" Schwartz asked.
>
> "Nothing really, sir. It sounds like they are trying to decide how to handle this thing. I think they're filling out a decision matrix on possible courses of action." I shook my head. "It looks like they are going to tell us to use MICLICs."
>
> LTC Schwartz said, "This is a brigade issue."
>
> "I don't think it's going to be solved at brigade," MAJ Donovan said, throwing his hands into the air and leaning back in his folding chair.
>
> I said, "MICLICs are not an option. It's too dangerous to pull them under heavy fire and they don't work well on roads anyway."
>
> "Ok, what else can we do?" LTC Schwartz asked calmly.
>
> "Well," I said, "We could try scraping with ACEs [armored bulldozers] but that's also risky and it's hard to keep the blade flat enough on the ground."
>
> "What else?" MAJ Nussio asked. "What about tank plows?"
>
> "Won't work," MAJ Donovan replied.
>
> MAJ Nussio said, "You're right, won't work at all," as if he knew it was a bad idea the moment he said it.
>
> "Could we try hitting it with Air Force cluster bombs?" MAJ Donovan was thinking of anything that might work or could be tried.
>
> The minefield had added a new level of difficulty to the whole plan and everyone was struggling with how to handle it. I could almost picture the 10th Engineer Battalion commander and his staff using every decision-making tool they possessed to determine the best course of action. I knew what our best option was, but I had an incredible amount of respect for the knowledge and experience of the men sitting with me, and I wanted to hear their ideas first.
>
> Then LTC Schwartz looked at me and asked, "Dave, what do you want to do about this minefield?"
>
> I knew LTC Schwartz was ready to make a decision. It wasn't his way to analyze it until everyone was confused about the real question

at hand. He respected the input and judgment of his company commanders. And he knew that if anyone was going to have input on how
to handle this, it should be the guy who's going to execute the plan.
I said, "Sir, we need to do a covert breach. It will work. I know it will
work."

Never ceasing to amaze me, LTC Schwartz replied, "Ok. Then
we'll do a covert breach. What do you need for the mission and what
time do you want to do it?"

"Sir, 0300. Those Iraqis will probably be asleep by then. I need
an infantry platoon, a scout team with LRAS, and the mortars in support."

He looked at me and said, "You got it."

Just that easily, the debate ended and the decision was made.

With Captain Burris's tanks watching over them, Hibner moved
his sappers up to the minefield.

"Dawg 26, move your breach team forward and commit. Keep me
posted," I ordered.

"This is Dawg 26, WILCO."

I watched what was happening almost in disbelief. We were pulling it off. It looked as if it was actually going to work. The scouts
started making jokes about the Iraqis. "This is Saber 2, I bet that
they're sleeping in their holes. Sound asleep."

"This is Dawg 6," I replied, "the MLRS strike scheduled in about
an hour will probably wake them up." SGT Cassady added another
line to his letter to Saddam. "Dear Saddam, thank you for letting your
soldiers sleep so peacefully at night. It has made breaching your minefields much easier and more efficient than if you kept them awake."

Down the road, through my night vision goggles I could see the
shadows of the sappers on the ground breaching the minefield. They
were working very quickly. SSG Guzman, SSG Oliver, CPL Meyers,
and CPL Vigil were making it happen. It all came down to those few
guys—the breach team. The Iraqis had put dirt over the mines for
some reason. We never did figure out why for sure, but it was probably
to slow us down. They checked each mine for booby traps, wrapped
a loop of engineer tape around each one, and then went back about
50 feet and pulled the mine to clear it of any anti-handling devices.
Then they walked up, picked up the mines and moved them to the
shoulder of the road.

We started the breach at 0346 and every minute that went by got
us closer to mission accomplishment. Time was not on our side, but
the sappers were working like mad to get the lane in the minefield.

Little by little they were getting the job done and the lane they were putting in was much wider than required for a tank.

At 0455 hours LT Szydlik reported that the breach was complete.

One hour later the 2nd Brigade began moving through the breach on its way downtown. Just ahead of the moving column, a short but intense MLRS and artillery barrage slammed into the Iraqi positions. Before the dust had settled, Schwartz's troop rolled through it, leading the assault into Baghdad for the second time. Hibner's engineers joined the column. No one was missing this ride.

Schwartz's 1-64 AR had learned a lot of lessons from the first thunder run. Foremost among them was "when you are going through hell don't slow down." When, almost immediately after passing through the minefield breach, his lead tank was disabled by two RPG hits, there was no attempt to get it going again. Without pause the rest of the column swerved around the crippled tank and continued north. The trail battalion would recover the crew and tank.

In a repeat of the first thunder run the Iraqis engaged the column from windows, roofs, spider holes, and bunkers. Perkins had assumed that every vehicle in the column would be hit by something and most were. However, every soldier interviewed from the 1-64 AR said that the fire, while intense, was nowhere near the levels they experienced on their first run through the city. Once again training and professionalism took over, and the radio nets became another continuous stream of targets spotted, engaged, and handed off. Reflecting after the war, General Austin said, "To get a feel for the tactical fight, I would often listen in on the radio nets of units in heavy combat. I was amazed that even while under heavy fire all of the conversations were as calm as if the speakers were sitting at their dinner table at home."

Less than a half hour after they started, Schwartz's lead platoon was at the third major intersection along Highway 8, where they turned east. The seat of Saddam's government was only a couple of miles away and resistance was slackening. Both the 1-64 AR and 4-64 AR roared under the famous crossed sabers monument and onto the ground of Saddam's government palaces. There they came under some small arms fire, and a few rounds from a 90mm recoilless struck the lead tanks before the defenders were dispatched.

The two tank battalions came in and spread out over an area the size of the mall in Washington, D.C. It was not long before the Iraqi forces in the city began to react, and for the next several hours both

Just prior to the start of Thunder Run II, 3rd ID engineers, directly in front of Iraqi forward positions, cleared a tank lane through thousands of mines laid on the road surface.

battalions constantly fended off small but determined counterattacks. Even while this continuous fighting was going on, Perkins remembered he had two wars to win. One was defeating the Iraqi army on the battlefield; the other was the information war. He had to make sure everyone in Iraq and even the world knew that he was sitting in the middle of Baghdad. Someone else was also thinking about the information war, and an order soon made its way from Kuwait through Vth Corps to 3rd ID for Perkins to find a statue of Saddam and destroy it, with cameras rolling. As one officer present remembers:

> Fighting was still going on and we are having pictures taken of us in the palace. Colonel Perkins was outside being interviewed on camera and there was fighting all around him. We were trying to get his attention and finally when the interview was done we briefed him and he jumped in his track to go watch us blow down a Saddam statue on a horse with an MPAT round.

A tank round obliterates a statue of Saddam in central Baghdad.

We had sent out an RFI to find which is the best statue of Saddam Hussein and 1-64 calls up that they found one at the parade field. It was great because we could get the crossed sabers in the background and the statue at Saddam's parade field. There was some debate over how best to tear it down, but a tank commander chimed in and said, "We're an armored brigade. We should shoot it with a main gun." Perkins agreed and told him, "Don't miss."

When that was finished 4-64 said they found a group of people that wanted to tear down a poster of Saddam. They asked if we wanted to do it without the media or wait. Colonel Perkins said, "We will be right there." When we got there it was at the department of interior building and it was a huge poster of Saddam, and Iraqi civilians were looking for tools to tear it down. We wanted the people to solve it themselves without any help from us. They were in the middle of doing this when someone told them where a number of refrigerators were stored and they all ran off to steal the refrigerators.

Perkins's 2nd Brigade was downtown, but now he had to decide if he could stay. Staying was not a matter of will, however, it was a matter of getting gas and ammo down Highway 8 and into Baghdad. For that to happen Lieutenant Colonel Stephen Twitty's 3-15 IN Battalion had to hold open the road. Perkins's decision was complicated by two factors: his TOC had just been hit by a missile and at the moment Twitty and his soldiers were fighting for their lives.

The Missile Strike

By 10:30 A.M., 2nd Brigade's battle was reaching a critical point. Two battalions were sitting in the middle of Baghdad and coming under increasing pressure as they spread out through the objective area. A third battalion was spread out along the entire line of advance, as it attempted to hold open a secure line of communications. Every battalion was calling for artillery, air support and resupply at the same time, and in the case of Twitty's 3-15 IN things were becoming critical. Back in the brigade's tactical operations center Lieutenant Colonel Eric Wesley, 2nd Brigade executive officer, was coordinating the entire support effort. It was his job to prioritize artillery fires and close air support as they became available, so that they went where they were most critically needed. While Perkins was up front making the decisions that could only be made by a commander close to the scene of the fighting, Wesley was operating the nerve center of the battle, trying to track and control those activities invisible to the commander.

With Perkins downtown, Wesley thought it was time to have a one-on-one chat with him and go over his impressions and future plans based on how he was reading the situation. Unable to reach Perkins by radio, Wesley went to his vehicle and grabbed his Iridium satellite phone. As he talked to Perkins, he began to wander around the compound. He had gotten only thirty feet from his vehicle when a powerful Abril missile hit it dead center. Wesley was knocked flat, while a soldier standing only a few feet from him was torn apart by the impact. According to Wesley:

> When I picked myself up all I could see at first was a lot of fire, smoke, and dirt. I was amazed at how quickly the surrounding soldiers responded and started triaging and taking care of the wounded. Many of them were running right through the flames to pull and carry the

wounded to safety. At the end of the day we had five killed and seven-teen wounded. We also had twenty-two vehicles destroyed, but quite a few were saved by soldiers risking their lives to drive them out of the spreading flames.

The explosion had sent a fireball through the TOC, setting the tent on fire and destroying vital communications equipment. For the time being the 2nd Brigade TOC was out of the war. All Perkins knew at this time was what Wesley had told him, "Boss, we've been hit." Thinking that a few rounds of mortar or artillery fire had hit the TOC compound, Perkins and the staff officers with him assumed its coordi-nation roll, while they waited for the TOC to get back in the fight.

By using equipment stripped off of the surviving vehicles, Wes-ley was able to patch together a makeshift TOC about three hundred meters from the original location. Forty-five minutes after the missile destroyed the original TOC, 2nd Brigade had a new one up and oper-ating. When Wesley got on the radio to announce that the TOC was back and taking over the fight, the first reply came from General Aus-tin: "Glad to know you're okay and welcome back to the war."

As Wesley worked to reestablish the TOC, the Headquarters Com-pany commander, Captain William Glaser, took charge of the rest of the response to the devastating impact.

I was at the battle board in the TOC and I thought I heard a low flying jet overhead and that's when the missile exploded. When I crawled out from under the wreckage I saw MSG Switzer our BDE S2 NCOIC lying unconscious next to a bloody body I could not recognize. By the time I got into the compound some soldiers had already established a casualty collection point and were conducting first aid on their bud-dies. I saw that they needed stretchers and I also knew the casualties needed to be evacuated and started off to my headquarters to make sure that happened. On the way I saw LTC Wesley and gave him a situation report. Wesley's leadership was crucial. When I saw him I had just been blasted off my feet and busted up my ankle a little bit; the fire, the flames, the bodies had turned my world to chaos. I don't even remember what he said to me, but it doesn't matter. Just his composed demeanor as he spoke convinced me he had everything under control. I calmed down a lot after talking to him. He was the senior guy present and he was creating order from chaos. His self-control was the model for everyone else there. It was a bad day, but Wesley let us know we would all get through it.

The 2nd Brigade tactical operations center immediately after it was hit by an Iraqi missile. The TOC was back controlling the fight only 45 minutes after this devastation.

As I continued to the front of the compound I saw PFC Camp walking towards the perimeter wearing his pants and one boot. He had shrapnel in his back and he was bleeding badly and was very confused. A female soldier was trying to convince him to go back to the aid stations with her. I asked Private Camp, "Where the hell are you going?" He said, "I have to pull security sir." The female soldier said, "I am trying to get him back with me but he won't listen." I said, "Camp, do you know who I am?" He replied, "Sir, you're the CO." I said, "Good, your CO is ordering you to go with this lady and do exactly as she says." He said, "Ok." She escorted him back to the aid station, from where he was evacuated, but returned to duty three days later.

This is the kind of thing that struck me most about that day. The motivation of the soldiers was awesome. Camp had just been blasted off his feet and wounded and his first thoughts were to go pull security and protect his fellow soldiers. There was a lot of that going on.

For the next hour Glaser continued to help fight fires, organize the evacuation of the wounded, and direct the response. Once he had accountability for all of the company personnel Glaser started worrying about the vehicles. "My first sergeant had already taken care of local security and the fires outside the complex when a team from the 4-64 AR TOC came to me and asked how they could help. I told them I had the soldier issues under control but could use some help retrieving vehicles. I did not see them again but I did see their M88 recovery vehicle drive through the wall of the compound to open a new way out for the trapped vehicles."

As a final note on those trying hours Glaser commented, "We had everybody in the area rushing to us to help us. I didn't have to get on the radio and call anyone. It was such a huge relief to be in a unit where people march to the sound of guns. It was one of the few times in my military career where I had more help than problems."

Moe, Larry, and Curly

As the TOC sorted itself out, Perkins had an even bigger problem on his hands. His ability to keep his brigade in Baghdad overnight rested almost entirely on the trail battalion's ability to hold open the line of communication back to Saints. If that could not be done, the fuel and ammo Perkins needed to stay downtown could not come forward and he would have to retreat out of the city. His daring raid would then turn into another opportunity for Baghdad Bob and his chorus in the international press to trumpet an American repulse. To ensure that did not happen, Lieutenant Colonel Stephen Twitty's 3-15 IN was fighting desperately in what would be the single most ferocious battle of the war, to open and secure Highway 8.

In the original plan Perkins and his staff had identified three major intersections along Highway 8 that needed to be held at all costs. From north to south these three intersections were named Moe, Larry, and Curly; they were given to the 3-15 IN to hold. Twitty remembers his thoughts as he organized for the mission:

> We planned our scheme of maneuver based on little intelligence information and the meager data found on our tactical maps. The best information I had about what awaited my men came from Lieutenant Colonel Schwartz, and we used this as the basis of most of our planning. A Company, commanded by Capt. Josh Wright, would seize

Objective Moe, while B/4-64 Armor, commanded by Dan Hubbard, would seize Objective Larry. Because Colonel Perkins requested two platoons to secure Objective Saints and his TOC, I had to detach Capt. Ronny Johnson and two platoons from his B Company for that mission.

As a result, I did not have a full company to seize Objective Curly. To fill the void, I combined B Company's remaining platoon with the battalion mortar platoon and an engineer platoon into an ad hoc combat unit. I put Capt. Zan Hornbuckle from my operations section in command and named the unit Team Zan. Captain Hornbuckle arrived in the unit just prior to our deployment to Kuwait and he had been my point man on several difficult tasks. I knew that I could count on him to accomplish any mission. I told my Command Sergeant Major, CSM Gallagher, that he would accompany Team Zan to Objective Curly and I would accompany B/4-64 AR to Objective Larry.[3]

Each company had a difficult challenge ahead, but Captain Hornbuckle's appeared almost insurmountable. Each of the other companies was going into battle with units that had been training and fighting together as coherent teams for many months. Hornbuckle, using Gallagher in the role of company first sergeant, had to pull three platoons who hardly knew one another into a single unit prepared to fight an infantry battle, and he had only six hours to do it.

In another of the war's surreal moments, just a couple of hours before the attack started, a Special Forces team asked Hornbuckle if they could join them on the mission. The Special Ops guys were sure that if they could talk with some of the locals at Objective Curly there would be no trouble. Hornbuckle welcomed them along, but wondered why they had such a radically different picture of what to expect than every other soldier in the brigade. Upon arrival at Curly the Special Forces soldiers immediately realized that talking was not possible, so they donned their combat gear and entered the fight. Hornbuckle would have reason to be thankful for their additional firepower.

His orders issued, and after the chaplain led the assembled officers in a prayer, Twitty went back to his Bradley to try and get some sleep.

---

3. Command Sergeant Major Bob Gallagher was already a living legend among the battalions troops, among whom he was affectionately nicknamed Blackhawk Bob. He had served in the Rangers for years and had been seriously wounded in Somalia in the raid made famous by the movie and book *Black Hawk Down*. Now, ten years later, he was the senior enlisted soldier in the battalion, who had a penchant for leading from the front. During the interview process for this book, more than a dozen officers mentioned that, if they could nominate the next Command Sergeant Major of the Army, Gallagher would lead their list.

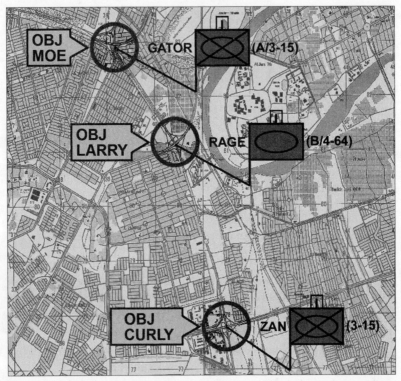

MAP 28. Moe, Larry, Curly

My adrenaline was at an all time high. I could not sleep, and the only thing that I could think about was the attack and the possible casualties that we might suffer. I picked up the radio and called Colonel Perkins to voice my concerns about the lack of troop strength due to B Company remaining at Objective Saints. Colonel Perkins responded, "Steph, if you need reinforcements, you got them. I will ensure that you have the forces to accomplish your mission." I trusted Colonel Perkins; I had served under his command for two years and knew that he was a man of his word and a highly capable leader. During our two years together, whenever I needed assistance he had always provided it. Our radio conversation assured me that he would do the same if I needed B Company once we launched our attack.

Racing up Highway 8, Twitty soon realized that the Iraqis had reseeded the entire route with fresh combat soldiers as the leading two battalions passed them. His lead company reported killing at least thirty of the enemy, and his other companies were reporting heavy contact. Still, his forces were able to fight their way onto each objective. There they became the object of ferocious Iraqi counterattacks. For Twitty and his men, the fight at each objective was both desperate and critical. Losing any of them could leave the rest of the brigade cut off without fuel or ammo, to be cut to ribbons after they lost the ability to maneuver or shoot back.

Though all of these battles took place at the same time, for the sake of clarity they will be recounted separately, starting at Objective Moe in the north. Captain Josh Wright tells his story of that fight:

When we came into Objective Moe the plan was to have a tank platoon to the north, to destroy any enemy coming out of the city. My mech platoons were positioned south of the tanks, with one facing east and the other west. Their task was to destroy any forces attempting to re-seize this objective area. I told my engineer platoon to constructing nonstandard obstacles from what they found on site. They did throughout the day and into the night by dropping telephone poles, building berms, felling trees, and piling up cars.

Almost immediately after arriving we came under sustained counterattack. To the southwest we were attacked by a company-size force of Saddam Fedayeen. To the east we fought off another company of Fedayeen mixed with fighters from Syria, Egypt, Palestine, and Jordan. To the north, we engaged two companies of Special Republican Guards in uniform. They arrived in civilian buses and attempted to deploy just in front of my tank platoon, which was not the best of choices on their part. We also were getting hammered by fire coming from a mosque at the edge of our perimeter. The Iraqis knew we were not shooting at the mosque, so they used it to rearm and refit their forces as we broke them. They would go to the mosque, get themselves together, and then come at us again.

Twitty, relates the company's arrival at Objective Moe:

Moe proved a veritable hornets' nest of resistance, and was constantly reinforced by the enemy. The entire company came under intense 360-degree direct and indirect fire. Several hundred enemy troops were in a trench and bunker complex among the palms and brush, and others occupied prepared positions in adjacent buildings dominating the objective. Additionally, armed enemy vehicles headed towards the cloverleaf. Iraqi troops swarmed into the area, boxing in the intersection.

Although he had not expected such strong defenses, Captain Wright realized that the best course of action was to attack immediately. His company launched a mounted assault that cleared the cloverleaf. But, finding the enemy growing in numbers against his flanks, and receiving reports of Iraqi tanks moving against him, Captain Wright decided to carry the attack beyond his assigned objective and deeper into Baghdad, by sending Second Leiutenant Van Kirk's tank platoon charging north, into the city, to destroy enemy forces massing there.

Following this attack, Wright settled his troops into defensive positions around the objective. While his combat elements continued to fend off determined attacks, the engineers blocked every enemy approach by cutting down light poles and using an armored bulldozer to push debris and burning cars into defensive berms. The engineers' work made it possible to stop a savage last-light attack that climaxed with a car bomb exploding just sixty meters from the perimeter. After eight hours of sustained and intense combat, a survey of the battlefield indicated that A Company had destroyed more than sixty vehicles and killed hundreds of enemy infantrymen.

For the rest of the day and night, Captain Wright and his small force fought off one attack after another. As other units had discovered at Samawah, Najaf, and other locations, the Iraqis did not lack for bravery. Hour after hour they continued to make suicidal assaults, only to be broken by hails of concentrated fire. After the war, one officer said, "Their attacks were as incessant as they were futile, but they were pressed home with such fierceness that many of my men believed the Iraqis were all on some sort of drugs." To beat them off, Wright had to call for more than twenty danger close artillery missions and another six danger close mortar missions. When, after eighteen hours, the Iraqis seemed to melt away it was discovered that the battalion had used up almost twice its normal basic load of ammo. If the Iraqis had continued to press their attack, in less than an hour the company would probably have had to resort to hand-to-hand combat.

At Objective Larry, Captain Dan Hubbard's company was fighting an equally ferocious battle. It was at this center intersection, three miles north of Curly and one and a half miles south of Moe, that Twitty placed himself. With his Bradley there would be a total of nineteen armored vehicles on the objective.

Hubbard assigned one of his tank platoons responsibility for the northeast quadrant while the other took the southeast quadrant. His infantry platoon was ordered to hold the entire west side of the objec-

A suicide vehicle rushes 3rd ID armor along the route for Thunder Run II. A moment after this picture was taken the vehicle was torn apart by 25mm cannon.

tive. Iraqis began pounding their positions with increasing ferocity from the moment they arrived. For the first several hours, the biggest threat Hubbard faced was a series of suicide attacks by vehicles racing towards his positions from the south. Filled with armed men, these vehicles raced towards the intersection with weapons firing out of every window or from the beds of the pickup trucks. Though the most ubiquitous suicide vehicle was the white and orange taxi, the Iraqis also threw city buses, dump trucks, and in one case a huge lumbering recreational vehicle at the company's positions. These vehicles were usually filled with so much explosives that the Bradley's 25mm gun would set off a tremendous secondary explosion. As the company's infantry platoon leader, First Lieutenant Mark Brzozowski, remembers it:

> As we rolled down to Objective Larry I was at 75 percent strength, with three Bradleys. Enemy in my sector was operating in two- to three-man RPG teams. They were using technical trucks and civilian cars

to maneuver and resupply in our sector. All told, there were between 150 and 200 enemy personnel in my platoon sector. All through the day we had heavy contact throughout our sector. Each of my Bradleys was hit by numerous RPGs and pelted by small arms. About halfway through the day, as my wing man unmasked to engage a ZSU-23 [anti-aircraft gun] that was firing on my dismounted soldiers, he was struck by two RPGs. One penetrated the Bradley's armor and lodged itself inside the vehicle without detonating. I had to order the soldiers to evacuate that Bradley, bringing my combat strength down to two vehicles. I moved both of them to high ground so that they could continue to dominate a pretty big sector.

Even after being reinforced with one tank and firing numerous indirect fire missions, I still was in great danger of being overrun. Unwilling to wait for that to happen, I decided to attack in sector. I executed a raid into enemy territory. We headed south down a side street and then cut west to flush them west of the highway. We found three large trucks loaded with RPGs, AK-47s, and small arms ammunition along our route. Since we did not have any proper demolition charges with us, Corporal Mishler, one of my team leaders, rigged an expedient charge with claymores, which blew the trucks to pieces. When the raid was over we had destroyed hundred of RPGs and driven the enemy out of the eastern portion of my sector.

We continued to have heavy contact in the western sector, however. Both myself and my platoon sergeant's track were hit numerous times by RPGs, destroyed everything on the outside of the Bradley, but did not get any friendly casualties.

Based on the continued threat to the west and the success of our first raid, I executed a second raid the next morning. I led that morning with a tank in overwatch to the west, covering down this highway. With two Bradleys I assaulted into the courtyard of a minaret from which we were receiving fire. Seven Iraqi defenders engaged us in the courtyard, but they were quickly suppressed. As I looked around the courtyard it became apparent that this was the main supply area for the Iraqi defenders. As I tried to decide how best to destroy the massive weapons cache we found there, a thirty-man Iraqi force counterattacked us. We fought off this attack as my men set the demo charge we had thought to bring with us this time. At one point, enemy personnel approached unobserved from around a corner and I was forced to kill at least one with my sidearm. But his return fire caused a premature detonation inside the cache, and I had to order a hasty evacuation of the courtyard. In the end we destroyed over 3,000 RPGs, 2,000 hand grenades, 30,000 rounds of small arms and

a handful of mortar and artillery rounds, without suffering any casualties. After this second raid, I was only fired on by one RPG over the
next four days.

Captain Hubbard was trying to control the overall company fight
while also engaging the Iraqis from his own vehicle. "As I was coming
up the exit ramp crossing the bridge I was hit by five RPGs but suffered only minor damage. That was a strong indication, though, that
I was receiving fire from every direction. Compounding that was the
problem of trying to decide who to engage, because the Iraqis were
often in civilian clothes. I saw some soldiers discard their uniforms
and appear to walk away, only to see them dart into a bunker or resupply point and come back and start fighting again. They were not given
a second chance to do that."

Hubbard, who had been a Marine infantryman in Desert Storm, was
the only soldier in his company to have seen combat before. Despite
the heavy pressure and chaos around him, his composure went a long
way towards keeping his men settled and focused on the immediate
fight. Though his own tank was continually hit by RPGs he maintained
an exposed position from which he could best control the defense of
the position. While he and his men fought the near battle, Hubbard
began calling for indirect artillery support, which he later credited with
breaking the Iraqis' will.

Lieutenant Colonel Twitty, positioned on top of the overpass in
the center of the intersection, was in the thick of the fight along with
all the others. Within two hours of his arrival at Objective Larry, he
had to resupply the 25mm ammunition he carried in his M2 fighting vehicle. His gunner was engaging targets on his own, while Twitty
maintained contact with the other elements of the task force, cleared
supporting fires, and kept Perkins updated. Eventually he estimated
that fifty to eighty enemy suicide vehicles were destroyed south of
Objective Larry.

At Objective Curly Twitty's makeshift company commanded by
Captain Hornbuckle ran into the fiercest resistance faced by any of
Twitty's units that day. Later it was discovered that the main enemy
force at Curly was Syrian Jihadists who had come to Iraq specifically to fight the Americans and were sworn to win or die.[4] They had

---

4. Hornbuckle's soldiers eventually captured thirty enemy prisoners of war. Of these,
twenty-eight were Syrian. After the battle ended, local citizens approached U.S. forces

been in position for two days and had dug trenches and built sturdy bunker positions amid the construction rubble surrounding the clover-leaf intersections. Twitty had briefly engaged them as he went past Curly enroute to Larry, and he had called back to Hornbuckle to alert him that there was a lot of dug-in infantry waiting for him.

As Hornbuckle's soldiers occupied their positions they were met by concentrated fire from the Syrian and Iraqi fighters occupying trenches and bunkers and firing from nearby buildings and retaining walls. According to Hornbuckle,

> They attacked from all directions. They attacked on foot and in commandeered taxis and civilian cars. Others would rush us in pickup trucks mounted with heavy machine guns on pedestals. They fired RPGs in volleys under the covering fire of light machine guns and AK-47 rifles. Throughout the day they would also often fire RPGs from long range, lobbing them high in the air to land among the U.S. defenders. Adding to the discomfort was mortar and artillery fire, firing pre-planned concentrations using three rounds at a time. They did not seem to be able to adjust this fire, but they repeated the fire missions often.

Hornbuckle's ad hoc team established a hasty defense with the mortar platoon's tracked carriers in a loose column on Highway 8; two mortars were aimed north and the other two were aimed south. The engineer platoon was given responsibility for the east side of the cloverleaf intersection, and the mechanized infantry platoon was responsible for the west side. Sergeant Major Gallagher remembers watching the Special Forces soldiers exit their vehicles and realize they were not going to get a chance to talk sense to anyone. "They just donned their combat gear as if nothing was going on. It was as if they expected to get this over with in an hour and get in a round of golf in the afternoon." After the Special Forces soldiers had picked up their weapons and ammo, they gathered some nearby infantry and charged the closest building. Gallagher said, "There was some fire inside the building and two of the SF guys were dragged out wounded."

As the Iraqi attacks intensified, everyone fought. Drivers and radio operators joined the infantry in clearing Iraqis out of trench lines.

---

at the road junction and asked for permission to give the Iraqi dead a proper burial. The local Iraqis took away the bodies of the dead fighters wearing army uniforms, but they refused to have anything to do with the masses of dead Syrians, expressing their disgust and hatred of them to anyone who would listen.

Medics picked up weapons and defended the wounded from Syrians who penetrated a hail of fire to get into the perimeter. At one point a severely wounded soldier being carried away on a stretcher grabbed a shotgun lying across his chest and killed two Iraqis who took advantage of the medics' distraction to get within a few feet of several helpless soldiers. Later in the day, Chaplain Stephen Hommel, a forty-one-year-old captain and former infantry sergeant, was walking among the wounded and realized the position was in danger of being overrun by Iraqis closing in on all sides. In a "moment of decision" Hommel picked up a weapon and began engaging the enemy.

All through the early fight Captain Hornbuckle moved from position to position; sand was kicked up all around him by Iraqi fire. At one point, an Iraqi just yards away drew a direct bead on him, so Hornbuckle did the same. Hornbuckle, who had a wife and new baby waiting at home, fired first and later said, "There was no way that bastard was going to keep me from going home."

Several times during the fight Twitty called to get an assessment of the situation. At first Hornbuckle told him that it was rough, but his guys were handling it. However, in the late morning Twitty could hear a rising crescendo of fire on the radio and thought he could hear increased stress in Hornbuckle's voice. In need of another opinion, Twitty called Sergeant Major Gallagher and asked what he thought. Gallagher, who was fighting while wounded, did not pull any punches, "Boss, we need help and we need it now!"

Alerted to the peril at Curly, Twitty called Perkins and asked that Captain Johnson's company, which had been left to secure the brigade's TOC and logistics base, be released to reinforce Objective Curly. Perkins immediately agreed.

Twitty got on the radio to Johnson and ordered, "Get to Curly ASAP!" Johnson, who had been listening to the radio traffic all morning and could hear the roar of fire just to his north, had anticipated the order. Just minutes after being told to bring his company into the maelstrom, Johnson and B Company were rushing north. They roared into the perimeter around Curly with every weapon blazing. Johnson's Bradleys moved to the trench line, where Hornbuckle's dismounted infantry were killing dozens of Iraqi, but still barely holding on. One infantryman later said, "It was awesome. I had never seen what a 25mm could do up close. They just started ripping the entire trench line to pieces, sending weapons and parts of Iraqis flying everywhere."

Corporal Warren Hall later said, "It was like watching the cavalry come over the hill. There was not one soldier on Curly who did not think they were going to die that day." Johnson's additional firepower began to turn the tide, but instead of giving up, the Iraqis seemed to redouble their efforts. The Iraqis no longer had the strength to overrun the position, but it was far from secure. For another half hour the combined firepower of Johnson's and Hornbuckle's companies, joined by artillery and close air support, continued to beat down the Iraqi resistance.

Both Perkins and Twitty were becoming concerned. There had been almost four hours of constant fighting all along Highway 8. Perkins had already ordered all of his tanks to turn off their engines to buy Twitty two more hours to secure his objectives, but the time for decision was rapidly arriving. Perkins called Twitty and asked if he could get the ammo and fuel forward.

Twitty, also worried that his own units were dangerously low on ammo, called Gallagher and repeated the question. Gallagher did a quick assessment and replied, "Boss we can get them through. It will be risky, but we can get them through." Twitty decided to accept the risk and ordered Captain J.O. Bailey, the unit S-4, to bring the R2 package forward. Bailey later said he wished he had the stature or guts to say no. Whatever his personal thoughts, Bailey soon had his convoy on the road, escorted by the unit's scout platoon.

They made contact almost immediately and took several casualties as they barreled north. Everyone in the convoy was acutely aware that they were driving flying bombs. Just one round or a piece of hot shrapnel would turn the 5,000-gallon fuel tankers or huge ammo trucks into moving Roman candles. After a harrowing thirty-minute drove, the trucks drove into the Curly perimeter and pulled into a tight coil on a piece of level ground where they hoped the terrain would mask them from the worst of the Iraqi fire. The troops at Curly immediately began unloading ammunition and passing it out to the forces dispersed around the intersection, who were still locked in heavy fighting against dismounted Syrian infantry trying to close in on the vulnerable supply vehicles.

It was inevitable that sooner or later one of the dozens of RPG round-streaking across the position would strike home. An RPG struck one of the ammunition resupply vehicles, which immediately began to burn. Efforts to unload the remaining ammunition and fight the fire did not prevent its rapid spread to four other vehicles. Drivers who upon arrival had left their vehicles in search of a safe place to hide now darted back to the undamaged trucks and moved them away from the raging inferno.

Emboldened by their apparent success, the Iraqis increased their rate of fire. Captain Johnson decided that it was no longer safe to keep the R2 package at Curly. He also knew that Lieutenant Colonel Rutter's entire 2-7 IN battalion, sent by General Blount from the airport to help the 2nd Brigade, was only minutes away. The 2-7 IN would soon take over at Curly and the defense would be able to spare his company. He decided to take B Company and escort the surviving vehicles north.

Twitty ordered Johnson not waste time at Objective Larry, but to move directly to Moe, where Josh Wright's soldiers were almost out of ammo. After a quick stop to resupply the troops at Moe, Johnson led the convoy to the center of Baghdad and to Perkins. All along the route, Johnson's men and the convoy vehicles pounded away at Iraqis who were making desperate final attempts to stop them.

Perkins remembers the scene as they drove onto the palace grounds.

> I knew they were almost here and I had already made the final decision to stay the night. But I could not believe it as the convoy drove in. The first vehicle in line was an ammo truck with only the driver on it. He drove in at fifty miles an hour and hit the brakes hard when he saw the protecting M-1 tanks around him. All of the glass in cab had been shot out. He was scrunched down behind the wheel driving with one hand and shooting his rifle with the other. When he stopped I jumped up on his cab to talk to him. He was only eighteen and his face was covered in blood. All I could think to ask was, "What made you do this?"
>
> He just looked at me and said, "Sir, we knew you needed this stuff."

25

Reflections

WHEN ASKED IF HE HAD ENOUGH SOLDIERS to fight the war and handle the later insurgency, General Weber, 3rd ID Assistant Division Commander, replied, "I don't know. I was only told to take Baghdad, and I had enough troops for that." For the 3rd ID, conducting stability operations in a post-Saddam Iraq was not even a consideration as they planned for war. As far as they knew, they would topple the regime and go home. It is therefore unfortunate that the insurgency that flamed up in the wake of the regime's demise has been allowed to obscure one of the most remarkable military achievements in history. In just twenty-one days a single division marched from Kuwait all the way to Baghdad in the face of fierce resistance all along the way. Even after being forced to pause by the worst sandstorms in fifty years and by the hesitation of higher headquarters, the 3rd ID still moved farther and faster than the Germans marched across France in 1940 or the Israelis blitzed across the Sinai in 1967. As it moved, the division annihilated thousands of fanatical Fedayeen, who were sworn to martyrdom if it would help them kill one American. Later, they encountered the vaunted Republican Guard and tore apart the Medina Division, and they also crippled the Hammurabi and Nebuchadnezzar Divisions.

Some commentators have made an issue of the fact that the Iraqi army was merely a skeleton of its former self and incapable of any coherent resistance. What truths there are to those beliefs are fully covered in this book. However, no one should lose track of the fact that the Iraqis had more tanks, more soldiers, and more artillery than the 3rd ID. The Iraqis were also well dug in and just waiting for the Americans to come into their field of fire. Though vast numbers of them up and ran at the first opportunity, just as many stayed and fought to the death.

There is no doubt that the Iraqis were severely outclassed by the 3rd ID and Coalition forces. They had no way to challenge the Coalition's overall air superiority or to match the technological resources that were brought to bear against them. But advanced technology is not the story of this war. Despite having deployed almost four-fifths of our national intelligence-gathering assets to the theater, the first information any 3rd ID commander ever had about the location of the enemy was when the first RPG round slammed into one of his tanks or Bradleys.

Technology helped, but the real reason the 3rd ID succeeded so brilliantly was that they simply outfought the Iraqis. In every encounter of the war the 3rd ID dominated their opponents, even after giving them the first shot. By any standard, this is a remarkable feat, considering that the average combat soldier was still in his teens and probably fewer than one in fifty 3rd ID soldiers had ever seen combat before. What made the critical difference was leadership. Without exception, every officer and sergeant rose to the occasion. Years ago a historian told me that "soldiers will forgive their officers any one fault except cowardice." When I returned from being embedded with the 101st Airborne Division, I wrote an article that mentioned that the officers I had encountered during the war seemed to have made a cult out of the concept of bravery.

As I learned more about the 3rd ID battles it became apparent that the "cult of bravery" was not limited to the 101st Airborne. Throughout the entire war, officers and noncommissioned officers ran horrendous risks under direct fire for no better reason than that is what their bosses, peers, and subordinates expected of them. If officers were not killed and wounded in much higher proportions than the soldiers they led, it was solely due to the vicissitudes of fate. Their bravery was contagious among the troops, who also ran almost immeasurable risks to win a fight or to help a comrade.

As many have discovered over the past two hundred years, the American soldier, when well trained and competently led, is a fearsome fighting machine. As a body, the 3rd ID units proved ruthless and without pity on the battlefield. At the same time, I came across hundreds of stories of individual kindness, often in the heat of combat. These stories ranged from the captain who carried a wounded Iraqi on his shoulders to an aid station while under Iraqi fire, to simply giving of their own limited water supplies to thirsty Iraqi civilians. Throughout the war the average Iraqi citizen had more to fear from the soldiers of their own army than they did from the invading 3rd ID.

Has there ever in history been an army like this one? It is almost impossible to think of another fighting force disciplined and compassionate enough to do what the 3rd ID and other U.S. forces did in Iraq. Try and place yourself of the eighteen-year-old gunner on a Bradley who had to hold his fire while being hit by deadly RPG rounds, because the enemy was hiding behind civilians. Consider how difficult it would be for a twenty-five-year-old company commander to resist destroying a mosque that the Iraqis have defiled by making it a defensive strongpoint but which is threatening the men he swore a silent oath to do everything within his power to bring home alive. Tens of thousands of Iraqis are alive today because soldiers and commanders decided to run risks no other military force in history would have countenanced, simply because they did not want to kill innocents when it could be avoided.

In a media atmosphere where every inadvertent civilian death was plastered on the front pages, nary a word was written about the soldiers who held their fire in order to give every person in civilian clothes on the battlefield a fair chance to leave the area (a humane trait that thousands of fanatical Fedayeen exploited in order to try and kill Americans). War is brutal. There is no escaping that fact, but no fair judge will ever be able to say the 3rd ID did not do everything possible to limit the war's impact on innocents.

Because this book is mostly a combat narrative it is of necessity the story of the maneuver units that made up the most momentous fights. This is unfortunate for several reasons. First, as I have said in my notes on sources, I was forced to leave out the independent stories of many engineer, artillery, and aviation units. Although these types of units are mentioned as they became critical in many of the 3rd ID's fights, this book does not do them full justice. It would simply have been impossible for the 3rd ID to do much of what was asked of it without the division's aviation units, which provided critical fire-support in almost every major battle. The same holds true for the artillery, which was almost constantly firing missions in support of the maneuver battalions or engaging Iraqi forces far beyond the 3rd ID front.

Second, I have left out most of the logistics battle. As this book often relates, there were many instances where units were low on fuel or where in the middle of a fight they became seriously low on ammunition. In truth, though, there was not a single example of a combat force running out of ammo or fuel during the entire march to Baghdad. To accomplish this feat, 3rd ID logistical units had to move tens of thousands of tons of supplies over a single road, often under the direct fire of the enemy. To say it was a logistical miracle is to understate the achievement.

In this regard, there is one man whose contributions do not receive proper attention in this book and that is Brigadier General Louis Weber. As the assistant division commander in charge of supply, it was his job to make sure that everything the division needed to continue the fight was available when it was required. Of all of the officers I interviewed, there was none who exceeded General Weber's desire to get into the middle of the fight, but that was not his job. Swallowing his own inclinations, he focused all his energies on keeping the division moving and shooting. Against almost insurmountable odds he succeeded.[1]

After the war, he wrote me and said that he was "supported by a lot of great soldiers who made me look better than I was." No doubt the first part of that statement is true, but I have a dozen senior commanders on record stating that "without Weber nothing would have gotten to us."

I hope that some future historian will continue this history with more focus on what the combat support and service support units accomplished, which made possible everything the maneuver battalions and brigades did.

---

1. Those interested in a thorough study of logistic operations during Operation Iraqi Freedom are encouraged to review the Rand Institute's *Sustainment of Army Forces in Operation Iraqi Freedom: Major Findings and Recommendations.*

In summary, I found research and writing this book one of the most humbling experiences of my life. Over the past three years I have met many of the men mentioned in this book personally, and there is no finer group of Americans anywhere. If those who fought World War II constituted our greatest generation, then the soldiers of the 3rd ID are surely worthy successors. As long as men and women such as these continue to serve the nation, the Republic is safe.

Index

Thunder Run II, 230–57. *See also* Perkins, David
Sherman, William Tecumseh, 10
Shiite uprisings, threat of, 157, 161. *See also* Al-Quds *and* Fedayeen Saddam
Shinseki, Eric, 6
Sistani, Grand Ayatollah, 89
Smith, Paul, 203–4
Smith, Robert, 51
Smith, Tom, 104
soldiers. *See* Iraqi army *and* U.S. soldiers
Special Forces, 26, 62. *See also* intelligence
special friends. *See* CIA operatives
suicide attacks, 65–67, 73, 97, 116, 137, 183; in Baghdad, 210–11, 250, 251; recruitment, 40–42
Sultan Hashim Ahmad al-Ta'i, 167
Sunday, Sean, 213
supplies: coordinating, 9, 232–33, 261; defense of, 57, 246–57; fuel, 21, 22. *See also* LOCs, battle of
Syrian Jihadists, 254

tactical operation center (TOC): attack on, 243–46; movement of, 20
tactics, Iraqi, 61–62, 65, 72–73, 74, 109–10, 148; during ambushes, 77–78
tactics, U.S., 56, 67, 73, 232–33; effects of: 58
Tallil Air Base, assault on, 24–33; Iraqi reports of, 84
technology, advantage of, 64, 65; limits of, 99–100, 259
Temple, Jim, 148–50, 154–55
thermal vision, 64, 66, 81, 117, 186. *See also* nighttime combat
3rd BCT: entry into Iraq, 17; isolation of Baghdad (Objective Titans), 220–28; isolation of Karbala, 132–34; Tallil Air Base assault, 24–33. *See also* Allyn, Daniel
3rd ID: reputation, 3–4
3-7 CAV Squadron, 44; battle near Najaf,

90; battle of As Samawah, 1–4, 47; relief, 116; taking Objective Montgomery, 178–87. *See also* Ferrell, Terry
Thunder Run I, 206–18; enthusiasm for, 229
Thunder Run II, 229–57
Time Magazine, 121–22
training, Fedayeen Saddam, 41–42
training, U.S., 19–21; utility in battle, 64–65
Trainor, Bernard, 5
trust, 10, 21
25mm HE, 100
Twitty, Stephen, 14, 169, 207, 246–57 *passim*

U.S. soldiers: accomplishments, 258–60; character of, 4, 10–15, 259–61; discipline, 142
urban warfare. *See* Blackhawk Down

vehicles: disabled, 80, 210–13; mechanical failures, 18–19; speed, 21
violation of laws of war, 110

Waldron, Dave, 30–31
Wallace, William, 121, 195: planning of Operation Iraqi Freedom, 7; Thunder Runs, 230–32
Washington, D.C., military and political leaders, 119
weather. *See* sandstorm
Weber, Louis, 9, 22, 112, 258, 261
Wesley, Eric, 22–23, 171–72, 215, 219, 243–44
Wheatley, Paul, 185–86
WITHCOM: explanation, 17
Wolford, Phillip, 127–28
Wood, McKinley, 136–37, 226–27
Woodward, Scott, 60–61
Wright, Josh, 128, 246, 249–50, 257

Yahya Taha Huwaysh-Fadni Al-Ani, 85–86

About the Author

Jim Lacey is a retired Army infantry officer who currently resides in Virginia, where he works as a military analyst and writer. During the 2003 invasion of Iraq he worked for *Time* magazine as an embedded journalist and was with the 101st Airborne Division during the march to Baghdad. He has been published in over a dozen major magazines and has written numerous articles and editorials on international and military affairs in many of the nation's leading newspapers.

The Naval Institute Press is the book-publishing arm of the U.S. Naval Institute, a private, nonprofit, membership society for sea service professionals and others who share an interest in naval and maritime affairs. Established in 1873 at the U.S. Naval Academy in Annapolis, Maryland, where its offices remain today, the Naval Institute has members worldwide.

Members of the Naval Institute support the education programs of the society and receive the influential monthly magazine *Proceedings* and discounts on fine nautical prints and on ship and aircraft photos. They also have access to the transcripts of the Institute's Oral History Program and get discounted admission to any of the Institute-sponsored seminars offered around the country. Discounts are also available to the colorful bimonthly magazine *Naval History*.

The Naval Institute's book-publishing program, begun in 1898 with basic guides to naval practices, has broadened its scope to include books of more general interest. Now the Naval Institute Press publishes about seventy titles each year, ranging from how-to books on boating and navigation to battle histories, biographies, ship and aircraft guides, and novels. Institute members receive significant discounts on the Press's more than eight hundred books in print.

Full-time students are eligible for special half-price membership rates. Life memberships are also available.

For a free catalog describing Naval Institute Press books currently available, and for further information about subscribing to *Naval History* magazine or about joining the U.S. Naval Institute, please write to:

Member Services
U.S. Naval Institute
291 Wood Road
Annapolis, MD 21402-5034
Telephone: (800) 233-8764
Fax: (410) 571-1703
Web address: www.navalinstitute.org